Praise for *Riding Out*

"Wonderfully relatable on so many levels. Simon's wanderlust, mental roller coaster and reactions to a fast-changing world had me enthralled in his journey, but very much reflecting on my own over the past few years. A brilliantly crafted book which holds a mirror up to the world we live in."

Mark Beaumont

"A truly inspiring journey that celebrates the healing power of adventure. A must-read."

Levison Wood

"If you've recently bought a 'lockdown bike' and realise you've not been using it enough, this inspirational, down-to-earth and touching book may give you a few ideas."

Tom Chesshyre

"Simon's cycle ride around his own country is a fine demonstration that adventure and transformation begins on your own doorstep."

Alastair Humphreys

"[Riding Out *is*] both hugely inspirational yet still relatable... Simon's vulnerability at times will show many readers – myself included – that they aren't alone in feeling lost these past 18 months. How he has managed this vulnerability with humour throughout the book drew me in, as did his ability to capture the spirit of the people he met along the way. His ability to describe challenging moments with honesty makes it feel like you're hearing an old friend regale the trip over dinner."

Alex Outhwaite

"In Riding Out, *Simon Parker holds a humane mirror to a fractured Britain as it adjusts to a strange, isolated new world.*"

Jon Dunn, author of *The Glitter in the Green*

Riding Out

RIDING OUT

An Hachette UK Company
www.hachette.co.uk

Summersdale Publishers Ltd
Part of Octopus Publishing Group Limited
Carmelite House
50 Victoria Embankment
LONDON
EC4Y 0DZ
UK

www.summersdale.com

Printed and bound by CPI Group (UK) Ltd, Croydon, CR0 4YY

ISBN: 978-1-80007-874-1

Substantial discounts on bulk quantities of Summersdale books are available to corporations, professional associations and other organisations. For details contact general enquiries: telephone: +44 (0) 1243 771107 or email: enquiries@summersdale.com.

Riding Out

A JOURNEY OF LOVE, LOSS AND NEW BEGINNINGS

SIMON PARKER

summersdale

Author's note

Everything you are about to read is true, and everyone I meet and talk about is real. On a couple of occasions I have changed the names of people, as a courtesy, to protect their identities.

To my friends

CONTENTS

riding out, phrasal verb
 ~ To survive or outlast
 ~ To come safely through a storm

PART ONE:

LOST

HOME:
SIMPLY SURVIVING

I hadn't slept in almost 80 hours, showered in 90 or left my pokey two-bed flat in well over 100. I had puffy bruised bags under my eyes and an incessant throbbing in my aching temples. I drank strong black coffee to feel up. I downed cheap red wine to come down.

We knew it was coming. "Stay at home. Wash your filthy hands. Repent your dirty sins." What had started as a few footnotes on the international news channels had quickly arrived in our living rooms.

For those first few weeks of lockdown, I did little more than watch disaster movies on Netflix while following every macabre narrative twist on Twitter. "Just going to do some work," I'd say to my girlfriend, Alana, before locking myself in the spare bedroom and doomscrolling for hours on end.

Of course, I hid the fact I was living this pathetic existence. Just a month before, I'd been in Cape Town interviewing Roger Federer for the BBC. I could never admit to my friends and family that we were forced to take a mortgage holiday and sign on to Universal Credit. My ego was far too big for that. Instead, I smiled my way through virtual pub quizzes and family Zoom calls I secretly loathed. "So, how was your week?" my parents would ask, as I contemplated downing another drink. My life was in freefall. Hardly any money, hardly any work. Things couldn't get any worse, surely?

But they could, and they did. On 13 April 2020 – two days before my thirty-third birthday – I received a phone call out of the blue that would throw my imprisoned life into chaos. "Simon?" said a quivering voice I hadn't heard for a decade. "It's Will. Joseph's stepdad. Joseph's died."

Joseph – or Joe as he was known to me and the rest of his friends – wasn't a 90-year-old pensioner with underlying health conditions, but a handsome 33-year-old father with a clean bill of health. He'd gone to sleep the night before, but never stirred the next morning. Gone. Forever.

Joe and I had been inseparable from the moment we met at secondary school. We danced at festivals together. We double-dated together. We grew from spotty teenage boys into scraggly-bearded men together. And although we'd barely spoken in the past year – like many adult friendships that flit and drift – news of his death made me smell the creamy smoke of his rollie cigarettes and the sweet scent of his hair wax.

I was charged with the grim task of breaking the news to about a dozen of Joe's oldest friends. Not over a few beers in a pub – they were all shuttered up for the apocalypse – but on the phone. I opted for a clinical bedside manner; quick, with shock and brevity rather than sugar-coating. Who wants to pass idle small talk about the inconveniences of a pandemic before then being hit with the news of a friend's untimely death? "Hiya mate, long time no speak," I'd say. "There's no easy way to say this, but…"

We still don't know exactly what happened to Joe. I'm not sure I want or need to know. The coroner recorded his death as sudden adult death syndrome, like a cot death. But regardless of what it says on a piece of paper in a filing cabinet somewhere, the final outcome remains the same. He's never coming back, and I'll never be able to persuade him out for one last pint.

What I do know is that his passing, at that exact moment, exposed ginormous cracks in defences I'd been holding up for my entire adult life. When we were 17, three of our friends died in quick succession. Dave, one of our best friends, lost his battle with cancer. Soon after, we arrived at sixth form to learn that Tim, by far the brightest boy in school, had been killed in an accident on his farm. Later that summer, as Joe and I sat together in camping chairs at Glastonbury Festival, we were told that Emma, a talented dancer with the world at her feet, had died suddenly of an asthma attack. Three young and ambitious teenagers gone, before their lives had really begun. Just a couple of months later, my sister's first baby, my first nephew, Joshua, was born prematurely and died within weeks. Not long after, my adoring godfather, Dennis, died of cancer.

At the time, I glossed over the pain and shunned the suggestion of therapy; choosing instead to anaesthetise those formative years with mountains of high-grade cannabis. Without it, I could neither sleep nor wake up. I left school with three terrible A levels, carrying a lump of raw, undigested grief deep in the pit of my stomach. Rather than starting life filled with hope and optimism, I couldn't shake the feeling that I had to live a handful of lives, as well as my own.

I blagged my way into university via clearing and then buried myself in books and films. I lived in the library. I would have slept there if I could. It became the longest and toughest slog of my life, but three years later, I staggered, wearily, out into the light with a first-class degree; a ticket to do more with my life than simply bum around north Oxfordshire smoking spliffs.

I gradually weaned myself off dope but the impulse to push myself, more and more, became so addictive that I made myself ill. I started to suffer panic attacks, a shortness of breath, insomnia and vivid nightmares about my friends and my nephew lying frail and helpless in hospital beds. I also became a hopeless hypochondriac. If I developed as much as a headache, I was convinced it was a brain tumour. A single bout of diarrhoea was always Crohn's disease. My GP notes became a thick ream of physical symptoms signed off as "overthinking". Eventually, I was diagnosed with generalised anxiety disorder but hid the shame from my friends and family.

In my early twenties I duped people into seeing me as a brave and intrepid travel journalist who sailed across oceans and visited dodgy borders. I dashed around the newsrooms of central London, then whizzed off to cover stories on the other side of the planet. I would work day and night in a bid to become "successful" as quickly as possible. I'd sleep in the office showers, drink ten shots of coffee a day and take every shift I was offered. It was distracting and exciting but the adrenaline merely plastered over angry teenage wounds that still festered beneath the surface.

Over time, I found ways to cope. Namely, alcohol and extreme exercise – I cycled across the USA and Europe, ran marathons and took on month-long hiking expeditions. For the best part of a decade, I managed to live with my anxiety in the background, suppressing it with the thrill of travel and adventure.

But when Joe died, coronavirus hit and borders were slammed shut, all the pain came flooding back. I was faced, day after day, with the image of hundreds of people in hospital beds, accompanied by an overture of wheezes and bleeps. I washed my hands until the skin blistered and sprayed our letter box with bleach until the door's paint began to leach.

I became haunted by the vision of Joe's lifeless corpse and obsessed by my own fragile mortality. Locked away in my flat – motionless for the first time in my adult life, rather than bouncing from place to place – I couldn't escape a deep sense of guilt. I felt ashamed that I was still living, and my friends weren't.

For a few socially distant summer months there were distractions, but life at home was far from perfect. One of my oldest friends, Nick, was supporting his fiancée, Sarah, through treatment for stage 4 bowel and liver cancer. She'd been diagnosed a few months before the pandemic struck, and at the age of just 37, with two young children, was fighting for her life behind a door we couldn't open.

All we could do was send our feeble love via WhatsApp and wait for updates on the outcome of her treatment. We didn't pray as such, but Alana and I would pause and hug, and hold her in our thoughts.

I found it impossible to come to terms with just how unfair life had quickly become. We were meant to be young and fit and in our prime, but sickness and death had now returned to the centre of my life, rather than being banished to its fuzzy periphery.

To make things worse, confusion, discord and frustration filled the newspapers and airwaves. Britain was no longer a united kingdom, but a collection of feudal states. Cornwall had told outsiders to stay away. The Scottish Highlands had been vandalised by marauding louts in camper vans. Greater Manchester was the Covid ghetto of the North. We were a plague island. A nation divided.

Britain was broken and I was, too. With no end in sight, I found it impossible to sleep, think and breathe. It felt as though I was on the cusp of an actual, proper, adult breakdown. All the psychosomatic symptoms that I'd hidden in my past were now bubbling to the surface and ruining my life.

My heart would beat so hard that it threatened to burst through my ribcage. My lungs drowned in carbon dioxide, as though they were being squeezed by elastic bands. I snatched breaths into my shoulders, rather than the pit of my stomach. From the moment I woke up, I was aware of every laboured inhalation – a hunger for air that could seldom be sated.

I needed counselling, antidepressants or both. But I'm a cynical hack with an addictive nature. The idea of talking to a therapist I'd never met via a webcam – while off my head on Prozac – seemed even more tragic than the predicament I was already in.

What I really needed was to feel like I was living again, rather than simply surviving. Because I wasn't just a travel writer, grounded. I'd become a miserable boyfriend, brother, son and friend who felt like he'd been wronged by life.

———

Our mortgage holiday was due to end at the start of November and with Alana's public relations business all but folded, it was looking increasingly likely that we'd have to rent out the flat and move in with our parents. I needed to try and make some quick money so we could keep a roof over our heads for the winter.

But by mid-September 2020 another national lockdown was being mooted and dozens of countries all over the world were shutting their borders to Britons. We were already climbing a new mountain of autumn infections, on course to look more like K2 than Scafell Pike. So, instead of setting my cross hairs on the far-flung islands, deserts and mountains where I usually plied my trade, I began fiddling around on Google Maps, waving a cursor over the squiggly contours at the edge of our isles.

I calculated that I could fly myself, my bicycle and a couple of panniers to the Shetland Islands for less than £200, then – at least in theory – cycle the length of the country before winter really set in. Rather than embark on a traditional John o'Groats to Land's End (JOGLE) route, which followed the most direct line from north to south, I liked the idea of seeing the fringes of Britain; the nooks and crannies of the country and the coasts and contours, where possible.

Beyond that, my plan was incredibly fuzzy; I still didn't know if I'd turn left or right when I made landfall at John o'Groats, or where I'd stay each night. I had less than £1,000 left to my name, meaning I had to be tight with my purse strings. I'd camp where possible but reward myself with a cheap hotel when the weather was really bad.

With the ten or so hours of autumnal daylight at my disposal, I figured I could cycle 40–70 miles a day, and do it all on my most expensive asset: a battered £2,000 titanium touring bicycle I'd been given to film a TV series four years before.

If all went to plan, I could sell enough articles to pay the mortgage for a few more months, and maybe have just enough money left over to fire up the central heating occasionally. But more importantly I'd get to feel rain on my face and wind in my hair. And instead of relying on the help of just one therapist once a week, I figured there were 67 million other people, out there, on Britain's beaches, in its small towns, on its farms and fishing boats, all with their own unique worries and concerns. Each of these people, I hoped, might help me in their own little way.

I don't think I ever asked for Alana's permission to leave. I just emerged from the garage one evening with my bicycle tyres pumped up and a sheepish look on my face.

"I feel like this is something I have to do. Not just for me, but for both of us."

"And you're going to find that in Shetland? In the middle of a pandemic?"

"I don't know, but I need to try."

"You know, you could just sell the bike?" she said, with tears building in her eyes.

It would have been easy to just forget the idea there and then. To let the bike gather dust and for my heart to steer my gut. But something deep down, in the pit of my stomach, was telling me to go. It was about so much more than money. I was leaving broken so that I could return in one piece.

FAEROES:
HELP ME HEAL

As I stomped over north Unst's rolling hills of sodden, spongy peat, the silver-grey Atlantic swept westward in silky ripples. The waning autumn sun fractured into low, rusty beams and where the sea melded with the sky, I could just make out the flatbed shadow of a distant oil tanker.

This was the furthest point of walkable Britain, and I was the country's northernmost human. Further north than St Petersburg or Stockholm, just Iceland and the Faeroe Islands lay between me and the North Pole. The air tasted cool, thick and green, like a dew-covered compost heap.

But I was still short of the very end of the line. I continued over a potholed headland, with just a few soggy sheep for company, then scuttled down a slope of pickled, salt-sprayed grass where a pair of jet-black ravens jabbed and slashed at a rabbit's mangled carcass. One misplaced foot and I would have plunged into the frothing sea or – a slightly better outcome – broken a leg tumbling into a concealed bog. I didn't have any phone reception, just an instinct that I was heading the right way. So, I simply walked and walked until there was almost no earth left to carry me.

Perhaps it was foolish to be out there on my own, but I couldn't bear the idea of cycling the length of the country and not actually clapping eyes on Britain's northernmost point. Even if that meant a stubborn prologue in the wrong direction.

Finally, after nearly 90 minutes, I saw what looked like a giant bowling pin perched on a pebble. Rising up from a serrated, slate-blue islet, it was the 64-foot-high Muckle Flugga Lighthouse. For over 150 years, "the Flugga" – as Shetlanders affectionately call it – had signalled the extreme north of our green and pleasant land. But as the rain sloshed in from the west, it seemed to sit precariously at the summit of a wholly different, uneasy country. A nation now divided by regional lockdowns, policed by millions of all-seeing eyes, peeking out over surgical face masks.

The Flugga was designed and built in 1854 by the engineering brothers Thomas and David Stevenson. It was originally used to protect ships during the Crimean War, and then in the twentieth century it became an optimistic maritime turning point at the confluence of the Atlantic Ocean and the North Sea. The lighthouse was automated in 1995, but until then it had been Britain's northernmost inhabited island. Lonely lighthouse keepers survived with little more than a radio – and their memories of home – for company.

The most famous of them, Lawrence Tulloch, had been a cricket devotee just like me. Growing up in the 1950s he used his pocket money to buy batteries for an old valve wireless, and then whiled away his blustery teenage summers listening to the clipped tones of commentators Brian Johnston and John Arlott on the BBC's *Test Match Special* radio programme. Between 1970 and 1979 he was not only Britain's northernmost lighthouse keeper, but he also proudly laid claim to the title of "Britain's northernmost cricket fan".

In August 2010 he appeared on *Test Match Special*, when England faced Pakistan at Lord's. On that hot summer's day, I remember being stopped in my tracks by his soft Scottish inflection, sprinkled with a hint of Shetlander-Scandi twang. For the first time in my life, I learned of a wind-ravaged squiggle at the top-right corner of the British map, the most socially distant household in the country.

Tulloch died in 2017, before I could get up there to try and meet him, but for a few solemn minutes I paused in the presence of his excited ghost.

Unlike the majority of the nation, he must have relished Radio 4's Test-match interruptions for the *Shipping Forecast*. I imagined him frantically dashing around his isolated seaside home, surrounded by curved bookshelves crammed with yellow *Wisden Almanacks*. As he prepared to get smashed by a storm rolling in from Bailey, Faeroes, Rockall or Hebrides, he'd be gripped by the closing moments of a Test match.

———

By the time I finally reached my bike, the sun was already teasing the south-west horizon and a hooley of my own was blowing in from the sea. I figured I had an hour before dusk and maybe 3 hours until pitch black, so I clipped into my pedals and began to roll tentatively south.

I'd managed just a couple of lazy "training rides" and felt hopelessly unprepared. My legs were heavy and awkward from the 3-hour hike and my shoulder blades hunched painfully toward handlebars already sopping with rain. Sitting on a hard Brooks saddle felt more like brutal torture than gentle exercise. During the American Civil War, Union guards used to suspend their Confederate prisoners over a blunt A-frame device called the Spanish Donkey and watch them writhe for days as the sinews in their groins split apart like slow-cooked brisket. As I fidgeted and squirmed from the perineum up, it felt as though my tough leather seat might do the same.

Way off behind me the Flugga's lamp had started its computerised nightly cycle, flashing every 20 seconds toward the Arctic and then back to Britain. But ahead of me, the Shetland Islands rose and fell in a low and long undulation, like the rippled backbone of a giant iguana. I had no idea where I was heading that night, so I just followed the lonely single-track road. South, south, wherever it may flow.

I'd been desperate for isolation and to be free of people. But all of a sudden, I was actually there, feeling hopelessly alone. I tried to focus on the road, but my mind drifted – to Alana, to Joe, to Sarah and Nick. I'd escaped, but they hadn't.

I'd naively envisaged cycling under a burnished Indian-summer sky, with Shetland ponies skipping beside me in breezy meadows. A few friendly locals would pop out to wish me bon voyage. The reality, however, was considerably and embarrassingly different.

The first house I passed was a derelict croft, more *Wicker Man* than *Last of the Summer Wine*. A dozen or so sheep couldn't even be bothered to muster a single "baa" between them. Then, in the first hamlet, Burrafirth, there was no sign of human life at all, apart from a laminated A4 sign on a fence post, advertising a two-bed house for rent at £275 a month. A cheap place to welcome in Armageddon, I thought to myself. Free up some extra cash for booze and strong opiates.

After half an hour of sweating and panting my way up a few gentle hills, I reached the small village of Haroldswick, where, at last, I spotted a postman holed up inside his bright-red van. "I'm trying to get south," I shouted from about 30 feet away, to which he responded with a look of wide-eyed horror. "I'm sorry, I can't hear you," I said, clip-clopping toward him in my cycling shoes while winding down an imaginary car window with my gloved right hand. As I edged closer, I saw that he was veiled behind a face mask, goggles and latex gloves. In almost full personal protective equipment (PPE), he resembled a brain surgeon moonlighting for the Royal Mail. "I wonder if you know the way south," I said again. At which point he shooed me away from his window, revved the engine a few times in neutral and then sped off into the distance.

My biggest fear had been realised within just the first couple of miles. And it had happened in one of Britain's most isolated corners. I'd wanted this journey to be about meeting new people and telling their stories, while selfishly rediscovering my own sense of intrigue and wonder in the world. I needed these people – to help me heal in a way I couldn't quite work out.

But they didn't need me. What if no one wanted to speak to me? I couldn't force anyone. Was I destined to spend the days alone on my bicycle, then my nights in a damp tent? I wondered if the whole silly idea was out of touch with the actual mood of the nation. I feared my actions might be brandished as egotistical, narcissistic and irresponsible. I cycled into a gloomy dusk while torturing myself with fictitious headlines. "Imbecile journalist revealed as Covid-19 superspreader." "Petrified postman speeds off remote Shetland cliff." "Cyclist abandons bike ride due to gangrenous saddle sores."

———

About 150 miles north of the Scottish mainland, spread across 100 or so islands, Shetland might be dismissed by some southerners as a backwater. The landscapes are mostly treeless and bleak. The wind can be unrelenting and the winters long and dark. Nevertheless, the island economy has been bolstered by the North Sea oil and gas industries since the early 1970s. Many Shetlanders like to remind visitors that oil paid for the best roads in Britain and I certainly couldn't argue to the contrary. At the very top of the country, I was cruising on asphalt smoother than in Mayfair.

With about an hour of daylight left, I took one final detour in the wrong direction. Not out of rank ineptitude, but because I found it impossible to ignore the Chernobyl-like structure on the next barren headland. I knew I shouldn't have cycled up there, but as soon as I saw a sign warning "RAF SAXA VORD: A PROHIBITED PLACE WITHIN THE MEANING OF THE OFFICIAL SECRETS ACT" in bold capitals, I gravitated toward it like a penny to a magnet.

From the outside, RAF Saxa Vord resembled little more than a disused arrangement of hangars and barbed-wire fences, encircling a bulbous dome about the height and width of a three-storey house. Boring in the flesh; more 1960s village hall than GCHQ. But the true story lay deep within, beyond what I could physically see.

The British government placed its first radar inside during the 1940s, at the height of the Second World War, then in 1957, during the escalation of the Cold War, used it to detect Soviet planes, boats and submarines that flirted with NATO's defences. It was closed again in

2006 when tensions thawed but reopened in 2018. In the preceding five years Russian military aircraft had approached British airspace on 69 different occasions.

Occasionally one of these interceptions makes national headlines. But with an average of more than a dozen stand-offs a year, most British newspapers can't be bothered to give them more than a paragraph or two. Much will depend on how jingoistic the country might be feeling at the time. Or if English clubs are faring poorly in the Champions League.

Nevertheless, the next time I see President Putin and the British prime minister shaking hands at Davos or the UN General Assembly, I'll study their body language a little closer. They may well have been scrambling jets somewhere off the coast of north Shetland just that very morning. In September 2020 alone – as Downing Street and the Duma battled to keep the coronavirus pandemic under control – Russian Tu-142 Bear anti-submarine fighter jets were intercepted by RAF Typhoons three times in just six days. The majority of us were none the wiser. Probably pissed out of our minds while the pubs were briefly open.

I knew I was pushing my luck being up there, and cameras were almost certainly trained on me. I especially didn't want to find myself in a humiliating Lycra espionage palaver. *Tinker Tailor Soldier Spy* meets Tour de France. So, I jumped back on my bike and finally turned southward. It felt good to be back on the road.

Until then, I'd walked and cycled 7 miles in the wrong direction and only seen one terrified human. The sun had disappeared into the Atlantic and by 6 p.m. twilight was fading fast. But for the time being, at least, the mizzle had eased and the wind was rounding perfectly to my back. The north of Unst is unofficially the windiest place in Britain. In 1992 a wind speed of 197 mph was recorded at Saxa Vord, a split second before the measuring equipment blew away into the North Atlantic. On the Fujita Scale of tornado intensity, that would be categorised as "severe", bordering on "devastating". As I pedalled forward for the first time proper, it was as though a supportive hand was pushing me on my way. It certainly helps to have the elements on your side.

I cycled as quickly as I could, desperate to bring my daily mileage to at least net zero. I rumbled across rusty cattle grids and zipped past the occasional roadside sheep. I'm not a fast cyclist by any wild stretch of the imagination, but thankfully the road was flat on the North Sea coast and I could trundle along at 10 mph quite comfortably.

———

My titanium bike was built for long-distance, heavily loaded touring, as opposed to the lightweight carbon-fibre varieties that are popular with middle-aged men in Lycra (MAMILs). If their bikes resemble fragile Lamborghinis, then mine looks and feels more like a trusty old Land Rover that can be slammed and bashed about. But durability comes at a cost; touring bikes are heavy.

On my first ascent into the barren centre of Unst, I calculated that I was hauling a 20 kg bicycle and panniers, 10 kg of clothing, 5 kg of overnight kit, 7 kg of technology, 5 kg of food and 3 kg of water. Add to that my 95 kg, and my two uninitiated legs were having to move 145 kg between them. That's the equivalent of two fully loaded kegs of beer.

But then the real weather hit. One moment I was bone dry, the next I was being lashed with sideways blasts of cold sleet. The polar wind was no longer behind me but whistling into my ear canals. It was about the same pressure you'd use to blast a particularly grubby garden patio in spring. "What the hell am I doing?" I growled to myself, as I kept pushing on, desperate to reach the bottom of the island by nightfall.

Soon, I was drenched and dishevelled, so took cover in a bus shelter, just to enjoy a brief respite from the hurricane that seemed to have burrowed deep into my brain. A torrent of water raged in front of me, transforming the road into a stream. Thick black clouds encircled the island on three sides, but to the south, a rainbow sprang from the Atlantic and curved a full 180 degrees into the North Sea.

After 5 minutes of noisy pitter-patter on the shelter's corrugated tin roof, I peeped out to see a grey-haired middle-aged man, dressed head to toe in glossy waterproofs, marching toward me in confident strides from the north. "Good day for it," he said, as he rummaged around in his rucksack.

"Ah, you know," I replied, trying to dream up a vaguely inspirational response. "Better than being stuck at home." He then produced a bottle of Lucozade and a flapjack and passed it from his bare palm to mine.

"This'll keep you going," he said, before making a prompt about-turn and marching back from where he came. For a brief warm moment, life felt wonderfully – pre-pandemic – normal. I watched him dissolve into the rain, longing for him to turn back and wave me in for tea and soup.

By the time I rolled into the small hamlet of Belmont at the bottom of Unst, the rain had finally cleared but darkness had set in. I half expected to find my MacBook and thermal long johns floating at the bottom of my panniers, but thankfully everything was dry. I had just enough starlight to pitch my tent on a half-moon beach about 300 feet from the small ferry port. I then strung a piece of farmers' baler twine between the top of the tent and my bike's handlebars, creating a rudimentary washing line for my sopping clothes.

The photo I posted on Instagram shortly afterward depicted a wild landscape devoid of human interference. But really, it was a clever camera angle. I was camping on a stretch of sand littered with detritus. Traffic cones, fishing nets and millions of shards of microplastic. Every half an hour the ferry would come and go, giving birth to a handful of commuter cars returning from the capital, Lerwick. Dozens of people returning to warm homes and happy families.

I don't know what I was expecting. Maybe a pub or a shop and a friendly face. Instead, there was just a lonesome ferry employee in a face mask, who gave me the occasional suspicious nod. Beyond that, the resounding highlight of that first night was sitting in a bright ferry waiting room out of the wind and drizzle while eating an entire eight-pack of fake KitKats and two portions of replica Super Noodles.

In a strange way, the stark, hospital-like light was a comfort, a reminder of home. But by 8.15 p.m. I was wrapped up in my thick down sleeping bag feeling damp and lonely, wondering if the few feeble sheets of lightweight nylon I'd pulled taut around me were capable of keeping me dry. Am I a "proper adventurer"? I wondered, while imagining Ranulph Fiennes in a bivouac halfway up Everest, wolfing down an Aldi Mars bar.

———

I managed 3 hours' sleep before desperately needing to spend a penny just before midnight. The night had turned a hard cold, and where my cheeks had been poking out from the top of my sleeping bag, the exposed flesh felt like chunks of defrosting ham. I wriggled toward the tent door like a caterpillar escaping a cocoon, but the commotion sent a shower of frozen condensation down the back of my warm neck.

With clouds of thick white steam streaming from my nostrils I was faced with an ultimatum – throw on damp clothes and traipse out on to the frozen beach or simply twist round on to my knees and piss into the grass under the awning of my tent. So, I did what any sensible man would do in that situation and opted to get back into bed as quickly as possible.

I woke up another 3 hours later – having managed my best night's rest in six months – accompanied by the acrid scent of frozen urine. Thankfully, the yellowy ice rink was just about hard enough to support my camping stove and the 300 g Italian moka pot I'd decided to bring with me. The choice had been either that or a 150 g deodorant and two extra pairs of pants. I could live with questionable personal hygiene, but the thought of starting the day without a decent cup of coffee was simply inconceivable.

The ferry between Unst and Yell only took 20 minutes, but it was just enough time to reorganise my already chaotic panniers and savour the warm sunrise. The surface of Bluemull Sound was as crisp as a freshly starched bed sheet. Lines of plastic oil drums bobbed across the water and beneath them, long gnarly ropes, bejewelled with clumps of dark blue mussels, plunged into a forest of olive-green kelp.

In a normal year, Scotland's mussel farmers sold 8,000 tonnes to British pubs and restaurants, often to be cooked in white wine, cream and shallots. When coronavirus struck in the middle of March 2020, that entire industry, like hundreds of others, vanished overnight.

Shetland's mussel farmers were particularly hard hit, because 6,500 tonnes are grown in their waters. Furlough wasn't much help either because most of them are self-employed, taking on extra seasonal labour when necessary. £10 million worth of stock was left hanging beneath the surface indefinitely.

As I rolled off the ferry on to Yell, I couldn't help but share a deep empathy with the men and women who had watched their livelihoods rot on their doorstep. I too felt abandoned by the government. I'd been left with no option but to survive on the couple of thousand pounds I had in savings and a tiny self-employed grant. Alana's limited company, meanwhile, had only been operating for a year and fell through the cracks with 3 million others. And Universal Credit, it turned out, was a total waste of time, too. We were entitled to £600 between us per month, but for every pound we earned, a pound was taken off that figure. We felt cheated by the system, while some of our friends on furlough were being paid £2,500 a month to sit at home in their pyjamas. As they spent money on new cars and home improvements, we were too embarrassed to admit we had nothing.

Unst had been covered in a thick coat of green grass, but Yell was much bleaker. Just a few flecks of purple heather interrupted a monochrome of singed brown. Rather than sitting on top of it, the road cut through the landscape. Shelves of peat had been sliced out and stacked in bricks to dry in the wind, like wedges of juicy chocolate cake. I stopped next to a pile for breakfast – a few hunks of damp bread, peanut butter and jam – as a school bus bumbled toward me. Alone on a windswept heath, I was desperate to exchange a wave or two with another human. Instead, a dozen or so little heads floated past without as much as a single raised gaze from an iPad.

As I pushed on south, I was learning that Shetlanders have an unwavering affection for scrap cars. Every croft was surrounded by half a dozen rusting heaps of junk and many of them had been amusingly upcycled. I passed a wiry silver lurcher curled up in a 1990s Ford Mondeo-cum-kennel. A 1980s Vauxhall Astra had been transformed into a garden shed, with hoes, rakes, pipes and chicken wire protruding from every jagged orifice. At one particularly windswept crossroads I stumbled across a bashed-up Citroën Berlingo that served as a waterproof local noticeboard. Tacked to the inside of the passenger window, an A4 poster read "Shetland stands wi Black Lives Matter".

Occasionally this commitment to wacky recycling would extend beyond automobiles. Someone was selling fresh duck eggs from an old microwave nailed to a fence post. I found an upright fridge-freezer that had been filled with old books and turned into a mini library. Every bus stop was jazzed up with a random collection of household furnishings, including pot plants, curtains and potpourri. Wires from old television sets, VCRs and stereos disappeared under grotty old carpets and then plugged into the soggy peat. Each colourful oddity provided me with a brief moment of joy on an otherwise yucky morning.

But perhaps what struck me the most was just how many crofts were surrounded by an acre or two of potatoes, kale and cabbage. Home-grown vegetables aren't just a trendy fad this far north but have been the key to a nutritious diet for hundreds of years. Cut off from the British mainland for sometimes weeks or months on end, a poor harvest could be the difference between full and empty bellies come Christmas.

Up until the mid-twentieth century, Shetlanders could only grow hardy root crops. The cold Arctic wind, filled with sea salt, was just too fierce and too corrosive to rear much else. But then, in the 1950s, the invention of polythene allowed Britain's northernmost gardeners to extend their growing season from just a few months to seven or eight.

In high summer, the sun barely sets in Shetland, providing enough twilight to read a book at midnight. Combine all this sunlight with the warming properties of plastic sheeting and strawberries, raspberries, figs and tomatoes will grow very comfortably on the same latitude as Siberia. During the Covid-hit summer of 2020, many islanders became so disillusioned with the weekly "travel corridor" fiasco preventing them from taking European summer holidays that they reinvested their refunds into yet more greenhouses and polythene. By September, Shetland was enjoying its biggest ever harvest of island-grown tomatoes.

———

It took me most of the morning to cycle the length of Yell, then another 20 minutes by ferry to reach Shetland's largest and most populous island: Mainland. It was greener and windier than the islands further north, with even more bedraggled sheep and cattle lowing on the treeless hilltops.

I passed peaty-brown lochs that resembled giant pans of beef stock simmering on a low heat. Very occasionally, a Land Rover or tractor would wait in a lay-by to let me pass. And as I'd roll on by, a ruddy-cheeked farmer would raise a lazy finger or two from the steering wheel before vrooming north in a cloud of hoary smoke.

After half an hour I spotted my first trio of Shetland ponies and felt compelled to pause and pet them. Standing no taller than 3 feet apiece, they chomped from a bale of soggy roadside haylage. As I nattered nonsense into their fluffy ears, their bushy blonde manes bounced up and down like the permed fringes of an 80s rock band.

I was now a day into my ride. And while the saddle certainly wasn't getting any softer, my pent-up tension was beginning to seep into the tarmac beneath me. The cycling wasn't too physically demanding either. I'd intentionally only set myself 30–40 miles a day in that first week, and I knew the distances would take care of themselves. All I had to do was keep pedalling.

It felt odd to have no other focus than simply moving forward. I knew this was one of the main reasons I'd wanted to do the journey: to become mindful and feel grounded in one place. But I was struggling to adapt to my new routine. My brain still expected the constant stimulation of emails, phone calls, radio, television and social media. With little more than livestock for company, I felt bereft of human contact. I'd craved being alone, but now I was on the verge of feeling lonely.

VIKING:
CONFUSED AND
BREATHLESS

Shetland was a world away from the turmoil unfolding further south, and I felt lucky to be there. The pandemic's summer lull had passed and infections were now on the rise again. 125.7 cases per 100,000 had been recorded in that first week of October, up from 63.8 per 100,000 just the week before. England was becoming ghettoised by a confusing tiered traffic-light system. Liverpool, Manchester, Leeds and Newcastle were waking up to strict local lockdowns while the House of Commons was still squabbling over what the new rules actually entailed.

As I cycled alongside gently trickling brooks and into seaweed-strewn bays, I imagined a not-too-distant otherworld of face masks and social distancing. It couldn't have been more different from my now rural isolation. I certainly needed a thick buff to keep the cold wind off my nose and mouth. But two-metre rule? More like two miles.

Across England, another nationwide closure of pubs, restaurants and non-essential retail outlets was looking more likely by the hour, but in Scotland, Nicola Sturgeon had already made her own contentious decision. Unbeknownst to me, at 6 p.m. that night, Scotland's pubs would be ordered to stop serving alcohol, closing most of them down indefinitely. I was now in a race against time because I was determined to savour at least one cold beer before last orders. But that was 6 hours away, and before I could even think of a fizzy lager, I had to survive an appointment at sea.

I met fisherman Richard Grains at Collafirth marina, an old Norwegian whaling station at the north-west corner of Mainland, as he and his small crew were offloading their morning's catch. "So, you're the mad cycling journalist that wanted to see me lobster pots?" he said, as I stepped cautiously aboard his slimy 30-foot boat. "I'll see if we can get us some mackerel, too. What are your sea legs like?"

Even in the calm of the marina, the men could clearly see that I was out of my depth, and I was. In 2016 I'd convinced the Clipper Round the World Yacht Race to let me sail across the Pacific and Atlantic in one of the fleet's media berths for *The Telegraph* and the BBC. Let's just say I covered myself in more vomit than glory. I'd barely stepped on a pedalo since.

But if I ever need to go to a fancy-dress party as "a fisherman", Richard's will be the blueprint I'll follow. Dressed in canary-yellow waterproof dungarees, steel-toecap wellington boots and elbow-high navy Marigolds, he clutched a dopey blue lobster in one hand, a snapping brown crab in the other and clamped a sharp-looking sailing knife under his armpit. The other men seemed more interested in their soggy roll-up cigarettes, but nevertheless, I felt safe in their fishy hands.

Just like the mussel industry, lockdown and widespread national unemployment saw Richard's business take a nosedive in spring 2020. With international freight on pause and nowhere for the produce to go, he was left with little option but to work through all the odd jobs his wife had been saving him for a rainy day. "We just stopped fishing altogether," he told me, as we began chugging out to the North Sea, flanked by a squadron of screeching seagulls. "March and April were really bad, but slowly things started opening up."

Two months is a long time for a fisherman to be stuck on dry land. It could be the profit margin between a good and bad year. Moreover, there is surely only so much DIY a man can be subjected to before the eddying open ocean becomes even more appealing.

Thankfully, trade began to recover in the summer, and even with a second national lockdown looming, he was confident of selling into overseas markets. His velvet crabs would be shipped to Spain, his whelks flown to South Korea and his lobsters couriered to France and elsewhere in mainland Europe. But after decades of stability, the incomes of a few far-flung families changed daily, depending on how countries were dealing with the pandemic on the other side of the world. One week a border was wide open, then the next it was slammed shut. Like most of us, Richard and his crew were left feeling helpless.

As we paused over a multicoloured blob of mackerel swirling about on the boat's echo sounder, I was in awe of Richard's quiet, reserved optimism, but also his shrewd business sense at an unprecedented time. Somewhere on the seabed beneath us he was hiding a cage filled with hundreds of lobsters for Christmas, when British pockets would hopefully feel a little deeper. "We collect them all year, then save them for December," he said. "They go up by about a tenner a kilo. But you can only get away with that up here. Anywhere else around the world and someone would steal them from right under your nose. We've had a tough time of it, but we've got to keep hoping that change is just around the corner."

A reel began to squeal and the water at the bow of the boat grew frothy with commotion. In the space of about 90 seconds, we landed two dozen silver-bellied mackerel, each about the size of a boy's forearm. They received a swift bonk between the eyes with a rounders bat and then twitched out their last few seconds in a bucket of dark blood. However harsh, sometimes we could all do with a reminder of how the food we eat ends up on our supermarket shelves.

With the sea building and our stomachs rumbling, we turned back to the marina to fire up a gas barbecue and eat Britain's freshest fish. In the buttery light of late afternoon, it was just about warm enough for a T-shirt and a woolly hat.

"You don't mind eating one-clawed male lobsters do you," asked Richard. "They get ripped off by angry females and I can't sell them to the restaurants. So, we'll have to do with these, I'm afraid." Shetland suddenly wasn't a backwater, but a British utopia, bursting with fresh food and open space.

———

By 4.30 p.m. I'd eaten a lobster and a half, a grilled mackerel, a dressed crab and about half a kilo of fresh squid fried in Shetland-grown garlic, lemongrass and red chillies. I could barely get up from the picnic bench, let alone lift my leg over the top tube of the bike. Seafood was practically oozing out of my ears and belly button. Nonetheless, I had 7 miles left to ride, so I waved a few burping goodbyes and began to climb out from the warm coast into Shetland's gusty interior.

I'd broken my first rule of long-distance cycling: never eat a big lunch, especially if you have miles to ride after it. The human body just isn't capable of digesting large quantities of food while simultaneously sending blood to its working legs. I felt light-headed, fatigued and queasy. I would cycle for 30 seconds, then rest for 30. When I could get away without turning the pedals at all, I'd simply let the wheels carry me along at 3 mph. It was just about quick enough to balance without falling off.

After about 10 minutes of following this pathetic routine, I stopped next to an old red phone box, its rounded, rusty lid catching the day's last winks of sun. It was one of the 21 that are still dotted all over Shetland but are now finally facing decommission. It's unsurprising, really. I took a couple of quick photos with my phone and noticed that I had 4G signal. I then lifted the old plastic receiver to hear a scratchy dial tone. I'm not even sure if it was capable of ingesting new 50p pieces.

I jumped back on my bike and cycled south for a few minutes up a softly pitched road. I then looked back at the bright-red phone box cast adrift in a sea of dusky green. I imagined broken-down crofters fighting their way toward it through shoulder-high snowdrifts. Or panicked fathers phoning ahead to the Lerwick infirmary as their wives endured contractions in the back of grubby 4x4s.

Strangely, though, its familiar contours made me think of home and the friends I'd left behind. I couldn't shake the feeling that I'd abandoned them when they probably needed me the most. Joe and his grieving family were rooted constantly in my thoughts. Had I let them down? Could I have done more to support them?

I worried about Sarah and her cancer treatment, the physical pain she must have been feeling and the fear of not knowing what horror was unfolding inside her. But in a strange way, I worried most about Nick, one of my oldest friends. Not only was he having to be a father, fiancé, driver and nurse, but also a communications and logistics manager, relaying constant updates to us all by phone and text while simultaneously fetching prescriptions and juggling cancelled hospital appointments due to Covid. It was inconceivable how he managed the stress. If the same thing had happened to Alana, I fear my own worries and insecurities would have selfishly overshadowed hers. Nick, meanwhile, was like the proverbial rock. Or at least that was how he seemed to me.

———

I followed a single-track lane for 4 miles, beside a saltwater loch that jutted inland from the Atlantic. It was filled with dozens of badminton court-sized salmon cages and hundreds of lines of mussels. About 100 feet above them I saw what I thought was a merlin – Britain's smallest bird of prey – jostling with what looked like an even smaller lapwing. They danced and lunged across the dark blue sky together, like wispy black floaters on tired morning eyes. And then, after a few frantic seconds, their silhouettes dissolved into the trembling sunset.

With rain and sleet forecast, I'd booked a room in the seaside village of Hillswick at the St Magnus Bay Hotel, a grand wooden house the colour of English mustard. I arrived at precisely 5.45 p.m., 15 minutes before Nicola Sturgeon would call last orders around Scotland. I tore off my helmet and barged through three pairs of heavy doors into a large but empty bar. There was only one beer left. The other dormant taps had upturned plastic glasses hanging on them like tombstones. Within 2 minutes I'd downed my first pint and the hotel's owner, Paul Bird, was halfway through pouring my second.

Paul and his wife, Andrea, wore the exhausted expressions of people who had already endured half a century in the hospitality industry. I know the appearance well; my parents display it, too. They looked as though they carried the weight of the world on their shoulders – fraught with worry, despite attempting to remain upbeat in the presence of their one and only thirsty patron. "I'm petrified by Covid," said Paul. "I've got a dodgy heart and asthma, but I'm now more afraid of what the future holds for us. I've got rates and insurance to pay."

For the first time in its history, Hillswick's only licensed premises would have to shut for winter, in a last ditch attempt to survive to see another year. A trickle of tourists would go thirsty, but much more significantly, the village would lose its one community hub. "I don't understand why I can't serve our guests a glass of wine with their dinner," said Andrea, as I sank one final pint. "Rules like these just make the trade even more untenable. We're on burnout, we can't afford the staff, so we're having to do it all ourselves."

Andrea and Paul felt as though the one-size-fits-all decisions passed down from Whitehall and Holyrood throughout the pandemic penalised Shetland unnecessarily. At the time, the islands had a Covid rate of just 4 cases per 100,000, whereas in Glasgow that number was well above 250. "Surely we can serve a few socially distant drinks outside?" argued Andrea. "Just to keep us – and the community – going." As an outsider passing through, I agreed wholeheartedly. Banding isolated Shetland in with Scotland's populous central belt felt like amputating a leg to save a toe.

The 30-room hotel had only me and one other guest, a birdwatcher called Jack Smith from Surrey, whom I met the next morning at breakfast. He was travelling with two twitcher friends, who'd rented a cottage around the corner from the local GP. Absurdly, the three of them were allowed to share the same hire car and dinner table, but it was against the law for their two households to rent a holiday home together.

They'd made a mad dash for Shetland following reports of a once-in-a-lifetime bird sighting. A singular 10 g Tennessee warbler had lost its way and then somehow ended up in a hedgerow on Yell. It was the first seen in Britain for a quarter of a century and Jack suspected it had been dumped in northern Britain by a storm.

I tried to remain enthusiastic about it while stuffing my mouth with toast and scrambled eggs. But if I'm honest, a quick Google search had revealed a rather boring-looking yellowy-green bird that resembled a radioactive sparrow. "I've been coming up here since 2010, and this is the best autumn's birdwatching I've ever experienced," said Jack. "This could be down to Covid, because it has drastically reduced the numbers of people travelling up here this year." Ironically, a terrible year for tourism had turned out to be a reasonable year to be a tourist. For the brave ones, at least.

With a belly full of bacon, beans and black pudding, I loaded my panniers on to the back of the bike and set off south-east into a dank sunrise. I'd dried out my wet clothes and tent and had charged every single battery I owned. Knowing that I was as prepared as I possibly could be, I sat a little prouder in the saddle.

When the sun poked out, Shetland glistened with muted beauty. The dark browns burned golden, and even the black Atlantic seemed to glow an optimistic, bluish mauve. But when the sun hid behind thick clouds, like it did on that drizzly morning, the landscape reminded me of the drab wasteland in Samuel Beckett's *Waiting for Godot*. There was a dreamlike dullness to the land, lacking detail – like a page of words without punctuation. I strived to remain upbeat, to concentrate on the glistening contours of the road rather than the transient and unpredictable whims of the healing sun.

I'm convinced that I suffer from seasonal affective disorder – it just hasn't been diagnosed. "You're a totally different person in summer," I'd heard a thousand times before falling into an autumnal funk, just after the cricket square has been put to bed. Perhaps it's a vitamin D deficiency, maybe it's a figment of my imagination, but deep in my subconscious, daytime, sunlight and warmth were life while night, the dark and cold symbolised death.

Looking back, my episodes of panic and anxiety almost always occurred in winter. Summer was too busy, too fun. But when the seasons drifted, so did I. With the days now shortening by a few minutes, exercise and forward motion were my only allies. For as long as I had a road to travel on and food for fuel, my mind and lungs were busy. When a squall roared in from the Atlantic and soaked me to the skin, I looked down at the asphalt I controlled, rather than up at the swirling clouds I didn't.

I followed the A970, the main road running down the spine of the island. The climbs were long and punishing and the road was grey and greasy. Occasionally a trailer-load of sheep would rumble past my right shoulder, leaving a trail of oily lanolin on the wind. I passed a couple of teenage boys doing doughnuts on quad bikes in a muddy field. I stopped to brew up a cup of coffee on a fence post and watched a khakied man – even more bonkers than me – sprint past with a heavy rucksack on some sort of sadistic military exercise.

By lunchtime I'd cycled 33 miles and had nearly reached Lerwick. From the heath rising above the small village of Tingwall, I could see a golf course squeezed into a vast gorge of peat. If I closed one eye, I could fit all 18 holes and a dozen tiny golfers between my thumb and index finger. To the east, in the North Sea's shallows, an oil rig the width of a city block and the height of a skyscraper was being dismantled. Gulls circled its rusty chimneys as angle grinders spewed out orange sparks like Roman candles.

Lerwick only has a population of 7,000, but as I entered through blinking traffic lights and past bawling toddlers, it felt like a heaving metropolis. People in face masks rushed through the wet streets, while dozens more formed socially distant queues outside almost every café, shop and restaurant.

Shetland recorded its first two coronavirus cases on 9 March 2020, four days after a local couple returned home from a long weekend in Naples, Italy. Attempts were made to contain the virus, but within five days the number of cases had risen to 15. At the time, Shetland had the highest number of Covid-19 patients in Scotland, relative to its population. Anxiety in Lerwick, in particular, grew. The islanders didn't have a single intensive care bed between them, and anyone who fell seriously ill would need to be sent via medevac to Aberdeen.

Unlike the rest of Britain, Shetland locked down early and quickly. Major annual events and ferries were cancelled. And as 250,000 people packed into the Cheltenham Festival, some 700 miles away to the south-west, the decision was made to close all of Shetland's schools. For several months, the only thing allowed in and out of Lerwick was food and oil.

The town's ferry terminal wouldn't fully reopen until 15 July. But even after it did, the summer was slow. Occupancy on NorthLink's North Sea voyages was halved from 670 to 335 due to 1 m social distancing measures. Over 100 cruise ships had also planned to pass through – containing 90,000 tourists – but for the first time since Shetland's tourism industry really kicked off in the 1980s, 2020 went by entirely liner-free.

For one unprecedented year, Shetlanders got their islands back. The Shetland Community Bike Project – a bicycle repair shop and charity in Lerwick – had already done 300 repairs by October, in contrast to the 200 it did in all of 2019. Electronic bike counters dotted around the islands recorded a 70 per cent rise in cyclists, and with the public pools closed, the wild swimming group – the Shetland Sea Swimmer Selkies – welcomed more than 50 new members.

They'd been keen to take me for a swim, but I was far too chicken to accept. Instead, I met one of their devotees, Emma Williamson, for coffee.

Her Instagram feed was a shrine to starfish, jellyfish and Shetlanders in wetsuits and brightly coloured swimming caps. But in the flesh, she was even more besotted by the sea than I'd expected. "It has become a cold-water adventure," she told me, her rosy cheeks dimpling behind her coffee cup. "I have met so many new people and galvanised existing friendships. Lockdown inspired so many people to take the plunge. We are all about nature and engulfing yourself in it. We've got nine-year-olds and over seventies."

When she wasn't swimming, Emma worked on the frontline of Shetland's health service. In normal times she'd be responsible for "packaging people up" with broken bones and arranging their flights to Aberdeen. Despite dealing with the unexpected, her life and shift pattern followed a predictable rhythm. In the very early days of the pandemic, however, everything changed.

"Logistically, it was new to everyone. If someone had meningitis, for example, we had a set way of dealing with that, but this was totally new. All we could do was our best. We didn't have enough scrubs for everybody, so people were making them out of old duvets. It was hilarious. We were absolutely spoiled. We were living on food and takeaways dropped off by locals." Without the wider community rallying around them, Emma conceded that she might not have made it through. "The NHS is a big wheel of business that's constantly turning, but at the coalface you've got folk who get up every morning and just want to do their job."

———

I liked Lerwick a lot, it was relaxed and quiet, with nodding yachts and calm waters. But I could never have lived there. As I sat and ate fish and chips on a damp wall in the harbour, I don't think a single person managed to walk from one side of town to the other without having to stop and pass idle chit-chat with someone they knew. I'm sure a lot of people would love that, but personally I enjoy being a grumpy git too much. If I lived there, I'd quickly grow agoraphobic, for fear of having to endure awkward small talk in the bread aisle at Tesco. Wearing a mask in places where I could possibly bump into someone I half knew was, perhaps, the one thing I actually enjoyed about coronavirus.

After a drizzly hour, I caught the ferry to Bressay, the chubby little island sandwiched between Lerwick and the North Sea. I spent all 7 minutes of the journey faffing around in my panniers, trying to scrape enough money together to pay the £5.90 fare. When the ferry made landfall, I had either £4.34 in assorted sticky change or a crumpled £20 note I'd been hiding under the sole of one of my old trainers. "Nae bother," said the teenage conductor, as I wheeled down the ramp on to the island. "You can just pay me tomorrow."

It was enough to give me a warm glow inside. I also now had a moral and economic obligation to break the slightly cheesy £20. So, I bought a four-pack of beers in the island's little shop and cracked one open in the company of a chestnut-brown Shetland pony. It was smaller than my bike but had big blue eyes the size of billiard balls.

I'd been invited to stay on the island by a man called Jonathan Wills, a former *Telegraph* and *Times* journalist who had made his name in the 1970s and 80s covering oil spills, sea rescues and helicopter crashes. He owned a bothy somewhere on Bressay's east coast and had told a friend of a friend that I could sleep in it for the night. There were, however, four minor hurdles that had quickly presented themselves: my phone was dead, I had no idea where he lived, it was getting dark and the drizzle was rapidly turning into a downpour.

A boy outside the shop knew of him but couldn't remember where he lived. I then asked a couple of dusty men in a builders' van, but they looked at me with blank expressions as though I was yodelling at them in Esperanto. And then a bloke walking his dog in a surgical face mask and latex gloves not only avoided making eye contact with me but was well out of earshot by the time I could even open my mouth.

After about 15 minutes of peering into the dark windows of gloomy bungalows, I was finally met by a jolly woman in a big, knitted cardigan, who pointed me in the right direction, albeit while giving the distinct impression that she was spinning the entire yarn off the cuff.

"So, you go down the big hill."

"OK."

"Then you go up the... no wait, you go round the small hill."

"Right."

"Then turn right at the big loch. Or is it left?"

"OK."

"Then stop at the smaller loch."

"Right."

"And then you continue along a very long and stony path for about a mile. Or maybe a mile and a half... You can't miss it."

I was perplexed. So, I just cycled in the last direction she'd waved her hand, and as soon as I came to a pathway looking vaguely long and stony, rode all the way down it until I could see a higgledy-piggledy whitewashed croft about a quarter of a mile away. It was, irrefutably, one of the most enchanting hideaways I had ever set my eyes upon.

The dying yellow sun washed over the North Sea, but the bothy was already shadowed by dusk. It had an oval loch – about twice the size of a cricket pitch – on its doorstep and a waist-high drystone wall protecting a vegetable patch from a dozen or so sheep. White smoke curled into the cold sky from a thin aluminium chimney, but a warm orange light flickered behind two skylights cut into its A-frame roof. It was the sort of fairy-tale setting where a hobbit might live.

I left my bike at a locked gate, jumped a stile and walked the last few hundred feet down a gentle slope of squelching mud. I found Jonathan rooting around in a shed filled with axes, sledgehammers, mallets, ladders and old mattresses. He had emulsion splashed across his boots and glasses, sawdust in his grey beard and dark peat under his fingernails.

"Welcome to the Gorie bothy," he said, as we both reached out to share a handshake, before recoiling sharply just before our palms touched. "This place is over 200 years old. We get lots of writers staying here who need to zone out and go offline. Maybe even you, one day."

For somewhere so remote, there was a surprising amount of activity. His wife, two adult sons, a daughter-in-law and a toddler grandson were filthy and exhausted from a hard day's graft. They'd been painting, digging, washing and cleaning in preparation for paying guests checking in the next day. "Make yourself at home," said Jonathan. "But don't touch anything. We've had to put the whole place through a deep 'Covid clean' – it's an absolute pain. So, you'll have to sleep in the bunkhouse. But please do have a snoop around."

Jonathan took over the tenancy in 2008 and set out restoring its crumbling walls and leaky felt roof. Slowly he transformed it into an off-grid bolthole, much more like an Arctic refuge than a self-catering cottage. In the kitchen there was a gas camping stove and an FM radio, a cupboard filled with half-drunk bottles of whisky, and a couple of USB chargers attached to a wire that ran outside, to a wind turbine spinning 30 feet above the potato patch.

One apex of the kitchen had been cordoned off to make a small toilet–shower and to the back of the bothy there was a cosy lounge with a small desk, a chair and a sofa. A pair of tin teapots warmed atop an old iron stove. A pile of woollen blankets spilled over a basket of firewood. A bookshelf was rammed with Dawkins, Darwin, Steinbeck, Burns and Bryson.

"We've always been particularly popular with birdwatchers and authors," said Jonathan, as a red-breasted robin skipped along the garden fence and then jumped off to join the sheep. "But these days, pretty much everyone is craving this sort of place. To escape humanity." He supported a stringent lockdown back in spring 2020 but feared that further lockdowns would do more harm than good. "It was the right thing to do at the time. We have an elderly population that we need to protect. The Scottish government didn't get everything right, but they told us what they were doing and there was none of the waffle you had to endure down south."

———

The "bunkhouse" where I was sleeping was really just a small MDF mezzanine constructed in the top third of a Victorian lean-to greenhouse. But it looked a lot drier than my tent and I had just enough light to climb up to the narrow platform and unpack my sleeping bag and roll mat. By the time I'd climbed back down, Jonathan's family had left for their house on the other side of the island, and he was about to do the same. "We would invite you for dinner," he said. "But we're not allowed a group of more than six. We also don't know where you've been. You see that paving stone," he added, pointing at my feet. "The last owner tried to lift that up one day and keeled over, right there on the ground where you're standing. But don't worry, there aren't any ghosts." And with that, he turned and wandered up the muddy hill, climbed over the stile and disappeared into the fug of dusk. All of a sudden, I was alone again, with the word "ghost" ringing in the silence. For the next half an hour the empty bothy seemed to creak and groan in a way it hadn't before.

As my phone charged on the breeze, I drank the rest of my beers and watched rabbits hop between the sheep. At least I had the FM radio for company, and I twisted through its fizzy airwaves, from Broadcasting House to Aberdeen, via Norway and a French trawler. But then the robin returned to the wall and whistled a little tune while Venus sizzled bright white in the dark purple sky.

By pitch black, my mobile phone was glowing, so I hiked out into the waterlogged field, feeling half-cut and desperate for news from the outside world. At first, I was met with an empty screen, but then a tiny sliver of reception popped up and a dozen missed calls and notifications flew in. I've been trying to call you all day, read a message from Alana. Where are you? Are you somewhere we can talk? It's Sarah. Sarah's died.

It was as though I'd been injected with a strong muscle relaxant. My shoulders, neck and arms fell into my diaphragm. Just a few seconds before, the inside of my mouth had been lubricated with bittersweet beer, but as I read the message, over and over, my sandpaper tongue seemed to triple in size and weight.

I stabbed so hard at the phone's screen that the undersides of my fingernails turned from blush pink to creamy white. I typed words. Then deleted them. Typed some more. Then deleted those, too. I didn't want to call Alana. I didn't want to call Nick. I wanted to walk back to the bothy and conveniently forget the past few minutes. I hoped I'd wake up in its dark kitchen, with *The World Tonight* crackling through the FM radio, and realise it was all a menacing dream. But it wasn't. And I couldn't.

I walked south, to the summit of a swirling hilltop, spellbound by my phone's reception bar. The display would jump from one bar to three, then disappear entirely. Every time I tried to make a call, all I heard was wind. I must have spent half an hour zigzagging up and down grassy sheep paths, my trousers, trainers and socks becoming sopping wet, before I returned to the reliable one bar of the hillside and mustered a few sentences to Nick.

> Alright mate. Hard to know what to say but know that we all love you like a brother. We will be here for you, always – and the kids too. We will love and support you and them and will be there for you through this. You would do the same for any of us. I'm sure the boys are rallying around you back home, but I'm only a plane away and will be back in a heartbeat if you need me. Xxxxxx

As soon as I sent the message, I read it back. It was pathetic. Eighty-one words of the same trite nonsense you'd find in a cheap greetings card. Were these the only feeble sentences I could muster? Back in the dark greenhouse, I slumped against my sleeping bag and yanked at tufts of hair on the crown of my head, ashamed.

I felt wired, haunted by the taps, knocks and creaks of the bothy. I was torn by how to proceed. If I threw in the towel and flew home after less than 100 miles I'd look like an idiot, and by selling just one half-baked article I'd barely break even, let alone make enough money to pay the mortgage for the winter.

But was going home what I was *meant* to do? Was it selfish of me to even consider continuing on this jolly while my friend planned the funeral of his future wife? Then again, if I did go home, what could I actually do? He had dozens of friends rallying around him already and we were banned from entering each other's homes. I couldn't even give him a hug. Legally, at least.

By the time dawn broke over the North Sea, I'd sat on the edge of every chair and pondered the horizon from every window. Confused and breathless, I'd not slept a wink.

FAIR ISLE:
THE CALL OF HOME

I didn't dare face up to the enormity of what had just happened. Not there, not alone. All I could do was leave and ride, in the vain hope that things would become clearer somehow, with distractions.

I paid the ferry man the £5.90 I owed him and was back in Lerwick by 8 a.m. It was a Sunday morning, and the streets were almost, but not entirely, empty. A lion-brown Alsatian dragged a teenage girl over the concrete, stopping to spray its fluorescent piss up the side of every bin. A bobble-hatted woman on a bench fed the seagulls chunks of stale bread big enough to choke an ostrich. Five middle-aged men in gaudy trainers and skin-tight leggings wheezed past me, their heels fluttering up and down along the pavement.

I cycled out of town and headed into the pebble-dash suburbs, then climbed into a drizzly hinterland of treeless peat moors and 10-acre lochs. Over my left shoulder, the North Sea sploshed into the ragged coastline, but to the south-east, a warm autumn sun peeked out from the horizon.

By the time I reached Sumburgh Head Lighthouse at the bottom of Shetland – 137 miles from Muckle Flugga and after three days in the saddle – it looked as though the entire northern hemisphere was bathed in a crisp golden light. From the top of the chalky headland, I could see across 24 miles of frothy Atlantic, all the way to Fair Isle, the southernmost of the Shetland Islands. I'd wanted to visit the 3-square-mile island on my journey south, but – like many things – Covid put a stop to that. Ferry and plane services had been reserved exclusively for the island's residents, and tourists were all but barred from visiting.

The closest I could get to making landfall was from the starboard smoking area of the Shetland–Orkney ferry that evening. As we rumbled southward, across the 100 miles of Atlantic separating Britain's two northernmost archipelagos, a few red and yellow lights flickered beneath a black sky busy with blinking stars.

I couldn't blame Fair Isle's 60 residents for wanting to stay safely cut off from the pandemic. I was jealous of their peaceful isolation, and most of the planet was, too. In the first half of 2020, estate agents in Sweden, Japan and French Polynesia reported a huge surge in interest for far-flung islands. In the Caribbean alone, enquiries quadrupled in the six weeks between mid-March and the end of April. Interest hadn't been as high since the days following the New York terrorist attacks on 11 September 2001.

If I lived on Fair Isle, I'd have ratcheted up the drawbridge and loaded a shotgun. Not only to keep out the sniffly birders and their grubby hands, but also the Russian oligarchs and Silicon Valley types with their big chequebooks and Learjets.

At times in 2020 it was impossible to flick through a British newspaper and not stumble across a feature entitled "How to buy a private island". Dozens of boltholes were bought and sold across Britain, and in July 2020 a particularly flush European buyer parted with £4.5 million for the 157-acre Horse Island off the west coast of Ireland. The anonymous person didn't even visit in the flesh but made the bid after viewing a short video on YouTube.

The travel supplements, too, ran page after page of "when this is all over" content, transporting armchair travellers to Svalbard, St Helena and Pitcairn. I should know, I wrote a handful of them myself. On the home front, Mull, Harris, Skye and Jura received more column inches than ever before. Only time will tell if this did more harm than good.

Locked in to our homes, we developed a perverse infatuation with remoteness. But at what cost? With our freedom of movement in a constant state of flux and Britons feeling wary of venturing too far, the most isolated – and often most fragile – corners of our nation became trendy like never before.

———

I rolled on to the tarmac at Kirkwall's ferry pier just before midnight and joined a motorcade of cars, vans and lorries through a channel of shipping containers and forklifts. An Arctic wind gusted in from the north-east, and as I cycled under a string of tangerine streetlights toward a grey town, the odour of rotting seaweed wafted in from a beach I could hear but couldn't quite see.

After a couple of miles, I arrived at a pretty little harbour, where two dozen or so fishing boats bobbed up and down in the water. Each boat's rigging whistled a slightly different pitch, and when I looked into the black around their hulls, I could see shoals of tiny silver fish flashing to and fro along their barnacled flanks.

My toes resembled frozen plums, my eyes felt raw and gristly. All I wanted to do was get into a bed – any bed – as quickly as possible. But when I arrived at the small harbourside guest house where I'd booked a room, instead of being welcomed with a warm cup of cocoa and the scent of potpourri, I was met with the waft of fortified wine and a smokescreen of Lambert & Butler.

Two men in their late twenties stood either side of the hotel entrance. They were so drunk it was a miracle they were still upright and not floundering around on the pavement. One of them had a long-dead cigarette in his right hand and a half-drunk bottle of Buckfast in his left. A trail of ash and purple liquid ran between the collar of his white T-shirt and the ankles of his grey tracksuit bottoms.

The other man was wearing a decades-old Kilmarnock FC shirt, Scotland football shorts and a leather tool belt with a single chisel in it.

He had a Jackson Pollock-esque blend of red, blue, white and green paint dried up his forearms and took deep drags on a nicotine vape. Neither man was wearing shoes.

"Alright lads, do you mind if I…" I said boldly, while wheeling my bike toward them.

"You English?"

"I'm afraid so. Is that allowed?"

"Do you want to have a drink with us?" At which point he scratched the end of his nose and gave me a suggestive, drunken wink.

There are few things in life more challenging than being in the presence of inebriated people when you yourself are sober. Especially when all you want to do is go to bed, and all they want to do is play repetitive dance music via their smartphones.

If I was ten years younger, I would have cracked open a can of Tennent's Super in a heartbeat. I just didn't have the energy to engage in any human contact whatsoever, let alone join them in their twin room at 1 a.m. on a Monday morning for a spliff and a couple of lines of novocaine.

"I'm actually feeling pretty rough, lads," I said. "Feels like I'm coming down with something and I could really do with a sleep, but thanks for the offer. Next time." They grinned at one another, then let my heavily loaded bike and me barge through to the small reception where the owner was waiting. She raised her eyebrows from behind a Perspex screen, handed me a room key, dipped her face mask and silently mouthed the word "sorry".

Thinking I was home and dry, I pushed my bike into a courtyard behind the kitchen and started unhitching the panniers. But then, the men reappeared through the front door in a plume of thick cigarette smoke and nicotine vapour. Think *Stars in Their Eyes* does the (paralytic) Village People.

"Nice bike, man."

"Aye, I bet that's worth a fair whack?"

"It looks a lot more expensive than it actually is."

"Do you not chain it up at night?"

"No. It has a special lock in the wheels." A lie. "And a GPS tracking device in the frame." Totally made up.

"What's that?"

"They're the brakes."

"How far are ye going?"

"Aberdeen."

I wasn't. But it was enough to pacify their inquisition for a few seconds as they began typing "Or-k-ney to Ab-er-deen dis-tan-ce" into Google Maps with their hash-stained fingers. I then did something I'm even less proud of, but it worked perfectly. I began coughing into my fist and sprayed a little of my very own vapour over the bike's saddle and handlebars. At which point the men took a few steps back, wished me goodnight and disappeared up a creaky staircase. "Proper weird bloke, aye," I heard one of them say as they stomped over the landing above.

A minute or two later I followed their smoky trail and tiptoed past a room where a Bluetooth speaker blared out the DJ Ötzi song "Hey Baby" (Uhh Ahh). I climbed another flight of stairs, then descended down one more. I zigzagged back along three corridors, pushed through half a dozen fire doors, then finally reached my own cosy room. It was directly below theirs.

The three guests in a 20-room guest house had been arranged one on top of another. Worse still, the floorboards creaked so much it sounded like a pair of elephants were enjoying a Zumba class 5 feet above me. Not wanting to waste a second, I threw my bags on the bed and made a rapid dash back down to the ground floor, where the owner was turning off the reception lights.

"Please, I beg you," I whispered. "Please can I have another room? I desperately need to sleep, and those guys are right above me. Please." She looked me up and down, took pity on me and then handed me a new key. In normal times I would have considered grabbing her by the waist and swinging her around. But all I could do was dip my face mask and silently mouth the words "thank you".

The next morning, I was showered, packed up and cycling around Kirkwall's flagstone streets by 8 a.m. A socially distant queue snaked around the exterior walls of Lidl. A gaggle of men in high-vis jackets sniggered over the screen of a mobile phone. Teenagers huddled outside a newsagent, their double Windsor ties poking out from the collars of their thick winter coats. Life looked quiet but sombre. Almost… normal.

Orkney confirmed its first case of coronavirus on 30 March 2020, a month after mainland Scotland, and for the majority of the first wave the infection rate hovered at just 4.5 cases per 100,000 people. In a population of 22,000 that represented less than one new case a week, one of the lowest infection rates in Britain.

But that's not to suggest that many Orcadians escaped the pandemic without experiencing the same crippling paranoia felt by a lot of Britons. Like Shetland, Orkney's biggest island, Mainland, is surrounded by 70 smaller islands, 20 of which are inhabited. Pockets of cut-off crofters had lived on them for hundreds of years, but when the pandemic struck, their isolation proved to be both a blessing and a curse. Most of the islands are at least a boat ride and a flight from the nearest intensive care unit in Aberdeen. Naturally, some residents grew wary of people travelling to and from their remote island homes.

This issue had been mostly hypothetical in the early stages of the pandemic but became a reality in the middle of August 2020 when a cluster of six cases was linked to a single fishing boat that arrived in Kirkwall from Peterhead. Contact tracers attempted to stop the outbreak in its tracks, but the head of NHS Orkney, Michael Dickson, warned that people with symptoms may have travelled to their islands, potentially putting other residents at risk. At her daily briefing a couple of days later, Nicola Sturgeon urged islanders to follow Scotland's quarantine rules as closely as those on the mainland.

Just like every other region of Britain, Orkney endured its fair share of scares and false dawns but by mid-October there had been only 26 positive cases. Many people put this down to the quiet tourist season. Just 50,000 visitors would visit by the end of 2020, in contrast to the 300,000 in 2019. Infections may have been minimised, but a shortfall of 250,000 visitors left a £67 million deficit in the islands' annual economy.

In order to survive, Orkney's food, fashion and craft brands centralised under the singular moniker www.orkney.com, and many local businesses sold their cheese, knitwear and jewellery online for the first time. According to the Royal Mail, during the first wave of the pandemic Kirkwall's sorting office was the third busiest in Britain, after Shetland and central London. The hospitality industry, meanwhile, wasn't quite so lucky. Heavily dependent upon seasonal footfall, a handful of pubs, restaurants and cafés put trading on pause while several businesses boarded up their windows entirely. Others, however, found innovative and pandemic-proof ways of staying afloat.

———

I cycled along to the Orkney Distillery, on the western edge of Kirkwall. The biting wind howled along its glass frontage, but inside the air was warm and thick, tinted with the scent of freshly ground coffee. Behind the bar, certificates and awards sat alongside litre bottles of clear spirit, labelled with trendy sans-serif fonts. "You're either an alcoholic or the journalist I'm looking for," said a ginger-haired man in a big blue Puffa jacket. "It's probably a bit too early for a proper drink, but how do you take your coffee?"

Before coronavirus, managing director and local entrepreneur Stephen Kemp had worked hard to turn his gin distillery into a not-to-be-missed stop-off on the Orkney tourist trail. Every afternoon in summer a procession of tourists would turn up from Kirkwall's cruise terminal with crisp £20 notes burning holes in their pockets. "We couldn't put the bottles on the shelves quickly enough," said Stephen. "But then Covid came along, and… well…"

Facing a summer without tourists, Stephen and his team quickly transferred their efforts from making 40 per cent spirit to 80 per cent hand sanitiser. "We only furloughed one person," he told me. "We ended up producing about 50,000 litres in a really short time and gave most of it to the RNLI. They work in a confined environment, and one positive case could put a whole lifeboat out of action."

Stephen was clearly an industrious and energetic chap. Besides the distillery, he owned a building firm and a handful of smaller sidelines. He was infectiously enthusiastic about creating new opportunities, not only for himself, but also the wider community. And despite the setbacks of the pandemic, he seemed excited by the prospect of being shaped by the "new normal" rather than persevering with the stagnant practices of old.

"After the first wave, we had to come up with a way of attracting business back," he told me, while proudly showing off the distillery's new Covid-inspired outside seating area, complete with patio heaters, dog bowls and faux grass. "I wanted to build a dog- and family-friendly garden. It's just not a normal thing for Orcadians to sit outside into autumn and winter. Culturally, we're more prone to crowding together in cosy pubs, but obviously that's not great at the moment."

There were many reasons why Britain had one of the highest coronavirus mortality rates in the world. The first lockdown was probably called too late and, unlike Australia and New Zealand, our borders remained wide open for the majority. But no doubt our often-dreary climate played its part, too. Many Orcadians, like most Britons, hunker down for the long winter and cosy-up until spring. In the most part, we are a stubborn nation of telly-watchers and sofa-sitters. Did we all stay out of each other's homes when we were told to? I doubt it very much.

———

As I cycled south-west out of Kirkwall toward Scapa Beach, rain lashed into my numbed cheeks and a mile-long sandstorm raged between land and sea. Wind turbines swirled on distant hilltops and a few cars teetered past, their fog lights on and wipers flapping. All I wanted to do was knock on someone's door and plead for a cup of tea, a towel and a cuddle. "I'm cycling the length of Britain. During the pandemic. By accident!" I'd tell them, like the famous scene from the 1987 film *Withnail and I*.

But, of course, that was wishful thinking. I was much more like a leper on a bike, to be admired at a safe distance. I shared a tip of the head with a farmer in a beanie, then exchanged a pursed-lipped nod with a couple and their soggy poodle.

Shetland had provided a clear A to B from north to south, but Orkney's Mainland was more like a big pancake surrounded by dozens of satellite splodges of batter. With no discernible point-to-point route, I continued along Mainland's southern coastline and pushed on into a thumping squall. I remembered the name Scapa Flow from one of the few GCSE history lessons I wasn't thrown out of. It had an onomatopoeic, exotic quality that demanded to be spoken and comes from the Old Norse *Skalpaflói*, which means "bay of the long isthmus".

The British Admiralty first took an interest in this 120-square-mile expanse of sheltered water during the Napoleonic Wars in the early 1800s, and then used it as a deep-water anchorage ahead of crossings to Baltic ports on the other side of the North Sea. Pub-quizzers will remember that Scapa Flow is the largest natural harbour in Europe, while many Britons will be familiar with its strategic importance during the First World War.

Protected on each side by low-lying grassy islands, it was first used as a training facility before going on to become the headquarters of the British Grand Fleet. While the rest of the navy was stationed in the English Channel, Whitehall could use it as a safe haven from which to launch patrols of the North Sea. In fact, it proved to be so tactically imposing that by 1916 German warships rarely ventured far from their own bases at Wilhelmshaven and Kiel on the Jutland peninsula.

At the end of the war, 74 German warships and U-boats were scuttled to Scapa Flow's sandy bed, and while some were later salvaged, dozens of wrecks still loom beneath the surface. Scuba divers from all over the world visit Orkney to swim within their mangled steel hulls.

I rode west into the wind through a channel of drystone walls separating me from a never-ending expanse of green fields rambling away on both sides. The corrugated roofs of barns rattled. Shivering lambs sheltered on the leeward sides of their doting mothers. Arctic terns and guillemots were tossed and lobbed with the gusts, like black and white football socks spinning around in a tumble drier.

Shetland's roads had risen and fallen, but Orkney's were mostly flat and skirted the rounded corners of the islands' dumpy coastlines. Occasionally I'd stop to peruse a lichen-covered standing stone, its jagged edges bathed in lemony light. Sometimes I'd pause to coo at a string of Shetland ponies, just to watch their big eyes blink. I brewed a pot of coffee with a herd of Highland cows. Spaghetti-like hay spilled from their mouths and formed a pile of second helpings at their fuzzy hooves. When the wind intermittently dropped, my ears rang, expecting sound. But all I could hear were their grinding jaws. That, and the occasional wet bovine fart.

Silence doesn't exist. There are always sounds. At the summits of the calmest mountains, there will always be a faint crack of ice. In the centres of the grandest, most motionless forests, you'll forever hear the distant snap of a branch. In Britain – home to 67 million noisy people – silence is just a word. But when the rain stopped and the wind calmed, the pulse in my temple drummed louder than the whole of the world combined.

However much I tried to subdue it, the call of home grew louder. Every time I stopped pedalling, I could hear the commotion of Sarah's death, the sound of muffled sobs and familiar voices cracking with emotion. I wanted to sob, to purge myself of something raw. But I couldn't. Just like when Joe, Dave, Joshua and Dennis died, the trauma was pouring inward, not out.

———

By 4 p.m. the sky had cleared, but the light was starting to fade. Muddy ponds glinted in the lowest fields, and Orkney's once manic wind turbines finally ground still. My toes squelched in their soggy socks and a pool of water, just about big enough to sustain the life of a very miserable goldfish, weighed heavy in the hood of my cagoule. As I headed north-west, the sun arched south-east behind me; its dying embers warmed my weary shoulders.

I'd arranged to meet a local journalist, Dave Flanagan, on the west coast of Mainland, where I planned to camp that night. And with the wind forecast to turn from a westerly to a north-easterly in the early hours, the Bay of Skaill, right next to the Atlantic, seemed perfect. There was a public toilet that reeked of urinal bricks, a patch of flattish sand dune to pitch my tent and a signpost that could double as a clothes horse. In the grand scheme of things, I'd found nirvana.

Like elsewhere in Scotland, most of Orkney's beaches and heather moors are free game to so-called "wild campers", providing they follow the "leave no trace" maxim. Unlike in the rest of the UK, Scotland's Land Reform Act of 2003 gives citizens the right to roam. A similar concept, *Allemansrätten* (everyman's right), encourages Scandinavians to take shared ownership of their great outdoors, too. It boils down to a simple concept: being outside is good for the soul.

I will, however, stubbornly continue to use inverted commas every time I refer to "wild camping", because the terminology annoys me. It implies that camping in a beautiful place is a treat that the great unwashed should forever be grateful for. The phrase perpetuates the notion that camping in a campsite, guide rope to guide rope, alongside hundreds of other paying customers, is somehow "normal camping", while simply yearning to spend a night under canvas in the wild is somehow quirky.

Whisper it quietly, but humans have been living and sleeping outdoors for a darn sight longer than they've been paying mortgages. It's the same with "wild swimming". What's next? Wild walking? Wild cycling?

Dave arrived with a bag of firewood and a box of beers just as I was hammering my last tent peg into the sand. In his mid-forties, he looked younger and fitter than most men his age. Lean and tall, he had a surfer's build and a bushy, badger-like beard, criss-crossed with seams of black and white. "I've been surfing this beach all summer," he told me, as tubular waves broke over the sand and I dropped a burning match into a pyramid of kindling and scrunched-up newspaper. "I've never seen so many tents on the beaches as I have done this year. There's been loads of camping, and campfires, and just hanging out. I think most local folk saw it as a chance to explore their own islands in a way they'd probably not done for a while."

Without the usual influx of tourists, Orkney's pandemic looked and felt different to normal. Being cut off from mainland Britain – even by just 6 miles – allowed the islands to take an unexpected fallow year. "Local folk had the opportunity to reconnect with the landscape," said Dave, as the fire flicked red sparks into the breeze. "In Orkney, the outdoors isn't something that exists separately from daily life, compartmentalised as a leisure commodity, only to be enjoyed at the weekends. The pandemic made all of us acutely aware of just how lucky we are to live here."

It was nice to hear that some people will remember 2020 for something other than death and hardship. In half a century, I too want to look back and cherish the new friends, skills and experiences I'd gained, rather than still be dwelling upon what I'd lost.

The dying sun appeared from behind a stripe of murky clouds and began to plummet into the Atlantic. A distant oil tanker revealed itself, like an outline developing on an iodine negative bathed in hydroquinone. The entire beach was washed in buttermilk, and the few whitewashed crofts on the surrounding hills turned from mossy brown to clotted cream.

Dave and I sat in silence as sets of humpback waves appeared as ripples out at sea, cascaded into Skaill Bay, then made landfall as messy whitecaps. To the west, there was nothing but ocean between us and the Hudson Strait, the entry to the North-West Passage on the shores of Baffin Island and Nunavik.

I found it impossible not to be carried away by this geographical fantasy. I was sat on British sand, just shy of 60 degrees north, with the taste of dark beer on my tongue and the crackle of burning wood in my ears. But if I were to slip my imaginary lines and never turn back, I'd have sailed around the southernmost tip of Greenland, then after about 4,000 miles wound up on a polar bear beach in the remotest corner of Canada.

We promised to meet again one day in the brighter future, but with tent and bicycle-shaped silhouettes growing longer in the beachgrass, Dave took off for dinner in a cosy family home somewhere near Kirkwall. I'm not sure who envied the other one more. As the sound of his exhaust grew fainter, I nestled a can of baked beans into the fire's orange coals, skewered three slices of bread with a desiccated branch of driftwood and angled them to toast in the warm smoke.

My cycling clothes had been wind-dried, so I packed them into a plastic bag, a makeshift camping pillow, and began preparing for the night ahead. This was always the most important hour of the day. I had just enough light to blow up my roll mat, arrange my head torch, phone and trainers close to where my head would be, and make sure my sleeping bag was ready to throw out just before bed. I gave the tent a final once over, tautening its ropes and shaking out any creases. By the time I was satisfied, baked beans hissed over hot coals and my makeshift toaster wasn't just burnt, but in flames. It resembled a medieval torch.

I was never a Scout, a Beaver or a Girl Guide. While some 16-year-olds spent their Sunday mornings working toward Duke of Edinburgh's Awards on the Ridgeway, I was most likely at a rave somewhere in the Cotswolds, skanking along to drum and bass as the rising sun singed a hundred washed-out faces.

When it comes to "adventure", I'm not ashamed to admit that I still have very little idea what I'm doing. I find it quite amusing that I've managed to find work as an "expert", when I've never read a tent's assembly instructions or lit a palm-full of tinder with a fire steel. If you were blessed with a lighter or a box of matches, why wouldn't you use them?

Television's obsession with ex-army survivalists has made living outdoors seem much more complicated than it really is. Why would you persevere with damp kindling when the petrol station down the road has dry stuff for three quid? Why would you eat sandy limpets while you've got a stock cube and 100 g of rice in your backpack?

If you've successfully navigated your way through life with just the occasional stubbed toe or paper cut, then you're more of a survival expert than Ray Mears or Bear Grylls. Jumping out of a helicopter and drinking your own urine isn't surviving, it's lunacy.

———

Two beers are never enough, but three are always too many. I remembered this for the umpteenth time as a globule of salty rain broke free from the furrow between my eyebrows and gurgled into my left ear canal. I'd fallen asleep, with my mouth open, beside the now smouldering fire. My tongue tasted of burned molasses and my lungs felt raw and bloodied, as though I'd been smoking on a chillum of old cigar tobacco.

I sat up, and a few tuppence-sized pebbles fell from my forehead into my lap. Goodness knows how long I'd been asleep, probably about an hour by the look of the fire. Dazed and confused, I bumped my fist against my grumbling ear and stabbed at the soggy coals.

A squall had blown in from the Atlantic and was already racing away inland. A blotch of grey cloud remained, but otherwise, the sky was crisp and clear and abuzz with bright white. All the way from the faint orange glow of Kirkwall in the south-east, to the Faeroe Islands and Canada to the north-west, billions of stars and planets blinked back at me.

Alone again on that empty beach, Sarah returned to my thoughts with a pang of hot sorrow, causing my Adam's apple to swell with grief. Behind the waves, I could hear her gravelly voice in my ears and the clink of glass on glass. In my mind's eye I could see her and Alana sharing bright-red lipstick at a festival. I could smell the chicken nuggets she'd cook for the two children she'd left behind.

But more than anything, I felt ashamed. Ashamed for not being at home when Alana needed me the most. Ashamed for not being there for Nick. Ashamed for fretting about my own mortality at a time when I should have been paying tribute to hers.

If I'm very lucky, I thought to myself. I might live for another 50 years. That's 600 months, 2,600 weeks and 18,200 days. After that, I'll rot into the earth and slowly turn into mud. Life always seemed so minuscule and insignificant when I broke it down that way. But when I considered something as grand as my one and only life, divided up into units of hours and minutes, it reminded me to savour – at least to try to – every bit of it, however wet, however cold. Even at its toughest and darkest moments, life was still living.

———

I managed a few more hours' troubled sleep, this time in my tent, but was awake well before sunrise and brewing coffee in the half-light of early dawn. Blue butane flames ripped at the base of the aluminium pot and a thick plume of steam dissolved into the sky. It was cold and misty, but dry and still. So, I threw on my clothes and combed the beach as the coffee soothed my throat.

A wave would wash away the top layer of sand and reveal tiny fragments of iridescent shell. Occasionally a nail or a rivet would appear, but before I could run and grab it, another wave would skim across the beach and wipe the canvas clean. I didn't find any lucky cowrie shells – known locally as "groatie buckies" – or one of the prized "sea beans" that occasionally drift all the way from mangroves in the Caribbean. Instead, all I collected was an instant noodle sachet, a triangular livestock tag and an Asda carrier bag.

The beach was spotless by global standards, but when you look for plastic, you find it, lurking in every dirty pore. The charity Ocean Crusaders estimates that there are over 5 trillion individual pieces of plastic in the world's oceans. By the most modest assessment, that's enough to strangle 100,000 mammals and choke a million seabirds a year. Even more depressing still is that, as a species, humans work their way through 500 billion so-called "single use" plastic bags every year. If you tied them all together, they would circumnavigate the globe 4,200 times.

The sun began to pierce the low, clotted-cream clouds, and where the flat ocean began to swell, a pair of seals flopped in and out of the surf, like chocolate Labradors chasing sticks through a field of wheat. I watched them for a few minutes, basking and playing, then flipped the few pebbles that wore the scars of my campfire. All I'd leave behind was a flattened imprint in the grass and three divots in the dune, where my bike's two wheels and kickstand had stood.

By 6.45 a.m. I'd cycled 8 miles to Orkney's second largest town, Stromness, and was waiting to board the ferry to the Scottish mainland. With my bum on the cold floor, and my legs dangling over the harbour wall, I watched a queue of vehicles edge slowly across the tarmac and disappear into its gaping steel mouth.

I was sad to be leaving so soon. I could have happily spent another week or two hitching between the outlying islands and camping on a dozen more beaches. But sadly, most were now off limits to outsiders and the morning's newspapers were, once again, starting to hint at another national lockdown.

For 5 beautiful minutes, I let the sunlight warm my rosy cheeks and waited to be called forward. A hockey stick-sized chunk of driftwood bobbed between a buoy and a seagull. A pair of fat mussels clung to a nub of concrete just beneath the surface. The scent of diesel and yesterday's fish hung in the air. They coalesced to create a smell that was – somewhat surprisingly – far more agreeable than most market-bought aftershaves.

Occasionally a small boat would rumble past me, escaping toward the sea. A few lashed-up RIBs and kayaks jumped up and down in its wake, like fledglings snapping at the talons of a departing mother. Otherwise, the water looked brittle and pure. To be admired from a distance, but far too delicate to reach out and touch.

Even at reduced capacity, walking on to a 12,000-tonne ship, alongside a few dozen cars and a couple of hundred people, was unsettling. Cycling and camping in Orkney had left me feeling like one of the last few people left on Earth, but all of a sudden, I was rubbing shoulders with articulated-lorry drivers, fish wholesalers and farmers transporting ewes to market. I wasn't particularly worried about any of the germs they might be carrying. I just wanted to be far away from their mess of chit-chat. In the vacuum of the ship's hull, I yearned for the swirl of wind.

Most passengers sat in the warm restaurant with their face masks on, but I opted to hunker down outside in one of the port-side smoking areas, with my nose and lips exposed to the icy breeze. At first the ship rumbled along at walking speed, sounding as though it was grazing along the seabed. But as we rounded the island of Graemsay, on the western approach to Scapa Flow, the captain opened up the engine and we began lunging southward across the Atlantic.

Most of the passengers had probably seen it a thousand times before, however I was left spellbound by the landscape unfurling in front of me. The island of Hoy rose dramatically out of the swell. It climbed toward the heavens and then flattened off to a tabletop swirling with late season seabirds. We must have been a mile or two out to sea, but the 1,500-foot cliffs loomed over us.

With my palms gripping the tubular steel handrail, and my face hanging out over the ship's edge, I was as close as I could get without falling in. Lush green moorland and glacial valleys marbled with peat ran away into a cobalt sky streaked with cirrus clouds. Then, as we rounded the island's north-west headland, and the Scottish mainland came into sight for the very first time, a red sandstone sea stack appeared, standing to attention like a sentry standing guard.

Rising to 449 feet, the Old Man of Hoy is the stuff of legend. Some say it resembles a human figure with a head, neck and shoulders, while I'm sure at least a few dirty minds have, like mine, looked at it and seen the shaft of an erect penis, complete with a bulbous head.

Whichever way you see it, it's impossible not to be left awestruck in its presence. Erosion has separated the stack from the rest of the island in just the past two centuries or so. And it could, at least in theory, fall into the Atlantic at any moment. Every single wave that crashes in makes its foundations ever so slightly weaker.

The stack was first climbed by mountaineers Chris Bonington, Rusty Baillie and Tom Patey in 1966, then a year later the BBC commissioned them to do it all again for a live outside broadcast that attracted 15 million viewers. Since then, it has become one of British climbing's most-prized ascents and about 50 daredevils reach the top each year. Someone has even buried a notepad in a Tupperware box at the summit, to keep an offline, uncorrupted account of the crazy souls that reach the crown of the Old Man's head, or – if you're otherwise inclined – the opening of its grassy urethra.

BAILEY:
RAMPING UP

An hour after leaving Orkney, the ferry grumbled into Scrabster, the small port just west of Thurso, and gave birth to a few dozen cars, a handful of lorries and me, the one and only cyclist. Forklifts buzzed and bleeped between pallets of tree trunks skinned of their bark. A crane dangled a shipping container over a flatbed trailer. A couple of men slid boxes around the deck of a greasy trawler stinking of fish.

It was now much gloomier than the early morning I'd left behind, and as I cycled out of the busy port, an RNLI lifeboat glowed bright tangerine in a soup of cold grey. After a few minutes I hit a crossroads. East toward John o'Groats and its famous signpost, or west in the direction of the Scottish Highlands, Cape Wrath and Skye.

I try not to confuse my travels with too much googling. If you're not careful you can live out the experience on a phone screen long before you actually visit in person. But on this occasion, it seemed essential, and the decision I made now would determine my route from here on in.

Part of me was desperate to see John o'Groats, however it was impossible to find a good word said about the place. In fact, I quickly discovered that Lonely Planet had described it as "a seedy tourist trap" in 2005, then in 2010 it received a Carbuncle Award from the magazine *Urban Realm* for being "Scotland's most dismal town". Neither accolade made an easterly route seem particularly appealing. I'd already schlepped to enough signposts, markers and borders in my life to know that it would have been a mostly joyless and underwhelming ordeal. And as for the wind? It was already tearing in off the North Sea and forecast to be a 30 mph south-easterly for the next three or four days. So, just like that, my mind was made up. I turned west and headed for another contentious tourist attraction: The North Coast 500.

The NC500 – as some people know it – was launched in 2015 by Prince Charles and his North Highland Initiative. The intention was to breathe new life into one of Britain's remotest and most economically fragile rural areas by creating a 500-mile loop of the Scottish Highlands. It was hoped that the NC500 would become one of Britain's bucket-list must-dos, like hiking Peru's Inca Trail or clapping eyes on Egypt's Great Pyramid of Giza, and at the beginning, it certainly achieved its goal.

A 2019 study commissioned by the government agency Highlands and Islands Enterprise found that in its first year, 29,000 more people visited than usual, contributing an extra £9 million to the local economy. Another 2019 study by the Moffat Centre for tourism at Glasgow Caledonian University discovered that room occupancy in the region's hotels increased from 52 to 78 per cent between 2014 and 2018, and in 2018 alone, the NC500 brought in an extra £22.8 million and created 180 new jobs. Great, one would assume. More tourists, more money, happier locals.

But these things are never as clear cut as they often seem, and while some people cashed in, there were many that didn't. A contradictory 2019 study – this time carried out by Stirling University – discovered that "the majority" of local residents viewed the NC500 negatively. Just 18 per cent of the survey's respondents agreed that the tourist route was positive for the area, while 40 per cent suggested that the region's roads, toilets, waste disposal and parking needed significant improvements.

Tensions were already pretty high, but then, in the spring of 2020, the Covid-19 pandemic struck, forcing 67 million Britons into lockdown. At first this meant the Highlands were much quieter than usual and the region's tourism industry was deprived of its spring windfall. For a change, the locals had only midges for company. But then, lockdown was eased in early July, at the same time as millions of overseas holidays were either cancelled or abandoned. A perfect storm was brewing. "How about the North Coast 500 this year?" said every husband, wife, backpacker, Scout leader, coach driver, tour guide, cyclist, motorhome and tent owner in Britain. "It'll be nice and quiet up there."

———

Just outside Thurso I stopped to buy breakfast: a bottle of fluorescent-orange Irn-Bru and a five-pack of Tunnock's caramel wafers. I was playing out a full-blown Scottish cliché, but I wanted to mark the occasion somehow. Moreover, the thought of haggis turned my stomach, battered Mars bars made my arteries wince and although I quite liked the image of a litre of auburn whisky catching the sun's rays in my bike's bottle cage, I couldn't imagine actually drinking the stuff.

Instead, I ingested 76 g of sugar in under 2 minutes, downing the fizzy liquid and practically inhaling the chewy chocolate bars. As breakfasts go it had all the nutritional value of one of those grotesque fatbergs clogging up London's sewers. Nevertheless, it felt good. Kind of.

I was relieved to be on the same patch of land as home, but I was also struck by how weary everyone now seemed. At times, cycling in Orkney and Shetland had seemed like paradise, with pursed smiles and friendly eyes. But all of a sudden, the atmosphere was different, cagier. "We got smashed by people this summer," said a shopkeeper, when I stopped to buy more biscuits and sweets. "It's the emptying of toilets that drives most locals crazy up here. These people rent camper vans for the first time but have no idea how to use them. They drive like idiots and then leave their rubbish in the lay-bys."

I continued west along the A836, the road that runs along the north coast of Scotland. I'd always wanted to visit this part of Britain. In my imagination it was a wild and jagged frontier, like New Zealand or

Patagonia. If you drew a straight line north on a map, there was nothing between this road and the North Pole. It must, therefore, be Mordor-like, with orcs and hobbits lining the route. Instead, I felt underwhelmed. Cheated, even. Was this potholed road really – as the national tourist board described it – "Scotland's answer to Route 66"?

Even in autumn the road was busier than I'd expected. A couple of cars a minute passed me on their way toward Thurso. It was hard to ride for a mile or two without an Ocado, Amazon or Sainsbury's delivery van choking me with its fumes. My soft tyres juddered in and out of sharp asphalt abrasions, like rubbery wheels of Edam grazing along the face of a cheese grater. Route 66? Never. More like the cobbles of Paris–Roubaix.

For a couple of hours, I cycled west, stopping from time to time to water the grass or chuck in a Hobnob or two. The cloud had lifted to reveal a wind farm to the south, spreading out across a chain of mossy-green hills, but nothing that resembled mountains. The road was almost pancake flat. In fact, I began to wonder if I'd taken a wrong turn, or suffered a bout of traveller's amnesia, and had accidently ended up on a lazy cycling holiday in the Netherlands.

I pulled in to a windswept car park surrounded by soggy green fields, where a woman in a hairy jumper was trying to persuade a golden retriever to do "a small wee" – a wee wee, if you will – on the grass.

"Excuse me," I said, "but is *this* the North Coast 500?"

"Yep."

"This," I said, pointing to the ground, "is the North Coast 500?"

"Yep. Why? What were you expecting?"

"Something a bit more, I don't know… not this." My shoulders sank and my forehead creased. I looked back in the direction from which I'd come, then out to the featureless horizon where the road dissolved. I made a conscious effort to straighten up a little and crack a smile, so as not to seem too rude.

"Don't worry," she said. "This is the flat bit. You'll wish you were back here soon. Just don't get run over by a camper van."

"Is there anywhere to buy food further west?" I asked.

"Aye, there's a chip shop a few towns over."

"Is it any good?"

"No, it's crap."

———

For most of the afternoon, icy gales blew in from the North Atlantic and rattled against my Gore-Tex jacket. It was a familiar but annoying sound, the soundtrack to many thousands of miles before. I wasn't quite cycling into a headwind, but if I was on a yacht, I'd have set my sails to a beam reach on a starboard tack and let the sideways wind wobble me forward. Sometimes I'd grip the extreme edge of my right handlebar and form a pronounced apex with my elbow. It felt cumbersome and unscientific, but there was a simple joy in watching the speed on my bicycle computer increase by 0.1 mph.

Left alone, on the bike, I did silly little things like this, just to keep my mind off serious topics like death and my dwindling bank balance. Doctors call it "distraction therapy" and it's often used on toddlers with things stuck up their noses. But for me it became a way to fill my mind with a physical action rather than the slippery tangential thoughts that I couldn't quite grip.

On one particularly boring stretch of flat, I challenged myself to do 100 mini squats in the saddle, something like a sitting trot on a pony. Later, I guessed the number of fence posts between two points far away in the distance, then counted them out as they became my here and now. On another quiet road, I unclipped my feet from the pedals, stretched my legs out to 45 degrees and wove in and out of the staggered lines in the centre of the road. It was fun to see how long I could roll along without giving in to the urge to clip back in again.

But most of the time I just savoured the primal thrill of simply being in motion. Eating up second after second, mile after mile. I pedalled. I looked. I breathed. I was. I don't think it matters if you're a British bloke on a bicycle or a Masai tribesman with a shield and a spear, all – or at least, most – humans, share a very common instinct: to move.

About 30 miles west of Thurso, the land finally began to undulate, and where the road occasionally meandered southward it carried me from a lush green seaside, into a natty brown moorland dappled in red and silver sandstone.

The occasional muddy Land Rover would rumble past me and then vanish into the toneless horizon. I was almost certainly the only cyclist stupid enough to be out this far north of Edinburgh and occasionally a car would give me a beep or two of encouragement.

But I wasn't alone out there by any stretch of the imagination. There were camper vans, lots of them. According to ITV, sales of motorhomes, camper vans and caravans rose by 71 per cent in July 2020 alone and 37 per cent of purchases were made by people who had never owned one before. In 2020 Volkswagen Financial Services (UK) saw the popularity of California vans increase by more than 600 per cent.

As I shivered on my hard saddle and contemplated which soggy bog would suit my tent best, it wasn't hard to see the attraction. Even on an unremarkable midweek day in a pandemic, there were camper vans filling up lay-bys and passing places for as far as the eye could see. In 1 hour, I lost count at around a hundred.

Some of them were pulling small hatchbacks or mopeds and had Sky dishes mounted to their roofs. One had so many bicycles attached to the back of it that it was practically a roving Halfords. In another, I saw a teenage boy playing FIFA on an Xbox, oblivious to his parents, and the mountains around him. Other vans were more like millennial stoner-mobiles, DIY Ford Transits, with tie-dye interiors and #vanlife bumper stickers.

At one scenic lookout there was a pair of vans, bumper to bumper like dodgems, blaring out Dire Straits. In one, a man was preparing what looked like a *salade niçoise*. In the other, his friend was uncorking a bottle of fridge-chilled Sauvignon Blanc. Their two wives – or mistresses, maybe – were taking duck-lipped selfies in puffed-up gilets and brand-new

Hunter wellingtons. When I stopped to take a few photos of my own, the four of them pondered my bike and me as though we'd just beamed in from the starship *Enterprise*.

A part of me was jealous, they looked warm and clean and well fed. But then again, I quite enjoyed being the smelly weirdo on a bicycle, rather than just another face in the crowd. They all seemed like lovely people, of course; childless aunties and uncles who had disposable income to spend on designer jeans and sports cars, rather than their snotty kids' trainers. But it was easy to see why camper-van owners were so often ridiculed. In their self-contained, glossy palaces, they were easy targets.

Most Highlanders don't like camper vans because the people that rent them have little or no idea how to drive them. The biggest bone of contention comes from them not turning into one of the thousands of bulged hard shoulders to let other vehicles pass. During 2016, the first full year of the NC500's operation, the number of deaths and serious accidents on the route increased by 45 per cent. In 2018 there were four reported incidents of sharp tacks being thrown on to the road to cause punctures, and goodness knows how many Londoners have been tutted at by farmers in flat caps.

By the end of July 2020, just three weeks into Scotland's Covid summer holiday, a local Facebook group had more than 3,700 members and several MPs calling for a camper van congestion charge. There had already been a surge in abandoned tents and human excrement found along the NC500, and even a dumped caravan.

But many people just don't like the sight of them blighting the landscape. And for that, some blame must lay at the door of their manufacturers, who often design them in a bright-white sheen instead of something more muted. As I cycled sharply upward, toward the first mountain pass of my trip, I looked back at an epic and jagged valley. It was clogged, from top to bottom, with dozens of chest freezers on wheels.

I made it to the village of Tongue just before dusk. Gnats and midges swarmed at head height and where the Atlantic jutted inland to form a sea loch, a dozen greylag geese were descending, eyeing up the glassy surface.

Tongue was a small, seemingly dead town, with a couple of pubs and a shop. The first pub was closed entirely and then, when I asked if I could have a pint in the one that doubled as a hotel, the woman in the empty reception took great delight in telling me that "the bar was for overnight guests only, sir".

"Can I not just have one quick beer?" I pleaded. "There's no one here."

"Overnight guests only, sir."

"How many overnight guests have you got?"

"I'm sorry, I can't tell you that, sir."

I seethed. Britain was in the midst of the biggest recession in its history, yet I was being prevented from pumping cash into its coffers. I didn't want to have a full-blown piss-up, I just wanted to buy a single pint of beer. I huffed and puffed, chewed the inside of my cheeks for a few seconds, then left her in peace to finish a crossword.

———

I'd cycled 45 miles since getting off the ferry that morning and, without really noticing, climbed 2,500 feet. But now that I'd stopped, I felt tired and groggy – as though my body was descending into a fever. I'd been on the road for almost a week and only showered once. When I moved, a film of dried sweat cracked between the hair follicles on my arms and legs. Out of the breeze, I reeked.

I'd intended to "wild camp" somewhere in the waterlogged moorland near the road, but when I noticed that the village campsite was still open, and I could camp, cook, dry my clothes, charge my phone and shower for £10, I was already stripped down to my underwear by the time the owner could take my money.

Scolding hot water ran through my matted hair, across my aching shoulder blades and into the tender spot between my arse cheeks.

A grimy stream of dust, pubic hair, biscuit crumbs and bike grease washed into the drain. I didn't have any shower gel, so I used hand soap. I then sprayed my humming clothes with half a can of Febreze Bathroom, giving them a chemically floral dry clean. After 20 minutes I emerged, pink and wrinkly, smelling a lot like a festival Portaloo, wondering if I should have gone the whole hog and brushed my furry teeth with toilet Duck.

I had just enough light to pitch my tent, brew up a couple of packs of instant noodles and drape my mangy clothes over a picnic bench. Half a dozen camper vans had filed into numbered spaces with electric hook-ups, but I had about a quarter of an acre of grass all to myself, just out of earshot of the chit-chat about jockey wheels and leisure batteries.

Despite the pandemic, the campsite had done well. "We were very, very busy. Busier than we could have ever imagined," said its owner, Stephen Macay. "It was especially tough because it was our first year. At the end of it all, I'll have to sit down and see where we're at, but it was certainly a very good two months for us in the summer."

Stephen and his wife also ran an adjacent hostel but decided that it was impractical to open under the circumstances. They'd have needed to clean the kitchen after every single use and impose strict social distancing guidelines. But with people outside, in their own biosecure bubbles, the swirling Highland air did the hard work for them.

"We like to welcome people when they arrive," said Stephen, "and a lot of people have told me that they should be in Florida, Benidorm or Tenerife, but they came to Scotland instead. That has meant a big increase in camper vans, especially."

"When you look back in a few years' time, do you think you'll have a positive or negative impression of this time in our lives?" I asked.

"On the whole, positive, I think," said Stephen. "People have come up here that haven't before. And when they do, they love the area. It might even move people away from going to other places too."

So-called overtourism has become a thorny issue all over the planet, and the NC500 has certainly come in for its fair share of flack.

But people have to go somewhere, especially during a pandemic with closed borders. In the grand scheme of things, I wondered if a few thousand extra people in the Highlands was anywhere near as bad as a hundred thousand on a Thai beach or millions of selfie sticks jousting their way through Venice.

———

It rained all night. A solid 10 hours. Thud, thud, thud on my sodden tent. Tap, tap, tap on the nearby Perspex roofs. I drifted in and out of sleep, imagining Alana back at home, alone in our big warm bed, curled up in a foetal position with lavender balm on her temples.

I was starting to forget the smell of her shampoo and the size of her hands in mine. While I was moving during the day, the routine of getting from place to place made me feel like I was achieving something worthwhile. But when I stopped at night – truly alone with my thoughts, squished into a damp tent – my journey seemed pointless, futile.

There was no escaping the fact that Alana was suffering, and I felt guilty that I'd abandoned her. In order for me to live out this selfish daydream, she had to endure being alone. I couldn't shift the thought that she'd wake up one morning soon and decide that I wasn't worth the hassle any longer. I worried I'd arrive home at the end of it all and find the locks changed and my clothes in bin liners. As my mind raced, the drops of rain grew heavier, like drumsticks tapping on a tambourine.

There didn't seem much point lying awake in a soaking wet tent for any longer than necessary. So, as soon as dawn broke, I had another hot shower, ate a can of cold baked beans and packed up. Almost everything I owned was heavy with water. My sleeping bag was damp on the outside and its down filling felt claggy and clumped. My cycling shoes were drenched through. My gloves sopped like kitchen sponges. The only half-dry things I had left were the precious "evening clothes" I'd slept in.

I looked at the skies around me. Directly above, the rain was thinning to a mizzle. To the north, a pea-souper was frothing over the Atlantic like off-white foam on a pint of Guinness. To the south, half a dozen lumpy mountains were shrouded in cotton-wool strands of cloud. But to the west, where I was heading, it looked bright, hopeful. Kind of.

I decided to keep my dry clothes on. It was a gamble, but if I wrapped my feet in plastic carrier bags and slid them into the wet shoes, I could, at least, keep my toes dry. I scrounged a black bin bag from the toilet block, ripped out holes for my neck and arms and wore it as a base layer. I wrung out my gloves, put on my helmet and rolled out on to the tarmac.

I was in the Scottish Highlands, surrounded by chirping blackbirds and trickling streams, but without sleep my mind was racing. People, places, memories and emotions flashed from one synapse to another. A TV skipping through channels.

I started fretting about biting my first girlfriend's lip while kissing her on a park bench 25 years before. Then I started remembering all the golden ducks I'd had playing cricket. Then I worried that my oldest friends didn't really like me. I thought about my dad having a heart attack and dying suddenly. I visualised my once living and laughing friends, lifeless and silent.

I only managed to cycle a few miles before I had to stop. My jacket collar was trying to choke me. My helmet straps had clamped tight like a vice. I unclipped my pedals and let the bike just fall to the road, bottles and biscuits bouncing off into the heather. I flung my hands high into the air, desperate for my chest to open. It felt as though I was being given a bear hug I couldn't escape from.

If I was honest with myself, I knew this moment was coming. I'd been "ramping up" ever since I heard about Sarah. It had taken a while, but the shock had slowly seeped from my brain into my body. First come the manic thoughts, then arrives the insomnia. Now I was experiencing a full-blown panic attack, in the middle of nowhere, totally alone.

When I first started having these symptoms in my early twenties, I was convinced I had a serious lung disease. My GP referred me for an ECG, an ultrasound on my heart, lung volume measurements and tests that checked the amount of oxygen in my blood.

To my immense frustration, every investigation revealed a fit young man, with no physical illness to justify why he couldn't breathe. I was furious that they hadn't found a tumour the size of a rugby ball hogging the space where my diaphragm should be, or at the very least diagnosed bronchitis or emphysema. Instead, my GP looked me in the eyes and said, "You know, have you wondered if this could be in your head?"

Begrudgingly, I dragged myself through six months of cognitive behavioural therapy (CBT) at London's Maudsley Hospital. I'd chain my bike to the railings next to the A&E and feel weirdly jealous of the people being unloaded from ambulances with proper, physical trauma – trauma that could actually be seen and quickly diagnosed. I'd then sit in a room 200 feet away and draw infantile mind maps with coloured crayons and felt-tip pens while a therapist with coffee breath said things like "and how did that make you feel?" and "what does this stick man mean to you?"

None of this made me feel any better; if anything, it compounded the problems even more, by making me hyper-aware of symptoms I couldn't fix. It took me years to even entertain the idea that I was experiencing panic attacks, because they were the humiliating episodes that sickly kids had at school with paper bags and inhalers. To me, anxiety was something celebrities talked about in their ghost-written books to try and make themselves seem less vapid. The "mental health crisis" was a catchy phrase thrown around on *Panorama* and *Good Morning Britain*.

I, meanwhile, wanted to be infallible, bulletproof – a brave adventurer type without flaws, because this was the hyper-masculine image portrayed in the adventure travel industry. Men scaled mountains and hacked their way through jungles. They didn't sit on chaises longues talking to shrinks about feeling anxious.

Stood beside that puddled road, I felt bitter that I wasn't one of these men. But with my lungs convulsing and my heart pounding, I was desperate to slow the speeding train. "Think what you see," I told myself, over and over, attempting to find focus beyond the walls of my pounding skull. "Think what you see... Road. Stones. Trees. Hills." I said, regressing from man to toddler.

If I was in a Southeast Asian spa, I'd have been coaxed down from the ledge by a guru with a soft voice, given jasmine tea and a head massage, to the soothing sound of whale song. Instead, I was all alone, in the Highlands, with my thoughts racing and my chest tightening. I'd need to improvise. Thousands of hours spent online searching "how to deal with air hunger" had thrown up few realistic cures, just a smattering of tools to help manage symptoms.

I'd forgotten to fill up my water bottles and coffee seemed like a bad idea, so I cracked open the only liquid I had: a bottle of Newcastle Brown Ale at the bottom of my pannier. I necked a third of it in one go and closed my eyes. It trickled over my raw larynx and washed through my veins, calming my fingers and toes.

I needed audio too – to distract me from the sound of my laboured breathing – so I clicked the first thing that popped up on the BBC Sounds app on my phone: the Radio 2 breakfast show. For 10 minutes I sat cross-legged on the floor, listening intently to whatever tune was played next. I tried to imagine being in a black tunnel, with no peripheral light apart from a tiny flicker in the far distance. I inhaled long breaths through my nose, then let them out as sighs through my mouth, challenging myself to do 100 before I could open my eyes.

A couple of cars went past in that time. I smelled their exhaust fumes and felt their drivers' confused eyes latching on to me. But if anything, it focussed my attention even more. It was embarrassing, but I felt pressured to calm myself down, before the next one drove past and shamed me some more. Somehow, miraculously, it helped. Sitting in a Buddha pose on wet grass, taking sips from a bottle of ale, humming along to Maroon 5, at 8 a.m., helped. It wasn't perfect, but if and when the panic set in again, I could at least try and turn to the holy trinity: breath, music, booze.

———

With my headphones in, I cycled on, around a finger-shaped sea loch. The road wove inland, through flocks of kamikaze sheep dozing on the warm tarmac. The "V" silhouette of 50 ducks raced across the horizon, and on a blue-green hillside, a herd of coffee-brown roe deer skipped away, their bushy cream tails rising and falling.

Where the road turned north again, toward the Atlantic, the asphalt was mottled in dinner plate-sized puddles. But when the sun peeked through, they flickered with an oily translucence, like shimmering peacock feathers. Millions of silver cobwebs coiled through the roadside heather, each immaculate strand hanging heavy with pearls of lucid rain.

By the time I made it to the outskirts of Durness, a village 30 miles west of Tongue, I felt hung-over and exhausted. Too exhausted to go on any further. Too exhausted to listen to another second of Bruno Mars, Ed Sheeran or Zoe Ball.

The sun was warm, so I pulled off the road and bumped down a gravel track to a white-sand beach with turquoise, Caribbean shallows. The swell was calm and crisp, it fizzed and zizzed rather than crashed and walloped. I settled on a dryish patch of seagrass and crumpled to the ground.

With my helmet for a pillow and a dirty old T-shirt as an eye mask, I slept, deeply. Deeper than I had in living memory. Too deep, even for dreams. The sort of sleep that other people have. Sleep to be jealous of. Sleep that disorients. Anaesthetic sleep. Sleep that leaves a crick in the neck.

I was dead to the world for anywhere between 5 minutes and a few days, but I awoke to the sensation of spots of drizzle on the back of my hands, like pins and needles. Black clouds were gathering out to sea and the wind was building from a whirr to a whistle. I packed up my bed and continued on, drowsy.

Durness was a pretty little village with a bobbly football pitch, a two-pump petrol station and a café selling buckets and spades. It was the sort of place that must be lovely during the early spring or dark midwinter, but that morning it was overrun with waddling tourists and patrolled by cranky locals.

If I'm totally honest, I found Durness hard to like. It had the feel of a music festival on a Monday morning, when all the vendors are trying to shift their stock at inflated prices to the stream of strung-out campers they'll never see again.

The industrial-sized bins outside the village shop overflowed with old coffee cups, banana peels, plastic bottles, sandwich packets, soiled nappies and fizzy-drink cans. Meanwhile, everything inside the shop was about three times the price it should have been. A little further up the road there was a van selling greasy "gourmet" burgers for about £10 a pop. Every other house was a holiday home, every other vehicle a camper van.

During the lockdown summer of 2020 the village had been overrun with people. Locals complained of smashed glass on the beach and dozens of tents a night being pitched "wild" on the nearby dunes. Even well into autumn there was a tetchy, weary atmosphere. In a lay-by a couple of – almost certainly – local men in flat caps and wax jackets scowled at a family of Russian-speaking picnickers, dressed head to toe in Gucci, Ralph Lauren and Porsche. Then, a little further down the road, I saw a shaggy cockapoo do a steaming shit on the kerb, only for its owner to stealthily kick the mess into long grass.

Durness resembled a tired model village, simmering with passive aggression. There was a palpable divide between the dawdling sightseers and the locals that wanted to milk them dry. Covid only further inflamed that peevish relationship. Short tourist seasons and closed borders had concentrated more people into a smaller space.

Before heading back into the lonely countryside, I stopped to get a cup of coffee at the "Craft Village" on the other side of town. At first, I had high hopes. The freehand painted signage gave the impression of a hippie commune-cum-Shangri-La, but in the flesh, it was really just a disused military radar station, dolled up to sell expensive trinkets.

Unfortunately, my arrival also coincided with the exact moment the heavens opened, and about three dozen other people pitched up with the same idea. It took me over half an hour to actually get inside the café, where two hair-netted women behind a plastic screen seemed to enjoy the sight of people rolling eyes in their direction. One of the women, almost certainly the owner, took even greater delight in yelling things like "two metres, please," and "no, I can't hand you a napkin. Due to Covid."

You'd think a business owner who depended upon seasonal footfall would have developed a routine that maximised her chances of keeping the electricity on through winter. Instead, it was as though she and her colleague were competing to see who could brew the slowest flat white.

I watched this charade play out for another 10 minutes, before finally receiving my lukewarm coffee. It was lashing down outside, so I stood in the doorway, dipped my face mask and took a small sip. "No drinking on the premises," she hollered, like some sort of omniscient Chris Whitty. "Keep your face mask over your mouth and nose until you have fully left the building. Due to Covid." I joined the road heading south-west, toward steep jagged mountains, and vowed never to return again.

It rained, unrelentingly. The sort of heavy rain that makes you wonder if your skin really is watertight and if you'll be a few kilos heavier when it finally abates. I followed a single-track road through a channel of drystone walls and rumbled across cattle grids almost filled to their rusted brims. Sheep huddled together behind hills, gates and oil drums, anything to keep an inch of wool dry.

At some lay-bys, the road was so narrow it was barely possible for my bicycle and me to squeeze past a hatchback. At others, Range Rovers edged through channels of tractors and quad bikes, nose to tail with minibuses and pickups pulling canoes and kayaks. I didn't see anyone not in a vehicle. Most of the roadside houses had signs taped to traffic cones plonked in the middle of their driveways: "No Parking. Private"; "Private Land KEEP OFF"; "The livers of English tourists make for the best haggises."

The grey road twisted through a vast, 40- or 50-square-mile-wide basin of dark brown peat and sprigs of tired autumn green. Sandstone paths began at my wheels and meandered for miles across the black earth, all the way to distant farms with steel barns and warm white crofts, spewing out twists of smoke. Beyond them, mountains, proper mountains, climbed into the dirty cloud, angled up steeply like sharp incisors, then levelled off in the far distance like soft-topped molars. For the first time, I could truly appreciate the allure of the North Coast 500. "Now this," I mumbled to myself, "this is proper Scotland."

Legend has it that the creator of *The Lord of the Rings*, J. R. R. Tolkien, dreamed up Mordor after visiting the very north-west corner of Britain. And as I pushed onward, and upward, part of me expected to get mugged by marauding orcs or stopped in my tracks by a white-cloaked wizard with a bushy beard and a long staff. "Thou shalt not pass…" he'd roar, in a puff of grey smoke, "without buying this overpriced North-Coast-500 bumper sticker!"

About 10 miles south of Durness, I was convinced I was taking a shortcut. But really it was just a track through a field. A muddy field. A very muddy field. A less stubborn man would have turned around after taking his first squelched footstep, but this one decided to persevere. Each stride sounded like that fart putty seven-year-olds get for their birthdays. Picture the Battle of the Somme, then colourise it, then insert a bloke pushing a bicycle laden with panniers. Pigs would have looked at this field and turned up their snouts. Or at the very least asked for armbands.

But I kept going. Stupidly, doggedly, I kept going. Transfixed by a gate at the far end of the field, smug in the thinking that I was taking "a shortcut". By the time I reached the road again I'd probably wasted an hour, dropped my bike three times and acquired a sticky mud-line just below my knees.

Remarkably, though, I wasn't hyperventilating any more. I'd been far too busy for that. My heart pounded, but satisfyingly, like at the end of a long run or sex. My lungs, too, took bites out of the thick, soupy air, rather than snatching nibbles from it. For the first time that day, my belly bulged when I inhaled.

I felt grounded for a change, centred and mindful of my surroundings. It was as though I'd lanced a boil. For a while, at least, I was determined to look outward, to a sea of luscious green.

HEBRIDES:
MY HEART JOLTED

Britain is big. Bigger than many of us often give it credit for. It's the seventy-eighth largest country, by area, on the planet. About the same size as Uganda. Twice the size of North Korea. Eight times the size of Belgium. Twelve times the size of Israel.

The true scale of Britain only fully dawned on me when I stopped to check my phone, about 5 miles south of Durness. Until then, I'd used Google Maps' route planner to get from one hamlet to the next, without giving too much thought to the bigger picture. But as I zoomed out, and out some more, my toes curled.

I'd been on the road for over a week but had only just rounded Scotland's north-west corner. I was more than 500 miles from the border with England and 950 miles (as the crow flies) from Land's End in Cornwall.

Scotland seemed even bigger, still, because it was just so empty. Of the 67 million people living in Britain's 80,000 square miles, just 5.5 million live in Scotland's 30,000. England is the most densely populated country in Europe, while Scotland is one of the emptiest. Only seven countries – Lithuania, Latvia, Estonia, Sweden, Finland, Norway and Iceland – have lower population densities. I zoomed in and out of the screen, unable to find much more than a few lochs and mountains. With my pockets running low on Hobnobs, my panniers stuffed with soggy clothes, and the "dry" ones I was wearing drenched through, the task seemed prodigious, beyond me.

Most people who cycle Land's End to John o'Groats take an 874-mile beeline right through the middle of the country. Many do it at the height of summer and have a support vehicle carrying their luggage from one hotel to another. I, on the other hand, had set off on a scenic route that was almost double the distance, in late autumn, lugging enough waterlogged kit to see out a winter in Antarctica.

I continued down the potholed road. It rambled away, into black, ominous mountains. Sheets of rain washed in from the west. Roadside brooks had burst their peaty banks. I couldn't stop moving again, every time I did, I froze. Did I have enough food? Could I really bring myself to drink from the puddles? What if I needed a poo? Did I have any loo roll? Where the hell was I going to camp?

———

After about an hour the rain finally stopped. The cloud had risen, but a cold, crisp twilight was setting in, filling the still air with busy midges. I could see further, but every patch of earth had become a quagmire. Pitching a tent would be more like launching a life raft.

I raced and raced. Forward, forward. Pushing my legs and the bike as hard as I thought they could go. I was desperate to find a village, a football pitch, a bus shelter, anything. Then.

SNAP.

CLUNK.

THUD.

Hard tarmac racing toward soft palms.

Shin smacked.

Ankle scuffed.

Elbow bumped.

Back tyre fizzing flat.

Suddenly, I was sat in the middle of the road, my eyes confused at being 6 feet lower than normal. I expected a broken bone or sprained joint to reveal itself and pain to travel from my limbs to my brain. But thankfully, there was nothing more than a few torn garments, a wonky helmet and a split fingernail.

One of the 10 mm bolts connecting my pannier rack to the bike had snapped off. The weight of my luggage had then slammed down on the back wheel with such force that the inner tube valve exploded, shooting the cap somewhere into the undergrowth. I was lucky the tyre hadn't been revolving in my direction at that precise moment, or it would have ended up in the underside of my chin.

I managed to replace the inner tube easily enough, but half of the broken bolt was still stuck in the frame. There was no easy fix, this was a vice-and-power drill sort of job. All I had was a bicycle multitool or a Swiss army knife with a corkscrew and toothpick.

A couple of camper vans slowed down next to me and perused from a safe distance, as though they were giving the lions a wide berth at a safari park. The light, and my hopes of pitching my tent in daylight, were fading.

After about ten minutes, a friendly couple stopped to offer a hand, but when they saw the pannier rack dangling loose, they just grimaced, then took a few cautious steps away from me.

"Do you need a lift?" the man asked, looking at my muddy feet, then back to his clean white vehicle.

"Probably yes, but no, thanks. I'll survive."

"Where are you going?"

"No idea. I actually have no idea. Somewhere south. Maybe another few miles, then I'll camp."

"I'll see what I've got in the van."

"Do you like biscuits? We've got biscuits," said the woman, excitedly, nervously. "I'll get you some biscuits."

They left me with half a pack of rich tea, a can of Fanta and a metre-long strand of gardening twine. I could see their confused expressions in the wing mirrors as they sanitised their hands and disappeared into the dusk.

Twenty minutes later, I followed them, with the pannier lashed to the frame and my gums claggy with crumbs.

———

I was so exhausted, wet and muddy that the idea of sleeping in my sopping tent filled me with dread. So, I begrudgingly parted with £80 to stay in the only B&B that looked open, a few miles north of Laxford Bridge. The owner, a smiley lady called Susan, insisted I remove the majority of my clothes at the door and ushered me toward the shower. I then passed out in a hot bedroom, with my shoes upturned on the radiator and my tent flapping on the washing line.

By 8 a.m. the next morning, I'd consumed so much "complimentary" breakfast my abdomen made a sloshing sound when I walked. Nevertheless, I took my first tentative strides south, as Susan waved me off in the direction of the next village, Scourie. "Scott Barnes will help you," she said. "If he can't, then you've no chance."

It was a brighter day than the one before. The surrounding hills blushed from a kiss of sun. They were greener, more alive, less bleak. Thick weeds rampaged through turmeric earth, then stopped dead at the blue-grey tarmac. The desiccated trunks of oak and beech trees snarled together, raced upward, then bulged outward, forming a lush tabletop canopy. I was caught in a windless, subtropical vacuum resembling New Zealand or Tasmania. I half expected a kiwi to emerge from the hedgerow.

I made it to Scourie after 90 nervous minutes. The garden twine had held firm, but I couldn't pass up the opportunity of a bike mechanic. A stocky man with thin brown hair and a thick plaid shirt beckoned me toward his garden shed, a trove of spokes, spindles, spanners and sprockets. "You must be the bloke," he said, then took one look at my bike and winced.

Immediately, Scott started performing keyhole surgery on my bike, throwing it from one vice to another, changing from one drill bit to the next. Hot orange sparks flew out of the frame and fizzled to ash on the dusty floor. "I'm going to be honest with you," he said. "I don't fancy our chances of getting this out. Are you going far?" This time, I winced.

Scott had once been a keen cyclist himself, but a serious spinal injury put an abrupt end to that. The damage also prevented him from holding down a "proper" job and fixing bikes was now his main source of income.

"Do you see many cyclists coming this way?" I asked.

"You're the 121st this year. And all of those have come in the three months since lockdown was lifted in July."

"How many do you get in a normal year?"

"I did 101 repairs last year, total."

And those were just the cycle tourists passing through, who happened to need help at the precise moment they were passing through Scourie. Scott's local repairs also doubled. "Usually, I sell a couple of recycled bikes a month," he said. "But this year I sold forty in six weeks."

He had a list of all the cyclists that had ever needed his help and he talked about bikes with the same affection many people do their children. Between whizzes of his drills, painstakingly grinding the stubborn bolt to tiny shards, he answered my silly questions.

"What's this for?"

"That's a Victorian tyre lever."

"What's this?"

"That's a saddle for a recumbent."

"What's the most gears you could fit on a bike?"

"Twenty-seven."

"Are there many hills south of here?"

"Oh yes," he laughed. "You're in for quite a ride."

After about an hour, and a lot of persistence, he'd carved out the steel, rethreaded the hole and bolted the pannier rack back to the frame. I was expecting him to charge me at least £50, but he insisted on £10, which seemed stingy, even by my standards. We settled on £20, and I headed off, panniers secure, tyres pumped, headset and handlebars straightened. "Give me a call one day," he shouted. "It's nice to know that everyone gets home safely."

For the next couple of hours, I felt lighter, stronger. As though I'd just spent an hour with a chiropractor, an osteopath and a psychologist. The mass of food in my stomach burned white hot and my knees bobbed up and down like pistons attached to a steam engine. I was now cycling due south, in a straightish line, rather than taking a slalom route. It was nice to think that I was biting chunks out of the map.

The sky cleared even more, leaving fluffy cumulus clouds on a canvas of matt blue. If I were a religious man, I might have believed I was cycling toward pearly gates. At times the road would climb and climb, at others it would fall and fall. The only flat patches of land had been swamped by tea-brown lochs. Some had little dinghies at their shores, but most just had a goose or a moorhen on guard.

The road was silent, serene. A car would pass about every 10–15 minutes. Otherwise, the only sounds came from me.

Breaths. Snorts. Farts.

———

I stopped for lunch in a lay-by shadowed by pine trees. A scent of sweet bark lingered in the still air. Part IKEA warehouse, part garden centre. I plonked myself in the mud, tilted my head back and strained to see the trees move. Nothing, nothing stirred. Alone. Biscuits crunching in my empty ears.

But then, my heart jolted.

I thought I was seeing things, dizzy from the exercise. But as four giant hooves clopped and grazed over the tarmac, I stopped chewing. About 30 feet away from me, a ginger-brown stag with a cow-like face stood panting in the centre of the road. Grinding something between his teeth, he took a few more steps, then paused again.

He must have been 8 or 9 feet tall. Two perfect antlers, the colour of coffee-stained teeth, splintered into four or five points each. The sun glinted over his fuzzy golden mane. He had a broad, testosterone-filled chest like a kangaroo buck, but svelte legs like a petite ballet dancer.

For about 20 seconds – it seemed longer – we shared each other's gaze. No man, no deer, existed anywhere else in the universe. Thick steam curled out of his wet nostrils and a string of gloopy slobber dribbled from the crease between his black lips. Instinctively, I reached for my phone. But even the thought was enough to spook him. Before I could even move, he was trotting off into the forest, hurdling fallen branches.

After that moment, the next few hours seemed insignificant. A blur of lochs, lay-bys and crumbs flew past my cheeks. I obsessed with the stag. His proud shoulders. His dominant strides. I was ashamed that I'd ruined a beautiful, ephemeral moment, by giving in to the urge to take a crappy photo.

The road carved through a pair of cold granite hills, each one about the length and width of a fallen skyscraper. Football field-sized wire nets had been pulled taut around them. They might have protected a car from falling boulders, but fissures still loomed precariously above me. I cycled faster, head down, flinching.

Out the other side, into the topsy-turvy hills, a telephone line ran from one pylon to the next. Triangular signs warned of ice, flash floods and imminent climbs. Eight per cent. Eleven per cent. Eighteen per cent. The road ducked and curved away from me. All I could do was concentrate on the patch of tarmac about ten feet ahead. My entire life had become the road.

In the sunshine, the landscape was an Eden. Thickets of dense birch resembled warm oases. A trout sunbathed in a muddy stream. Two ducks rubbed necks on a mirror-calm loch. Wild and never-ending, I could have been in Vancouver, Patagonia or Lapland.

I stopped at a viewpoint to admire a vast, seamless forest sprawling away to the east. For a few minutes I was alone. Then a car vroomed in, a couple jumped out, took a selfie, jumped back in and drove off. I'd seen slower Formula-One pit stops. Cycling on, I wondered what might come of that photo. Would it get them 100 likes on Instagram? A dozen comments on Facebook? Or would it just eat up a few megabytes on a smartphone, then linger forever in a kitchen drawer?

The road plunged to sea level, skipped across a narrow spit running between the Atlantic and Loch Gleann Dubh, then climbed up again into a boggy plateau criss-crossed with pure streams and stagnant ponds. Mountains loomed to the east and west, but a cold wind whistled in from the north, pushing me south-west toward the sun.

I dropped down to the north shore of Loch Assynt and passed the crumbled ruins of Ardvreck Castle. I probably should have stopped to take a closer look, but there was already a scrum of Gore-Tex at its grassy base and a pair of ratty dogs yapping in the shallows. I just kept going, around the loch, through the hamlets of Inchnadamph, Elphin and Drumrunie, and followed the A835 toward Ullapool.

If I squinted, I could deceive myself into thinking I was alone in a landscape devoid of human interference. But when I stretched my eyes wide open, I saw crisp packets, ring pulls, plastic spoons and tin cans. I passed one lay-by spilling over with nappies and strands of toilet paper streaked with skid marks. Then the detritus got bigger. A mattress. A refrigerator. Two broken bin bags filled with rubble. Seven car tyres.

I looked at the chaste, wholesome mountains, then back to the piles of rubbish. It was hard to comprehend what sort of cretin would spray shit up the side of a bin or drive out of their way to deposit a lawn's worth of grass in a ditch. Nevertheless, these people existed. Somewhere, out there over the horizon, these people were going about their lives, without a second thought for the mess they'd left behind.

———————

By 5 p.m. I'd reached the small town of Ullapool and was knocking on the door of a garage that echoed with the swish of sandpaper. "Hello," I shouted, not wishing to startle the person inside. "Hello, anybody home?"

I'd been invited to stay with the parents of Peter Dawson, a teacher I'd met in Caracas, Venezuela, five years before. Peter had helped me with a report for the BBC World Service looking at product shortages and hyperinflation. We hit it off, and the expenses weren't great, so I ended up spending a week on his sofa.

By a weird coincidence, my route went right past his family home and he'd offered up his old bedroom for the night. A lovely gesture, apart from the fact that he wouldn't actually be there himself. Peter and his Venezuelan wife, Carla, were now living and working in South Korea. "Come in, Simon," said a voice from the garage. "Come and have a look at this." Peter's father, Topher, was covered from head to toe in fine sawdust and running his palms across the smooth hull of an upturned rowing boat. "A little lockdown project," he said. "I'll hopefully get it out on the water one day soon. It's been nice to have more time for things like this."

Within 5 minutes I had a glass of hoppy home brew in one hand and a slice of fruit cake in the other. "Just help yourself to more," said Peter's mother, Jan, before pointing me toward the shower and throwing my fetid clothes in the washing machine. "These have certainly seen some action. Maybe an incinerator would be more appropriate?"

The transition between the empty road and their warm home left me discombobulated. One moment I was alone, slogging my way up a lonely hill, the next I was in Peter's bedroom, surrounded by teenage football trophies and school certificates. As the smell of home-cooked food wafted in from the kitchen, I felt like an imposter. A charlatan, stealing cosiness I didn't deserve, while Peter and Carla holed up in their one-bed apartment in Seoul.

South Korea had been one of the few countries in the world where they could both get visas. They'd been working for two years, getting ready to return to Britain to make their case for residency. But then the pandemic struck, leaving them stranded on the other side of the planet while the Brexit clock kept counting down. Despite being married to a Briton, Carla could only visit for a three-month holiday. "Where does that leave them?" said Jan. "It's hard to know what will happen."

Topher, Jan and I sat around a kitchen table scratched with 40 years of family life. "You can see the marks of the kids' beer bottles from their Christmas drinking games," said Topher. "Do you fancy a shot of this Togolese moonshine Peter sent home for my birthday a few years ago?"

As steam rose up from plates piled high with salmon, pastry, potatoes and carrots, it was hard not to worry about Peter and Carla's future. Like billions of people before them, two people had fallen in love. One just happened to be from Britain, a country that was clamping down on immigration. The other was from Venezuela, a country tormented by unemployment, debt and political upheaval. Two lives had collided, but now, as one, they were stranded, impeded by events out of their control.

My bike ride seemed a lot less important. But with my tummy bulging and my lips red with Merlot, Topher began pulling maps from the bookshelf and plotting landmarks ahead of me with pepper grinders, pastry crumbs and dessertspoons licked clean of rhubarb crumble. "You can take the flatter, more dangerous inland route. Or the much more scenic road that takes you deep into the mountains. You'll have about ten miles in the morning to decide which way you want to go."

Unfurled in A2, Britain spilled over the sides of the kitchen table. I'd only cycled the length of a carrot. "I can't say I'd fancy either route," said Topher, delighting in my mammoth journey playing out in miniature. "It's really beautiful out there, but both ways are likely to be pretty busy. There aren't many toilets, either."

By another stroke of serendipity, I'd ended up staying with a man who was as enraged by roadside defecation as I was. Throughout the pandemic, Topher, a local councillor, and a team of equally committed locals had made it their mission to clean up the Highlands' lay-bys. "More vehicles, Covid and decreased availability of toilets created a perfect storm," he told me. "My emails were buzzing with angry messages from upset locals. It became evident that many people who normally might go to Greece or Spain were camping without the skills. They became known as 'dirty campers'. So, we put up signs in the hundred or so lay-bys in our area and equipped each sign with a plastic trowel. That way, if people got caught short, they could at least bury their business. The idea got a lot of publicity, but the Scottish *Daily Record*'s headline of 'Trowel motions' was fairly typical."

———

The next morning, I awoke from a short but deep sleep, comforted by the thought of other people waking up around me. A father, mother, friends. People that gave a shit, about other people's shit. They waved me off with a flask of coffee, four apples and a sandwich wrapped in tinfoil. It felt like my first day at school. "Take this," said Topher, handing me a trowel of my own. "Just in case."

The skies were blue and clear, specked with swirls of seagulls. A cool breeze whipped in from the shores of Loch Broom, but when it dropped, the sun felt warm, life affirming. At first, the road meandered along a whitewashed promenade of pubs, tea rooms and youth hostels, but then it climbed steeply south-east, through a tree-lined suburb of big houses, hotels and B&Bs. Panting and sweating, I wanted to turn around and climb back into bed.

After an hour I reached a crossroads. I could either go south-east down the A835, setting myself on the course that I'd been warned was dangerous. Or north-west on to the A832, toward Skye and the Applecross Pass, a mountain route so steep that there are dozens of videos on YouTube showing people how to drive it safely.

The thought of hauling myself and a fully loaded bicycle over a road that made gearboxes quiver and pound signs spin in the eyes of local mechanics didn't sound particularly attractive. It would have also added about 300 miles on to my trip. So, I decided to take my chances, and set off toward Inverness.

The tarmac felt smooth and silky. There was ample room for cars to pass me safely. I cycled past a handful of Topher's lay-bys, where trowels dangled on ropes like wind chimes. Geese ran and splashed across the surface of kidney bean-shaped lochs. Every hour or so I'd stop to brew up an espresso or have one-sided conversations with cows or horses. I felt light. Mindful of my surroundings and awake to the zip of my tyres flying over the asphalt.

The road cut through a valley flanked by distant mountains, but my path was true and flat. I had a train track on one side of me and a river on the other. For as long as they were in sight, I knew I could cruise at 14 mph without breaking sweat. To drivers and MAMILs, that might not sound like a lot, but as I zoomed through villages, leaving dog walkers in my wake, I could have been falling at terminal velocity.

By the end of the day, I'd cycled 70 miles, successfully given Inverness a wide berth and had a sunburned nose that was hot to the touch. Perhaps "dangerous road" was relative, I thought. Or maybe I'd just got lucky.

Just as the sun was setting, I cycled into Drumnadrochit, a tourist town on the north shore of Loch Ness. Every shop sold the same made-in-China tat. Fridge magnets, mugs and pens, festooned with cartoon "Nessie" monsters. I had the briefest of looks around, but the place made me feel nauseous. I feared I might throw up and then have to reclothe myself in a "My friend went to Loch Ness and all I got was this lousy T-shirt" T-shirt. Instead, I bought a bag of steaming chips, two bottles of beer and a few reduced-price sandwiches, and cycled out of town on the A82, the main road running east to west, parallel with the loch.

After a mile or two, the stark street lights faded, leaving just a distant orange aurora. I pulled in to a lay-by and descended a muddy track, probably traipsing through a summer's worth of human excrement. The gap between the water's edge and the road was only about 50 feet wide. It was a terrible place to camp, but I was exhausted and didn't fancy cycling through the night again. I pitched my tent on a flattish crag, pegs jutting out from between the slippery pebbles and guide ropes lashed to mossy boulders.

Willow trees and ferns drooped over the damp tent, but on the far side of the loch a few yellow lights twinkled and a faint scent of burning beech tinged the cold air. By 8 p.m. I was cocooned in my sleeping bag, with a tree root sticking into my ribcage and a twig jabbing into the back of my head. Every few minutes a car would pass and illuminate the trees through the canvas, shining brief, creepy shadows into the canopy, like inky Rorschach tests. The breeze was growing, causing the trees to creak and the loch to splash. I found it hard not to catastrophise. I pictured cars sliding off the road and squishing me in my sleep, or floating away and drowning in my tent. The more I thought, the more I suffocated.

I had 3 per cent of phone battery, so I called Alana.

"Where are you?" she asked.

"I've found a really cool place to camp, next to Loch Ness. You'd love it. Any luck with work?"

"Nothing. I just don't…" Her words shrieked a little as she gulped, then stopped. She sniffed, blew her nose, tried to talk again, but couldn't.

"This will all be over soon," I lied. "I promise this will be over soon."

"You know it's Sarah's funeral next week? Are you coming home?"

I paused for a moment that seemed to last an eternity.

"I promise. Whatever happens, even if I have to give this up, I promise I'll be there." I started to move the conversation on, but then, my phone died.

For the rest of the night, I drifted in and out of a troubled sleep, busy with a million dreams. All alone, with no one but myself for company, it was hard not to transfix upon all the other funerals I'd been to and the young lives that had been cut short. How could life be so unfair? This question had plagued me for almost two decades.

Every now and then a car would rumble past, turning the inside of my tent as bright as day. I'd jolt awake, ready to fight or fly, but then darkness would return. I was sure I could sense something out there, watching me. A human figure standing over the tent. I was too scared to leave, so I pissed into my empty beer bottle and poured the warm contents under the awning.

As soon as I could see the outline of my hand in the first mauve of dawn, I packed up. My eyes stung and my ribs ached, but I couldn't lie there for a minute longer. I had to move. An ethereal, smoky mist floated over the loch; scattered with logs, twigs and leaves, it was easy to see how a monster might have come to life here.

For the first hour, the road was empty and dry. The ditches were littered with leafy brown, but high above me the branches held tight to their golden summer glint. As the tunnel of trees grew thicker, so too did the feeling of being watched, followed. A red dog fox with a paintbrush tail skipped away in the distance. Half a mile further on, a pair of rabbits darted into a muddy bank. As sunlight washed over the loch, a shiny cock pheasant strode out into the silent road and let out a bossy caw.

But then the first lorry zoomed up behind me, and the heavens opened. I looked back briefly and wobbled out into its path. The beast grumbled, dropped a gear, then gurgled on, leaving a trail of diesel in its slipstream. This was the "dangerous road" Topher had warned me of.

Soon I was being stalked by a long line of vehicles. Parents on the school run, builders racing to site, farmers rushing to a field. I tried not to look back, all those annoyed people, huffing and puffing. Without a hard shoulder to hide in, all I could do was narrow my shoulders, hold a steady line and hope to be seen.

Short of throwing my bike into the loch and swimming, there was nowhere else I could go. So, I accepted my fate, and cycled on, past signs warning of a "serious collision" and "fatality here".

I busied myself by trying to guess what type of vehicle was about to overtake me, based on its unique sound. Tractors rumbled in a low pitch, like snoring lions. If they rattled, too, I knew they were pulling something heavy, deadly. Small cars had a higher engine tone and whined in first gear. Lorries sounded somewhere between the two, but vans were wild cards, impossible to pick.

Then came their unique smells. Most of the time it was just petrol fumes, but every now and then I'd be hit with something surprising. A builders' van drove slowly past and flooded the few square metres around me with the citrusy hum of delicious cannabis smoke. Half an hour later a truck rumbled through, pulling hundreds of sweet pine trees. A cement mixer reminded me of school playgrounds. A baker's van gave me daydreams of croissants. But just as I was about to pull over and google "patisseries near me" a refuse lorry made my stomach turn, leaving the pong of umpteen bins in its wake.

With Loch Ness over my left shoulder, and a convoy of vehicles behind my right, this pattern played out for 45 mostly flat and rainy miles. All I could do was concentrate on the tarmac ahead of me.

I didn't want to give the "dangerous road" another victim. And while I certainly preferred the open roads further north, sometimes these routes were good for focussing the mind. With two dozen frustrated eyes burning into my back, I probably cycled 5 mph faster than usual.

———

By 3 p.m. I was in the Fort William Wetherspoons, surrounded by lonely, half-drunk men, drowning their sorrows at £1.79 a time. As warm as a sauna and smelling of fried bread, it reminded me of my grandparents' council-house kitchen. It felt like the place I needed to be. With my clothes drip-drying on the backs of half a dozen chairs, I scrolled through my phone, skimming my Twitter feed.

I abhorred social media. It seemed like a tragic waste of time in lives that were so finite. Every time I scrolled, I felt worse, less significant. I'd stop on a post from a rival journalist and seethe at the sight of their new TV show or newspaper column.

On this trip, however, my phone quickly became a crutch. Without it, my tent would have felt colder and the road a lot lonelier. It was also nice to know that people were following along, vicariously riding with me from the comfort of their own homes.

One such person was Mary Ann Kennedy, a folk singer that started showing an interest in my journey while I was still in Shetland. She lived with her music-producer husband, Nick Turner, a few miles from Fort William and had offered me a place to sleep for the night. All I had to do was find them.

By the time I left the Wetherspoons, I'd charged my phone and laptop, drunk a £1 coffee, helped myself to two free refills, used the toilet three times and dried the majority of my clothes. I was practically a salaried member of staff. But I'd done enough freeloading for one day and I wanted to make a good impression, so I bought a £12 bottle of red wine from the Co-op – so as not to look too cheap, or too flash – and set off for the harbour.

It was hammering down again. Everything was grey. Soggy pigeons pecked at a few spent fag butts. A car flew through the traffic lights and sent a wave of dirty water across my shoes. Drenched and exhausted, I threw my bike and panniers on to the roof of a small boat and gladly left Fort William behind. "You've no chance of seeing Ben Nevis behind all this rain," said the captain. "But it's over there, behind the town, to the east." I nodded along, looking at a mass of white cloud. "It's quite the picture, when you can see it."

We crossed Loch Linnhe and landed in the hamlet of Gaul, where a grand oak tree towered over a small concrete jetty. The rain still blew in from the direction of the Atlantic but there was barely a sign of life. A defunct phone box, a dilapidated bus stop, a few old bottle banks. Then, a deer. Another deer. Dozens of deer, ripping at green sprigs of lichen on the pebbled beach.

I continued west down a single-track lane at the base of a toffee-black mountain topped with creamy mist. Grey wings flapped between the branches of moss-covered trees. A rabbit lunged out, just as I was about to freewheel over a cattle grid, causing my arms and wheels to flinch. My heart skipped a beat, but I just managed to pull the handlebars straight and stop myself from face-planting the iron rungs.

There were a few whitewashed bungalows away to my right, but I still hadn't seen a single human. Wild and empty, the landscape reminded me of those in Danny Boyle's zombie film *28 Days Later*. Perhaps the locals were hiding in their barns, counting rifle rounds, loo rolls and tins of tuna. Or maybe I'd been lured there as bait.

I eventually found Mary Ann and Nick's place thanks to their clear instructions: "turn right at the rusting fairground dodgem filled with green plants, next to the multicoloured wheelie bins". I was drenched and nervous, but they welcomed me in like an old friend, thrusting a cold beer into my hand and pointing me to the shower.

I'd stayed with hundreds of "strangers" over the years and met some incredible people. In the United States I slept on the porch of a Lutheran pastor, camped in the back yards of Vietnam veterans and crashed in the pool house of tech billionaires. I'd stayed with Christian evangelists, recovering heroin addicts, frat boys and widowers.

Only once had accepting these invites turned out badly, when a tattoo-covered neo-Nazi offered me his couch, positioned under a swastika in a room that reeked of crack cocaine. "So, what do you think about Brexit?" was the first thing he said to me, before offering me a slug of bourbon. I politely stayed for a beer, mumbled some apologies and camped in a nearby forest, startled by every crack of a branch.

Luckily, Mary Ann and Nick didn't seem to hold any far-right beliefs, and the only things hanging on their walls were bass guitars and mandolins. Instead, my biggest worry was trying to form coherent sentences after a long day in the saddle. By the time I got halfway through a second glass of wine, I'm pretty sure I was already slurring my words.

In a big house, surrounded by thousands of acres of deserted moorland, I'd assumed that life hadn't changed much for them during the pandemic. As the rest of the country locked down, surely, they were living the dream. But to my surprise, they admitted to finding life a struggle. "I couldn't sing or play at all to begin with; my brain just wouldn't do it," Mary Ann said, as she carved a leg of roast lamb. "I couldn't even listen to the tsunami of living-room performances online, it just felt so intrusive. The work disappeared overnight; it was really scary."

In a normal year, dozens of musicians would rock up and record albums in their music studio. For the first time in their adult lives, however, they were alone, struggling to fire creatively and keep their heads above water financially. "We're a really spread-out community up here," said Nick, pouring me a glass of red wine. "But that actually makes us even more connected, in a weird way. As musicians we're so used to living a life with people, nearly all the time. We need people to bounce off."

In a desperate bid to kick-start their artistic engines, Mary Ann decided to think outside the box. For 151 days straight she took the same photo of Ben Nevis from her front door, just to feel like she was still an artist. "Gradually, I came out of the funk I was in," she said. "I translated *The Lion, the Witch and the Wardrobe* into Gaelic and we filmed and streamed the book, chapter by chapter, for kids stuck at home. It became a valuable connection between me and my mum, in isolation in Glasgow. We'd spend three or four hours a day on the phone, going through the translation, editing and refining it. It was better than talking about shopping and sanitising."

After riding out the lean patch at the start of the pandemic, things picked up. They curated online music festivals and collaborated with artists as far away as India. "Strangely, I think I've worked with more people over the last six months than I have in the last six years," said Mary Ann. "It must be something about needing to stay connected, about solidarity. We threw barrel-loads of mud at the wall and just waited to see what stuck. It made me less precious about new ideas."

At some point, probably much earlier than it felt, I stumbled off to their recording studio and flopped on to a sofa bed surrounded by harps, pianos, drums and microphones, the tools for noise, frozen in eerie silence.

With their instruments taunting them, it was unsurprising that Nick and Mary Ann had struggled to stay positive. Just like me, their entire identity had vanished overnight. And as we struggled through an unprecedented and seismic ordeal, was it any wonder that many of us had suffered?

As I lay beneath the sheets, I tried to imagine what rousing melodies had been dreamed up between those walls before. Those times would return, I hoped, as I drifted into a fuzzy sleep.

I left early the next morning, my temples throbbing and my tongue resembling a dirty bar towel. Thankfully, the skies had cleared, and Ben Nevis loomed high above Fort William, its doughnut summit dusted in icing sugar. I caught the first ferry across Loch Linnhe, wolfed down a petrol-station bacon roll and cycled for 4 solid hours, sweating out Rioja all the way to Connel.

I was now faced with a significant decision. Shave 100 miles off my route and head inland on the busy A85 toward Loch Lomond, The Trossachs National Park and Glasgow. Or take the longer, scenic route down the Kintyre peninsula, spend a night on Arran and hop over the Firth of Clyde into Ayrshire.

As cars roared past me, it became a no-brainer. I hummed Paul McCartney's 1977 hit "Mull of Kintyre" and set a course for the seaside.

MALIN:
THUMPING TEARS

South of Connel, the road became a thin strand of tarmac, stitching its way through a tapestry of lush grass and ginger heather. I climbed to the summits of small hills, descended into the wells of V-shaped valleys, then hauled myself back up again. Up and down. Up and down. The afternoon felt like a roller coaster. In 3 hours, all I saw was a donkey, a shire horse and a flat-capped farmer; three rebellious pigs short of the entire cast of George Orwell's *Animal Farm*.

I had no idea where I'd stay that night, so I just rode, desperate to hit a respectable mileage. I was now determined to cycle as far as possible before Sarah's funeral. The closer I could get to the border with England, the easier my journey home would be. I knew I'd only be another face in the crowd, but the more time I spent on my own, the more I knew I had to be there. I needed to pay Sarah my last respects, I needed to show Nick that I cared. But perhaps more than anything, I couldn't live with the thought of not being there at the moment Alana needed me the most.

Alone on the road, I was stalked by the image of a black hearse. I remembered Joe being lowered into the ground less than six months before. I could still taste the stream of salty tears I shed on that drizzly April day and smell the white rose I dropped on his coffin before turning away for the last time. I buried myself in the miles, pushing the bike further and faster. The aches in my legs were nothing in contrast to the pangs of grief still drifting through my troubled mind.

About 60 miles south-west of Fort William, the sun started to set and I pondered a patch of flat grass on the eastern bank of Loch Melfort. In sight of the Slate Islands and the Inner Hebrides it would have been a wonderful place to camp, but according to my phone, "heavy rain" was due overnight, with winds of 40 mph. Curiously, the weather nearly always seemed to follow my mood. It felt foolhardy to ignore the forecast, so I hastily scrolled through cheap local guest houses on my phone.

The pandemic had made accommodation tantalisingly cheap. Hardly anyone was travelling at the time and I could find hotel rooms for as little as £20 a night. By the time they'd washed the sheets and replaced the teabags, I wondered if they were turning as much as a few pounds in profit. As the consumer, however, that wasn't my problem, and after a few nights in a tent eating 20p noodles or sleeping on someone's sofa, I figured I could splash out occasionally.

I settled on a 200-year-old country estate a few minutes away and crept up its leafy driveway as dusk descended. Tall trees loomed over me; gravel crunched under my tyres. From the outside, the three-storey house looked grand and ostentatious but its closed attic curtains, dank porch and black front door made me feel uneasy.

Before I had the chance to flee, I was met by a squat man with a hunched back and no neck. He reminded me of Quasimodo, in Crocs and a gilet.

"How many guests do you have tonight?" I asked, as we climbed a flight of creaky stairs with gargoyles carved into the banisters, looked down on by portraits of Victorian children with wandering eyes.

"Oh, just you," he replied. "You'll probably be our last guest before the winter."

A degree in film history has proven to be a blessing and a curse. On one hand, it's made me a dab hand at the movie rounds in pub quizzes, but on the other, a module in horror has given me an imagination that can run wild. The dim hallways resembled those in *The Shining*. The bed could have been straight out of *The Exorcist*. Even the shower curtain reminded me of *Psycho*.

"See you tomorrow," said the man, before shuffling away to a distant room.

I waited for a few seconds, then opened all the cupboards, looked under the bed, checked the paintings for secret peepholes, locked the door and leaned my panniers and a chair up against it. An hour later I was curled up on the lumpy horsehair mattress listening to the wind rattling the windows. "Happy thoughts," I mumbled to myself. "Happy thoughts."

It was a fretful night and I packed up and hit the road as soon as possible. Thankfully the morning was bright and crisp, and frozen puddles glinted like broken glass. Feeling cold, but dry and clean, this was always the best time to be on a bike. I had 10 hours of daylight ahead of me and the prospect of hitting Arran by nightfall.

After 9 miles I stopped at the eastern corner of Loch Craignish and brewed up a strong espresso. It was once an Iron Age landing point for settlers travelling between Ireland and Scotland's Great Glen. Celtic missionaries moved into the area in the seventh century, followed by Vikings a hundred years or so later. These days there are more expensive-looking yachts than longboats, but the view was as raw and wild as it must have always been. As I took my first hit of caffeine, a few balloon-shaped clouds bubbled up in front of the sun, dappling a dozen wooded islets in dark black spots.

The best mornings often seemed to follow the worst nights. I passed one perfect camping spot after another, wondering what might have been. Nevertheless, it felt like a morning to cherish and I sat a little taller in my saddle, excited for every loch and beach ahead of me.

In the small village of Cairnbaan, I joined the towpath of the Crinan Canal. Opened in 1801, as a shortcut between the river Clyde and the Inner Hebrides, it was the Panama or Suez of its day, saving mariners a detour around the storm-lashed Mull of Kintyre.

Unlike the canals I'd cycled alongside in southern England, busy with narrow beams and Dutch barges, Crinan was mostly filled with sailing yachts. Some of them could have, at least in theory, slipped their lines and sailed around the world. There was something quite magical in thinking *Old Rosie, Dragonfly* or *Carpe Diem* might one day round Cape Horn and end up in Pitcairn or Samoa, rather than rusting out their final days in a Glasgow scrapyard.

The canal ran into Loch Gilp and the towpath merged with the A83, the coast road running along the east side of the peninsula. Once again, it was beautiful and easy. For 15 miles I had browning trees on my right and a seaweed-strewn beach to my left.

I was starting to think I'd fluked a flat stretch. According to my bicycle computer, I'd climbed less than 1,000 feet all day. But then the road turned inland and started to rise steeply. It took me 2 hours to cycle 10 miles, adding another 2,000 feet to the tally.

By the time I finally made it to the jetty at Claonaig, every inch of my skin was covered in a layer of rapidly cooling sweat. I changed into dry clothes, then followed half a dozen cars on to the ferry heading for Arran.

———

I'll remember the 20-minute voyage across the Firth of Clyde for as long as I live. For starters, the water was as calm as a garden pond and to my relief the contents of my stomach remained *in situ*. But most memorable of all was the sheer grandeur of the island unfurling ahead of me. A green and mountainous otherworld encircled by a halo of cream clouds. It felt as though I was heading for a new planet entirely.

I'll also remember that journey for the puncture that revealed itself as I rolled down the ramp into the village of Lochranza.

"Where you headed?" said a voice from behind a face mask in a parked car.

"Campsite, I hope."

"Jump in. I'll give you a lift."

"Don't be silly, I can walk."

"Nope, I insist. We'll just open all the windows, and you can sit in the back left. That's *basically* two metres."

I hated the idea of cheating a lift, but before I could protest too much, the man was pulling off my panniers and throwing my bike in the boot of his car. What would have been a 20-minute walk, with my back rim grinding over tarmac, became a pleasant 2-minute drive. Sitting in the back-left seat with the windows down, I felt like a head of state, being chauffeur driven in the tropics. If we'd passed another person, I may have even practised my royal wave.

I spent the night at the Lochranza campsite, a place where horny stags outnumbered tents by five to one. Until that night I'd only ever heard crass Australian men use the term "chasing tail" but in the half-light of a full moon three antlered males rushed from one fluffy hind to the next. My plan had been to camp, but the owner was so impressed by my journey – and slightly concerned for my welfare – that he let me sleep in one of his small wooden glamping huts. It was only about the size of a Mini, but with a double mattress, a power socket and an electric heater, it felt like the royal suite at the Ritz.

The next morning, I awoke to the sound of 200 deer hooves thudding around the campsite. I loved that they were there and hadn't been fenced off somehow. This was their territory, and I was just squatting in it temporarily. I pulled back the curtains to reveal a red sun climbing through a horizon glistening with frost. The does packed tightly in scrums, steam rising from their backs like a smouldering pile of ash. Meanwhile the stags ogled them from 30 feet away, saliva dribbling from their mouths. They looked exhausted, close to death.

I fixed my puncture, completed a stubborn loop of the campsite – in order to make up for the distance I'd hitched the night before – and set off for the day. I knew almost nothing about Arran, and I liked it that way. When I first started travel writing, I obsessed about research, arriving on location with reams of printed pages, novels and guidebooks. But over time, I realised I was carving out a narrative in my mind, long before I'd given a place and its people a chance to carve one for me.

With only one road to follow, the morning was perfect for zoning out and trusting the compass. I climbed out of Lochranza and headed toward the island's uninhabited interior. A patchwork of burned heather and lush greens scrambled away from the greasy tarmac then rose up as distant peaty mountains. At times the road was so steep I could barely turn the pedals. I growled and spat, head down, inching my way up in the easiest gear.

At the top of an hour-long ascent, I looked back at what I'd achieved. I'd traversed a ceaseless bruised slope now enveloped by dense charcoal clouds. My red panniers popped brilliantly against the murky skyline, but a storm was now chasing me.

Within 10 minutes I was drenched again, but in a weird way, I enjoyed the rain. It seemed like the most fitting way to experience the island. I descended on to Arran's east coast, and into the seaside village of Sannox. I'd once read about a fabled cricket club in this most unlikely of places, and I rolled from one green field to the next, desperate to find familiar signs of life.

At first, all I could see was sheep, but then I spotted a shed-like pavilion next to a pile of mouldy boundary ropes and a rusting lawnmower. I marched toward them, fascinated. A pair of heavy iron rollers had been abandoned in the centre of what was once the wicket. Two ewes nibbled grass at square leg, another at long on and three more had successfully infiltrated cow corner. Wonderfully familiar, yet eerily deserted, the field felt solemn, like a graveyard.

Sannox Cricket Club had played on this bobbled oval since the 1960s, but dwindling interest saw them fold in 2018. The summer of 2020 was meant to be their comeback year but Covid stopped play before a single ball could be bowled. I cupped my hands around my eyes and peered through the pavilion's grimy windows. Scorebooks, bats, stumps and pads, strewn around a plywood mausoleum; a cricketing Pompeii, covered in owl and pigeon shit.

By the time I reached Arran's biggest village, Brodick, most of the rain had disappeared in the direction of Northern Ireland and a double rainbow now perfectly encircled the town's crazy golf course, lending it a grandeur it didn't really deserve. I scoffed down fish and chips and watched half a dozen families attempt to maintain social distancing while moving cautiously from one hole to the next.

———

Later that afternoon I boarded the ferry bound for the Scottish mainland and watched Arran grow smaller behind me. I was sad to leave, but the Firth of Clyde was as calm as it would ever be. An hour later I rolled into the harbour at Ardrossan, joined a puddled promenade and continued southward.

I cycled past a few teenage lads sharing an acrid-smelling spice spliff and wove around a snail-like woman pulling a shopping cart. A man on a park bench guzzled a can of Special Brew. A hooded figure with odd trainers waited impatiently outside a chemist. Then, in Irvine, I stopped at traffic lights and a V8 Range Rover pulled up beside me; its tinted window came down, a cigarette butt flew out and then it sped off down the road.

In the 15 miles between Ardrossan and Troon I counted 12 golf courses, in a coastal channel no wider than a mile. The car park at Royal Troon Golf Club could have been plucked straight from a Saudi palace. A single round of its Old Course cost £260 per person, over half the average Scottish weekly income.

Troon was well out of my price range, but with the wind howling and the rain lashing in again, I snagged myself a four-star hotel room at Ayr Racecourse for £40. I walked into the reception, dripping gritty water all over their spotless carpets.

"How much are these rooms usually?" I asked the suited concierge.

"Normally over £200."

We shared an embarrassed look, then I headed off to make a dent in the biscuits and bubble baths.

———

I left early the next morning. I had just two full days until Sarah's funeral and the only way I could keep my mind off it was to fill every waking hour with cycling. Miraculously, I'd now covered almost 600 miles but was still somehow 150 miles north of the border with England. More rain was set to arrive on an Atlantic storm, and the route ahead would be mostly scenic and mountainous, cutting through the wilds of Dumfries and Galloway. I was nervous for the days ahead.

But before I could leave Ayr I'd been invited for tea. My randomly plotted route around Britain had, once again, thrown up another strange coincidence. The cycle path that ran along the Ayrshire coastline passed the front door of the parents of a friend, Mark Lambert.

In their late eighties, Bob and Liz had been stuck at home, shielding from Covid-19. My arrival seemed to be one of the most exciting things to happen all year. "We usually watch the dogs playing on the beach," said Liz. "This really is a wonderful surprise."

We sat, socially distanced, in their breezy porch, while they fattened me up at arm's length. With no news of a vaccine and the UK and Scottish governments hinting at a second national lockdown, they seemed resigned to another year in isolation.

"The worst thing of all is not seeing my grandchildren," said Liz. "We're luckier than most, but that doesn't stop us feeling all the same human emotions as everyone else."

They were fascinated by the idea of a journalist cycling around Britain. They didn't like the idea of all the rain and dirt, but I could tell they were travellers at heart.

"Good for you," said Bob. "If I was fifty years younger..." At which point Liz let out an amused yelp.

"You never know," I said. "You two could get a tandem?"

Married for 56 years, with three sons and eight grandchildren, they'd lived and worked in Nigeria, Jersey and Singapore. After retiring, Bob fought off prostate cancer. Life must have felt even more precious after overcoming such a hurdle.

"We keep busy," said Liz, parachuting a plate of cake and sandwiches into my lap. "We have a family Zoom a couple of times a week and Bob has been speaking to a lot of old friends. We have to remain thankful for what we have. There are so many people worse off than we are."

"It could be worse," said Bob.

I could have happily chatted to Bob and Liz for hours. Warm and generous, they were the archetypal grandparents. They made me miss my own. I rolled out into the drizzle with half a kilo of ginger cake, a flask of vegetable soup and two boiled eggs.

"I'll see you again," I said. "When this is all over. We'll celebrate."

Pushing inland, into a sea of dark green spruce, I couldn't shift Bob's parting words: "It could be worse." Before the pandemic, this was something my dad would say if Oxford United were losing 5–0 or if his van broke down on the way to work. It always struck me as upbeat nihilism, repackaged as optimism. But as the pandemic rumbled on, I found myself saying it too. "It could be worse" – it was a typically British catchphrase, as relevant to lockdown as it was to the Western Front.

Stuck at home, seeing the world through the prism of social media and rolling news, it was easy to think that a hospital bed, then death, were the worst-case scenarios. But on the ground, moving at 10 mph, I could see that millions of lives had disintegrated in so many different ways. I certainly didn't want to take consolation in other people's suffering, but when I saw men drinking alone on park benches, or pensioners locked up in their homes, my own problems seemed a lot less extreme.

⎯⎯

Bar northern Scandinavia, Dumfries and Galloway was the greenest place I'd ever been. Millions of birch and elm trees sprawled southward for 300 square miles, forming Britain's biggest woodland, the Galloway Forest Park. Home to red squirrels, red deer and long-haired goats, it felt wilder than the Highlands. As I cycled deeper into its shadowed heart a pair of red kites whistled and circled above me, hugging a warm autumn thermal.

This empty corner of Scotland was handed "Dark Sky Park" status from the International Dark-Sky Association in 2009, putting it in an exclusive global club alongside Joshua Tree in California and the Grand Canyon in Arizona. In a normal year, around 800,000 tourists arrived to hike, camp and marvel at the Milky Way, but as I ventured further, down a tunnel of 100-foot-high pine trees, I could have been the last man on Earth.

I'd set up a quick meeting with David Warrington, the resident astronomer at the Scottish Dark Sky Observatory, a multimillion-pound telescope and planetarium built on the Craigengillan Estate. It had taken much longer to get there than I'd envisaged, because it was, perhaps unsurprisingly, positioned at the top of a ginormous muddy hill. The detour added 10 miles and 2,000 feet to my day, but when its domed white roof finally came into view I felt as though I'd stumbled across a nuclear bunker.

With 90 per cent of planes grounded during the first lockdown, David watched the skies clear above Britain. This resulted in crisper stars, free from the "noisy" contrails that usually distort the view. "In the past we've observed comets, explosions of supernovas and helped with the search for near-Earth asteroids," said David, as we looked down on the sprawling forest canopy. "But with everyone stuck at home all of a sudden the stars were clearer than usual. We obviously couldn't get people up here, but we still wanted to have some sort of outreach. It was more about giving people something to do beyond watching Netflix. So, I set the telescope up when the moon was visible and live streamed it on Facebook and Twitter. People could take part in virtual stargazing."

According to Ofcom, British adults spent 40 per cent of the first lockdown watching television, therefore the idea of a few people tearing themselves away from *Tiger King* and *Normal People* filled me with hope for the human race. "The lockdown killed our plans," he said, standing next to a telescope the size of a motorbike. "So, we had to completely rework how we ran our events. There was a massive surge in interest for space, so I broadcast a lot of talks online and helped people see planets from their back gardens."

Astronomers are, obviously, night owls, and David had been up late, so without wishing to outstay my welcome I left him to tinker with a computer and began my descent of the muddy hill. I was fascinated by the surprising new trends that the pandemic had created. Baking, home fitness and TikTok had boomed, but who would have predicted astronomy? Who knows, I thought, this tumultuous period in our lives could have inspired the next Stephen Hawking or Carl Sagan.

I cycled until dusk, then disappeared into a dense conifer wood somewhere north of Castle Douglas. As I traipsed into the darkness, a carpet of soft green moss squelched underfoot. I was used to having wet feet, but by the time I found a dryish place to pitch my tent, they were practically swimming in their respective shoes.

I found "wild camping" both exhilarating and terrifying. I was overnighting in a green tent, in the middle of a vast expanse of trees, without phone signal. I felt invisible. But if I'd broken a leg out there, no one knew where to find me.

Thankfully, the night passed without a hitch and I slept deeply for 4 unbroken hours under a billion throbbing stars. It was still well before dawn when I decided to pack up and leave, but free from man-made light, I could see for what felt like miles. The forest was bathed in a noirish, chiaroscuro sheen, and the tree trunks resembled silver pencils. I cycled for the first hour of the day without lights. There didn't seem much point in wasting the batteries.

———

Most of the morning fizzed by as a green blur, but by lunchtime I was cutting through Dumfries. It always felt strange to enter a town from the wilderness. I felt like an imposter, one of those weirdos raised by wolves.

People looked at me like a hobo, rather than a living, breathing human. This must be how homeless people feel, I thought, as a mother shielded her children from my gaze. "I'm a journalist, with a mortgage and a degree!" I wanted to shout at every person that gave me a dirty look. But then I caught the reflection of a grubby, bearded man, with bruised bags under his eyes, in the toilets of Costa Coffee, and conceded that I'd have probably crossed the pavement to avoid me, too. After the green, clean forest, I couldn't get out of Dumfries quick enough. It looked like a perfectly nice town, but my nostrils stung from the exhaust fumes and the voices in the streets seemed louder than ever.

I followed the river Nith for about 10 miles, then joined a country lane that cut through emerald farmland specked with dirty sheep. Golden leaves clogged the dykes and the trees looked gaunt and ready for winter. It was a relief to be back out in the windy, drizzly silence, but my chest was already tightening, and my lungs snatched at air. Part of me was annoyed that I'd made such good time and the border with England was now in sight. I wanted to slash my tyres and, maybe, an Achilles tendon.

I reached Gretna by late afternoon, checked into a £30 motel and spent half an hour stood under a burning shower. I emerged pink, with the taste of metallic phlegm on my lips, and spat a globule of bright red into the sink. I'd drawn blood. By gnawing away at the inside of my cheek.

Gretna was another grey splodge, famous for elopements and discount Levi's. Britain's attempt at Tijuana, just with worse food, fewer prostitutes and a lot more drizzle. Bored and restless, I sat in bed and drank a cheap bottle of red wine, then drifted off to sleep with the *News at Ten* whispering tales of death into my ears.

By lunchtime the next day, I'd crossed the border into England and was chaining my bike to the railings outside Penrith train station, hoping it would still be there when I returned from the funeral. Since setting off from the top of Shetland two weeks before, I'd cycled 800 miles, just 75 miles short of the traditional Land's End to John o'Groats distance. This was always going to be a significant milestone in my journey. But instead of feeling elated, the station swirled around me in a hazy, frantic fuzz. Pausing my journey felt like cheating, but to not return home and see my friends would have haunted me forever. My silly little bike ride was a vanity project in the grand scheme of things. I knew that Sarah would have done the same for me.

For 4 hours, England flashed past in fast forward – the antithesis of my sluggish norm. Preston. Wigan. Wolverhampton. Stafford. Birmingham. Thousands of people, every single second. By the time the train rolled into Banbury I felt seasick and stumbled off, straight into Alana's trembling arms. Warm tears ran from her swollen eyes on to my chest. The platform was empty by the time we came up for air.

The next morning, we lined the rain-lashed streets of Chipping Norton, shoulder to shoulder with hundreds of others, hiding our faces under a sea of multicoloured umbrellas. Black puddles collected on the same pavements that we'd stomped along as a mob of friends. Then, as a stream ran between our shiny shoes, a hearse arrived, carrying a wicker coffin covered in flowers.

For the first time since Sarah's death, I cried. I cried thumping tears. It felt as though my eyes might detach from their optic nerves and fall to my sodden feet. I couldn't find the strength to lift my head and look up at my friends. I just focussed on a finger-long twig about 2 feet ahead of me and listened to the sniffles and whimpers.

A few minutes later, Nick emerged from their family home, smiling broadly, full of incomprehensible strength. He hugged a few of us, then proudly revealed a small pin badge in the shape of a red-breasted robin.

"Just before she died," Nick said to us, "Sarah told me she'd come back as a robin. So, every time you see one, she hopes you'll think of her." He then thanked everyone for coming, apologised that Covid had prevented us from attending the funeral, took a deep breath and joined Sarah on her last adventure.

As the hearse disappeared, I became rattled by Nick's words. "Robins, robins, robins," I said to myself, unable to work out why that bird seemed so significant. "What is it with robins?"

I then scowled through the notes on my iPhone, speed-scanning thousands of words of nonsense. It took a few minutes, but finally I found what I was looking for.

"Shetland day 3. A robin skips through the bothy garden."

Less than an hour later, I found out that Sarah had died.

IRISH SEA:
LIFE HAD PURPOSE

By 7 a.m. the next morning, I was on a train destined for Penrith. At every station, I pressed my forehead against the window and searched desperately for little brown and red birds. Heavy chrome clouds weighed down on Middle England, but despite a pounding hangover, I felt lighter and brighter than before.

It would have been better if my first rest day had come out of cheerier circumstances, but my mind – if not my body – was certainly grateful for the respite. I already knew I was drinking too much but getting blind drunk had seemed like the right thing to do. When Joe passed suddenly, we didn't get the chance to give him a boozy send off, and I was convinced it prolonged the grief. Going home for Sarah's funeral had been as much about finding closure in the pub, as it was sobbing in the rain.

Thankfully, my bike was still where I left it and I rode out south, toward the Lake District National Park. My legs were well rested, but my spine felt twisted from spending 8 hours contorted on a train. I'd cycled 800 miles and climbed the equivalent of a Mount Everest, but somehow put my back out sitting still. Every few minutes a spasm zapped through me, so painful I had to stop and punch the burning muscles between my vertebrae.

The rain fell harder and louder than at any point on the trip. Muddy water whipped up from the bike's tyres, and soon my ears ached from the sound of a million icy droplets clattering against my helmet. Nevertheless, just to be living and moving felt like the ultimate privilege. I craved to be in motion, terrified of stasis. I fixated on the road, hypnotised by the sound of my turning wheels.

———

Celebrated Cumbrian authors William Wordsworth, Beatrix Potter and Arthur Ransome conveniently left the rain out of a lot of their work. The Lake District depicted in *The Tale of Peter Rabbit*, for example, is often bathed in a warm and cuddly yellow light, ideally suited for a child's bedtime. The reality, however, is significantly more nightmarish. Cumbria is officially the wettest county in Britain, with more than 200 days of rain a year.

By the time I hit the northern corner of Ullswater, sections of the lakeside road were submerged under a foot of muddy water. But despite the deluge, the rambling green fells emitted a bucolic charm unlike anything I'd seen in Scotland. I wanted to jump over every stile and run my palm across the lichen-encrusted walls. I felt the urge to tussle the dreadlocked topknots of Highland cattle and march to the summits of their waterlogged paddocks.

And herein lies Cumbria's biggest problem. Even in the pouring rain, it's too beautiful for most people to leave at arm's length. Each year, 47 million tourists arrive, and inevitably some of them end up straying from the footpaths or letting their dogs loose in fields of sheep. The result is an often-fractious relationship between the tourism industry and local farmers, who are forced to share their country lanes with thousands of surplus townies.

When the pandemic hit, some campaign groups and politicians suggested a London-style congestion charge. There was also a surge in abandoned "wild" campsites. The local police force went out on nightly patrols, handing out fines to campers who had encroached upon private land. Unlike in Scotland, where the Land Reform Act of

2003 legally permits responsible "wild camping", no such law exists in England.

As I cycled deeper into the national park, I felt conflicted. On one hand I sympathised with the landowners cleaning up after the tiny, irresponsible minority, but on the other, it seemed like a travesty that so much green space was off limits. Sometimes we forget that human beings are animals, too. Surely, we need fresh air just as much as cows and sheep do. Moreover, one in eight Britons doesn't have access to a garden.

It was hard to travel along the thin road, surrounded by hundreds of thousands of acres of private land, and not feel slightly ripped off. Under normal circumstances I would have thrown caution to the wind and pitched my tent under a tree somewhere, but I felt like I had to do things by the letter of the law. My trip was being followed by thousands of people on social media, and in the court room that is Twitter, I was only ever one tweet away from a virtual pile on.

Luckily, the rain was so intense that I couldn't have contemplated camping without a life vest. In fact, by the time I reached the small village of Patterdale, at the southern end of Ullswater, the Met Office had reclassified the downpour with an amber weather warning. According to the official advice, people travelling in such conditions should "be prepared" and "avoid any unnecessary travel". Simple enough in a car, but on a bike, I had little choice but to continue. Soon I was as wet as I could ever be, and I just continued, doggedly, with the hope of finding a B&B before nightfall.

An even bigger problem, however, was the random route I'd plotted. In order to avoid the M6 and its many adjacent A-roads, I was following the A592, a straightish-looking road that rounded the north shore of lake Windermere. Serious cyclists would have done a lot more research, but I was so eager to make up the ground I'd lost due to the funeral that I continued, oblivious to what lay ahead.

The road started out flat enough, weaving through a channel of 6-foot-high drystone walls, but within half an hour I was climbing, steeper and steeper with every turn of the wheels. Unbeknownst to me, I was hauling myself up the Lake District's highest driveable mountain pass: Kirkstone, known locally as "the Struggle". Imagine lugging a heavily loaded wheelbarrow up the infamously long and steep escalator at London's Angel tube station. But rather than a measly 90 feet, enduring the pain for 1,489 feet, and up a gradient of 20 per cent. Even in my lowest gear, standing out of the saddle, I was lucky if I could move at 2 mph. I should have turned back.

The rain soon became so ferocious that I couldn't see more than a few feet ahead of me. Even Cumbria's hardy sheep huddled together in flock-sized scrums, like Antarctic emperor penguins shielding from the polar freeze. The deluge grew so intense, and the wind so fierce, that beads of painful rain stabbed into my exposed cheeks with the unforgiving sting of a thousand tattoo guns. About three quarters of the way up, I passed a man and a woman in a warm camper van, sensibly sitting out the storm with a Thermos flask. "What the fuck is this idiot doing?" I lip-read the driver saying to his wife, before he took a photo of me through his steamy windscreen.

It eventually took me 2.5 hours to reach the summit, an underwhelming patch of flat grey tarmac. Scafell Pike, England's highest mountain, was somewhere away to the west, but I could barely see a few tufts of grass on either side of the road. The only other sign of life was a recently deceased cock pheasant that had been pummelled out of its chestnut-turquoise plumage. Stripped clean of its outer shell, it was now more meat than bird. All I'd wanted to do was reach the top, but now that I was there, I couldn't wait to get off it. My sodden clothes must have weighed an extra 5 kg. Steam seeped out from my collar and sleeves. I inhaled a handful of soggy Hobnobs and set off down the other side.

Gritty water washed between my wheel rims and brake pads, producing a scratchy, evil squeal. And despite clasping the brake levers as tight as physically possible, I descended at 15 mph. I unclipped my shoes and dragged them along the road. Anything to slow me down. In just 5 miles I dropped 1,000 feet, and by the time the land flattened out again, my knuckles were bleached white, criss-crossed with bright-blue veins.

It was a relief to eventually reach the north shore of lake Windermere. The rain was still crashing down, and I took shelter under the first trees I'd seen for hours. I rooted around for something to eat, but then, out of nowhere, I heard my name.

"Simon!" said a strangely familiar voice.

I thought I was hearing things, so ignored it. But then it came again.

"Simon!"

I looked out into the lay-by, where an estate car with swishing windscreen wipers was flashing its headlights in my direction.

"How's it going, mate?" said a voice from within. "We thought you could do with some Kendal mint cake."

It took a few seconds for my brain to catch up, but inside the car was Rich Evans, an old flatmate from university. I hadn't seen him for 12 years, probably since the day we graduated. Yet somehow, here we now were, two grown-up men, face to face.

"We've been stalking you on Twitter and thought you might appreciate the extra calories." At which point he handed me a bag of sugary snacks.

On holiday with his wife and two young children, Rich looked clean, dry and contented with fatherhood. I, on the other hand, caught my reflection in his wing mirror and saw a gaunt man with sunken eyes and chapped lips.

"Did you just come over Kirkstone?" he asked, clearly displaying a better knowledge of the region than me. I nodded.

"You crazy bastard."

We chatted for 10 minutes, quickly drifting back into our student patois. He gave me a brief overview of married life, then, despite my shivers, I tried to give the impression that I was living the dream. It was a heart-warming interlude on an otherwise rotten day, but with his children growing restless, Rich departed to a nearby chalet, and I squelched off down the road, my teeth chattering between mouthfuls of mint cake.

As I cycled along the banks of Windermere, with Rich's life fresh in my frazzled mind, I felt jealous of him. Jealous of his fatherly calm, while all I wanted to do was rush to the next place. In Cumbria, in Britain, in life.

As the rain clattered down around me, I wondered if I was chasing something, or really just running away. I knew that Alana wanted to have a family sometime soon. And I knew it would mark a junction in our life together. Either we went in the same direction, or we diverted to our separate ways with broken hearts. I could imagine myself cradling a son or daughter in my arms, but part of me also still hankered to be young and carefree. Single, alone.

———

By the time I reached Kendal, the rain had stopped, and a few rays of buttery sunlight pierced the sludgy grey. I celebrated with a hot pasty and cup of coffee in one of those farm shops where everything costs about 50 per cent more than it should do, then spent the rest of the afternoon on the hard shoulder of a busy dual carriageway, weaving around shredded tyres and lorry-butchered venison.

I only stopped once in 2 hours, to speak to the drive-time show on BBC Radio Cumbria. "So, how's it been out there?" asked the enthusiastic presenter, from the comfort of her warm studio.

"Incredible," I lied.

"You've had some pretty serious weather."

"I've loved every minute of it."

I finally made it to Arnside, a seaside village on the north-eastern corner of Morecambe Bay, just before dark. A pair of black guillemots scratched and stabbed at stubborn limpets under the town's Victorian promenade. The street lamps clunked on, and away to the west, a fishing boat steamed in from the Irish Sea. I'd dissected the Lakes, but on one of the wettest days in living memory. A month's worth of rain had fallen in just a few hours. I was dripping wet but feeling surprisingly chipper.

I then saw the front pages of the day's newspapers and my heart sank. Their headlines were unanimous: another national lockdown could be just days away. Worse still, I was now on a collision course for Lancashire and Greater Manchester, which were already under Tier-3 restrictions. In theory, I wasn't allowed to pass through, unless I was travelling for work. So, I rooted around in my panniers for a damp business card and rehearsed my best "this is an essential journey" spiel, just in case I was stopped by the police.

Cycle touring has never been straightforward. In fact, it's the unknowing that makes it all so addictive. But travelling during a pandemic ratcheted up the stress levels even more. I'd need to complete a 100-mile dash across Tier-3 Lancashire the next day. By first overnighting on the southern edge of Tier-1 Cumbria, I could at least sleep within the boundaries of the law.

Thankfully, there was a spare room available in one of the guest houses overlooking the sea. And as I sank into a hot bath with a cold beer, I sketched out my grand tour of the north-west: Preston, Wigan, Bolton, Runcorn, Crewe. I could hardly contain my excitement.

Later that night I had dinner with the owner of the guest house, Lesley Hornsby. She seemed determined to put on a brave face, despite feeling weary from lockdowns and cancellations. "Although Cumbria has been in Tier One, we're surrounded by Tiers Two and Three," she told me. "This means that most of my customers, who live in Lancashire, can't actually visit. The taps were turned on in summer and everyone was busy, but then – suddenly – they were turned off again."

Arnside, like a lot of Britain, enjoyed a few months of post-lockdown buzz, and most local businesses had scrambled to make hay while the sun shone. The promenade was packed with twitchers, spotting curlews, waders and woodpeckers, while the west-facing pubs enjoyed deep-red sunsets. Nevertheless, by the time of my arrival Cumbria's tourism industry had only contributed £1.7 billion to the county's annual economy; half what it does in a normal year. "It's grim," said Lesley. "I don't know the answer."

But a bad year for tourism wasn't necessarily a bad one for the village. The low summer tides made Arnside's mudflats a hub for socially distant water sports. "Our membership increased by fifty per cent this year," said Alasdair Simpson of the Arnside Sailing Club, who popped in for a cuppa later that evening. "We've almost quadrupled our membership since 2015."

Paddleboarding became particularly trendy, with 162 people taking lessons. In fact, unlike the depressing picture of rising unemployment nationally, in Arnside at least one new job was created. "We were able to employ an instructor full-time over the summer," said Alasdair. "In a normal year they would have been working for the [temporarily closed] outdoor centres inland."

———

I cycled out the next morning wondering how Lesley had found the motivation to keep going. She'd invested her life into a business that could be opened and closed at the whim of men in suits, 300 miles away in Westminster. While Cumbria remained in Tier 1, she wasn't permitted to claim the same benefits as people living just a few miles away in Tier 3. Therefore, unlike me, she was hoping for a national lockdown.

I had 10 hours of daylight to get somewhere south of Liverpool. It wasn't raining, which was always a small bonus, but the task ahead of me was daunting. I would need the day to pass without a single hiccup, while cycling further than I had done in years.

Thankfully, the first 10 miles whizzed by, winding through little seaside villages along the sludgy banks of Morecambe Bay. Covering an area of 120 square miles, the estuary was once only ever known as a holiday destination, but ever since 5 February 2004 it has been remembered as the site of a cockle-picking tragedy that claimed the lives of at least 21 illegal Chinese immigrants.

The group of mostly young men in their twenties and thirties had been trafficked halfway around the world to collect shellfish at a back-breaking rate of £5 per 25 kg. They didn't know enough about the local tides and when the water raced in, they became stranded and drowned.

For most of the morning the brown bay had festered under an inky black cloud, but as I turned south-east the sun finally broke through, lending the mud a brilliant shimmer, something like a Bolivian salt flat. I wanted to stop and soak in the vitamin D, but I knew I had to make ground. I joined the Lancaster Canal and pushed on. And on. And on.

In the space of a few hours, the towpath carried me 30 miles, from a quiet green corner of Cumbria to a noisy grey sprawl. Towns and cities blurred into one, and suddenly, the world reeked. Of cigarette smoke and grease. Of petrol and fried chicken.

For 800 miles I'd felt almost invisible, moving through Britain like a ghost. But then, somewhere north of Preston a white van zoomed past me, so close the passenger-side wing mirror grazed my right shoulder. "Prick!" I shouted instinctively, struggling to stay upright. I thought nothing more of it, until I then saw the shaven-headed driver stood in a bus stop about 500 feet ahead of me. As I got closer, he got bigger. Built like a rhinoceros, with biceps bulging out of a tight T-shirt, he had a swollen green vein zigzagging through his sweaty red forehead.

He looked capable of crushing my bike and skull between his finger and thumb, so instead of making eye contact, I dropped my chin and looked down at the road. As I cycled on, I could hear him following me, revving his engine in first gear. This went on for at least a mile, before I turned sharply down a bridleway and left him to pick a fight with someone else.

Professional cycling teams invest millions into psychologists, analysts and dieticians, just to achieve tiny gains on their rivals. But perhaps they should simply employ an angry northerner with road rage to berate their riders from a moped. Thinking I was about to be bundled into a Transit van and disposed of somewhere near Blackburn, I cycled about 3 mph faster. I didn't feel safe until I hit the pedestrianised streets of Preston's city centre.

Like much of the north-west, the city was under lockdown, and devoid of human buzz. Subway napkins, McDonald's burger wrappers and dead autumn leaves swirled in the doorways of nail bars and pawn shops. I sat on one of those riveted benches, deliberately designed to be uncomfortable, and inhaled a sausage roll, two meat pies and a slab of lardy cake. An old man with silver hair and sellotaped thick glasses dragged a grubby little dog along the pavement. I was pretty sure it was a bichon frise, or perhaps just his kitchen mop.

I only paused for a few minutes, but just as I was about to leave, a woman about my age appeared with a filthy duvet draped across her skinny shoulders.

"Have you got any money, mate?" she asked, in a Scouse accent.

"No, sorry," I replied, instinctively, harshly.

She looked at me and my bike, then turned and stumbled away. I watched her slowly walk down the street, picking up cigarette ends and looking in the bins. Every step she took, I felt more and more ashamed. It had become so easy to think that I was the most hard-done-by person on Planet Earth, but really, I'd become just another privileged white bloke on a navel-gazing bike ride. In a feeble attempt at redemption, I took £10 out of my overdraft at the nearest cash machine and cut her off at the top of the road.

I escaped the deserted city in a sombre, reflective mood. Deepdale, the 24,000-seater home of Preston North End Football Club, sat eerily quiet. A cold wind rumbled against its corrugated grubby shell, but the thought of a noisy, singing crowd was all but a melancholic fantasy.

I flew through one suburban splodge after another. Leyland, Bamber Bridge, Clayton; all seemed to simmer with tetchy energy. Then, just outside Chorley, I cycled through the dying embers of an angry row between two red-faced dog walkers.

"I've got you marked," yelled a man in jeans and a shiny Adidas jacket, clutching the collar of his snarling Staffordshire bull terrier.

"Oh, piss off, you pleb," replied the other man, wearing chinos and a Barbour, before lobbing a tennis ball for his doting Labrador. Meanwhile, a socially distant melee took photos from a distance.

—

In Scotland's rural corners, life hadn't seemed all too different at all. The fields still glowed pre-pandemic green, and the cows mooed none the wiser. But in England's bottleneck north-west, where dozens of motorways roared between prefab Matalans the size of power stations, the atmosphere felt claustrophobic. The cycling infrastructure was also the poorest I'd experienced anywhere in Britain. In fact, to describe it as "infrastructure" would wrongly suggest a cohesive network. One minute I'd be flying along at 15 mph, then, all of a sudden, I'd be cut off by a busy dual carriageway.

In order to avoid Wigan and Bolton I had to squeeze through a heavily fly-tipped rural channel, where shifty men sat bumper to bumper in blacked-out Audis. They were either dogging or dealing. Regardless, neither was my business, and I just looked straight and kept on moving.

By 3 p.m. I'd cycled 50 miles. I was on course to reach Tier-2 Shropshire by nightfall and my brain fizzed with adrenaline. When I had a very clear goal to achieve, my mind and body were too busy to manifest the physical symptoms of anxiety that had crippled me further north. As I twisted through the gears, fixated on the prospect of a warm shower and a comfortable bed, even the roar of the motorway fell silent. I had no idea where I might stay, but I knew that the alternative was bleak: pitching my tent in a littered wasteland somewhere near the M6. I rode and rode, maniacally turning the pedals.

But then, on a cycle path somewhere north-east of St Helens, my back tyre was flat. I was furious, but with the sun setting, every second was precious. It took me almost half an hour to fix and left me with the palms of a coal miner. But after less than a mile, the tyre was flat again. I didn't have the energy to start over, so I walked, very slowly, to the nearest town, Haydock.

It wasn't hard to convince a four-star hotel that I was travelling for work. "I don't really care, mate," said the teenager at reception. "If you say you are, then you are." The room cost me £30 – their only booking that night – and I must have consumed at least that in hot water and Nespresso pods. Warm, clean and buzzed, I spent the rest of the night fastidiously inspecting the inside of my back tyre while eating 20p packets of instant noodles out of a teacup.

After the psychological problems that had plagued my ride further north, it felt as though I was enjoying a rare purple patch. Sure, there were logistical hurdles and inconveniences to overcome. But nothing was as bad as the feeling of suffocating, constantly. Now that some order had been restored – maybe just momentarily – it was important that I savoured it. Feeling "normal" wasn't a given but a sensation to cherish when it came along.

I set off early the next morning, desperate to get out of Lancashire. No rain was forecast, and a tailwind gusted from north to south. The first half an hour passed without a hitch, but a few minutes after crossing the river Mersey, just south of Warrington: POP. Another puncture. Always the back wheel. Always when I was making progress.

With no major town ahead of me for at least 100 miles I had no choice but to backtrack. I hated going in the wrong direction, but something sinister was causing the punctures and I knew it would waste even more time to keep fixing them. So, I trudged back to Warrington, taunted by the sound of a rubber tyre squelching flat across the pavement.

Every bike shop was closed, apart from one independent outfit, Cyclehouse, and thankfully the owner, Simon Owen, was as friendly as every bike mechanic I'd ever met. "Get all the bags off, help yourself to a coffee and I'll see what I can do," he said, before putting the bike through triage. Ten minutes later he announced that he couldn't find a specific problem but suggested my patchy inner tubes were probably to blame, and began fitting new ones, just to be sure.

I knew that the pandemic had triggered a cycling boom, but I was fascinated to find out what that meant for the people working in the industry at ground level. "Up until coronavirus hit, the bike trade was pretty much on its knees," said Simon. "The big chains had caused a lot of problems because they ran at a loss for years, gradually killing off the independent trade. Then coronavirus came along and it gave the independent stores an adrenaline injection."

Between April and June 2020, when the government allowed people to escape their homes for essential exercise, cycling's popularity surged by 250 per cent. By the end of the year, a million more people had taken to the roads than in 2019, and bike sales had contributed an extra £2.2 billion to Britain's flailing economy. "Before the pandemic, many independent shops had mountains of debt, but now a lot of us are in a much better position. It's certainly helped level up the playing field."

I loved the idea that small independent bike shops had been handed an unexpected lifeline. Especially considering that, on the whole, the pandemic helped the world's richest people get richer and plunged its poorest further into poverty. Better still, it was nice to think that a third-generation bike-shop owner like Simon could pay himself a good living wage, rather than simply having to persevere because he had no alternative.

British towns need bike shops, not only to provide annual services and sales, but because they're cultural hubs, just as important as football clubs, markets and pubs. They smell of rubber and coffee, and echo with the clip-clop of muddy cleats. I've never walked into a bike shop and not felt immediately at home. And, true to form, this one had swallowed me whole. "Any problems, just come back," said Simon, as I rolled out into yet more heavy rain.

It was Halloween, and Boris Johnson was set to address the nation that evening. A second national lockdown looked imminent, but all I could do was keep pedalling. Nevertheless, I found it hard to muster the motivation, knowing that my end-to-end could be cut short, just as I was approaching the home straight.

———

I'd never been particularly interested in the "further, faster" clique of adventure cycling. There was far too much willy- and flag-waving for my liking. Furthermore, racing through somewhere as quickly as possible seemed far too much about the rider and his or her inflated ego than the place and its people.

I did, however, have a weird obsession with my overland journeys beginning and ending at geographically satisfying points. When I was 19, I hitch-hiked between the northernmost and southernmost points of New Zealand. When I was 27, I drove a rickshaw from the top to the bottom of India. When I was 28, I sailed and cycled from China to London. And when I was 30, I cycled from the North Cape in Norway to the southern end of the Scandinavian peninsula in Sweden. In my mind's eye, this journey through Britain was always meant to begin and end at its two extreme points: the Muckle Flugga and Bishop Rock lighthouses. Not a random Burger King car park on the outskirts of a Midlands provincial town.

It took most of the afternoon to escape the incessant hum of Manchester, and it was a relief to finally glimpse the rambling farmland of north Shropshire. The familiar scent of silage hung in the wet air, and rather than old mattresses and paving slabs, the road was littered in jewel-like conkers and silver-red leaves that glinted like £50 notes.

I was now only 10 miles from the Welsh border and my original plan had been to add on a 500-mile detour by following the Wales Coast Path, all the way from Chester to Chepstow. I'd wanted to pass through Snowdonia, Anglesey and Pembrokeshire, and document how Wales had managed the pandemic, but the country was already under a national lockdown and there were reports of police cars patrolling the main roads in and out. I was tempted to cycle on all the same, but with every hotel, pub and café closed, a week sleeping rough, and illegally, wasn't quite what I had in mind. I'd also done well to reach the age of 33 with a clean criminal record, and the last thing any travel writer wants is a black mark against their name. So, I continued deeper into Shropshire.

On the official tourist-board website, the landlocked county is described as a "secret", and under normal circumstances, this would have set alarm bells ringing. In the travel PR world, "secret" is often the spin that really means "no one bothers coming here" and should be taken as seriously as an estate agent describing a property as "cosy".

Secret Shropshire, however, was a revelation, and when the rain finally abated, a lush sprawl of green emerged from beneath the cloud. There were robins chirping in the hedgerows and the smoke-tipped wing feathers of magpies clinging to the roadside brambles. In the 2 hours I spent cycling along the country lanes between Winsford and Whitchurch, I counted more sheep than cars.

———

Via a friend of a friend, I'd been invited to stay at Soulton Hall, a bed and breakfast 3 miles east of Wem. I hadn't checked the website and I expected to find a run-down country home but was startled by the sight of a sixteenth-century red-brick manor house, surrounded by kitchen gardens and 500 acres of farmland. I crunched up the gravel driveway, under a pair of spooky oak trees. The silhouettes of cows and their calves melted into the purple dusk, and behind the hall's single-glaze windows, an open fire flickered warm orange. As I leaned my bike beside a pair of stone owls, the warm sweat on the back of my neck seemed to freeze even quicker than usual.

Thankfully, Soulton's owner, Tim Ashton, emerged from the gloom and immediately put my mind at ease. About my age, with a warm smile and muddy wellington boots, he handed me a cold bottle of beer before I could properly catch my breath. "Before it gets too dark, let's get out into the fields," said Tim. "You can follow me in the tractor."

The hall had been in Tim's family for 450 years; however, it was immediately clear that he wasn't a snooty lord-of-the-manor type, but an entrepreneurial young farmer who was battling through the pandemic just like everyone else. Until the virus, his home had been a successful wedding and conference venue, but when that trade disappeared overnight, he was forced to come up with new business ideas.

The most popular was an outdoor – Covid-friendly – amphitheatre called "The Sanctuary", and in the dwindling half-light we tiptoed around its waterlogged stage, surrounded by two semicircle grass banks and a JCB-dug moat. Tim had been inspired by the story of Shakespeare's acting troupe, the King's Men, who had visited Shropshire during the plague of 1603, with the intention of keeping British culture on life support.

"It was vitally important to do this, this year, because live performances had been stopped," said Tim. "This was about taking civic responsibility and providing local communities with access to culture. We also wanted to set an example that other people might follow."

Despite suffering a broken tibia in early 2020, and needing to adapt to the ever-changing guidance on live events, Tim hosted 14 performances in total, welcoming over 1,000 people to watch open-air shows, ranging from *Horrible Histories* to *A Midsummer Night's Dream*. "I know of five landowners that saw what we did here this summer and are planning their own events next year," he told me, as a full moon began to rise. "But now let's get back to the hall for roast lamb and mashed potatoes. You could also do with a wash."

Amid unprecedented societal disruption, Tim had been determined to muddle through in the best way he could. He reminded me of every farmer I'd ever known. Calm, placid and mollified by the inevitable passing of the seasons, despite the calamities of the human world unfolding around him.

In that sense, there was something very similar about farmers and cyclists. Perhaps the revolving tyres of a bicycle and the spinning blades of a combine soothed the human soul just like the rotating rims of a Buddhist prayer wheel.

An hour later I was clean and settled in a grand candlelit dining room. With beech embers spitting from the open fire and meat piled high on my plate, every gravy-soaked mouthful delivered protein to my aching limbs. I was glad to be off the bike, but I knew that when morning eventually came, I'd be itching to get back on it again. All I wanted to do was ride. When I was riding, my life had purpose, direction.

But then, at 7.30 p.m., the prime minister appeared on the nation's television screens, bearing a solemn and exhausted expression. "Now is the time to take action," he said, staring into our living rooms, "because there is no alternative. From Thursday until the start of December, you must stay at home."

LUNDY:
FOUR MEASLY DAYS

I now had just four days. Four measly days, to complete a journey that was meant to take another two weeks. I'd cycled over 900 miles, but I was still 400 miles short of Land's End at the south-west tip of England. In order to get there, I'd need to travel further and faster than I had done at any point on the entire trip. I felt fit, but Devon and Cornwall were infamously hilly. Attempting four consecutive 100-mile days felt not only foolish, but probably impossible. I was in the wrong place, at exactly the wrong time.

This trip had been about slowing down and seeing things more clearly, and I'd reached a moment when this was finally happening. My lungs felt free of stress and pain, and I could sleep deeply, for a few restful hours, at least. What might pushing myself to such an extreme level do to me both physically and psychologically? I was wary of risking a state of hyper-adrenaline – the very chemical that had caused me so much discomfort. But despite all that, my ego was still urging me to suck it up and crack on. After everything that had gone before, the fear of failure was an addiction more powerful than any.

While I'd been ambling along at 50–70 miles a day further north, the pandemic had constricted me. I felt cheated that my journey was being impacted on, but another side of me felt guilty for seeing things so selfishly. There were people lying in hospital beds, saying their laboured goodbyes to loved ones via iPads, yet there I was, ruminating over the pathetic injustice of having my silly little bike ride cut short.

My Twitter followers were, somewhat predictably, unanimous in urging me to have a stab at reaching Land's End. These things are, however, always simpler in 280 characters, and it was easy for my confidence to grow with every incoming message of support. Alana, meanwhile, was more ambiguous. "If you try and do it, you'll make yourself ill," she said. "But then again, if we're going to be in lockdown for another six months, you'll be stressing about it all winter. And I'm not sure that will be good for either of us."

I rolled out early the next morning, exhausted from worry. The sky was thick with sooty clouds, so heavy they threatened to suffocate the earth. But thankfully, the road was mostly dry and clear. Just a few random patches of golden leaves and a couple of piles of shiny nitrous-oxide canisters, dropped off by the gremlins of the night.

With the wind at my back – for now, at least – I tried to enjoy the miles as they whistled beneath me. There were ponies in rugs and sheep with sopping woollen fleeces the colour of tobacco-stained hair. Six scruffy crows followed me for a while, got bored, then heckled from the branches of a hawthorn, drooping with a thousand glinting rubies. The air was cool and crisp, flavoured with a pinch of earthy silage.

But by 10 a.m. I'd only cycled 15 miles and could already feel myself falling behind. It was soon impossible to think about anything but the final finish line. Chocolatey fields whooshed past me in a haze. I stopped to scoff a banana beside the ruins of Moreton Corbet Castle, a medieval stronghold north-east of Shrewsbury. Under normal circumstances I might have spent half an hour mooching among its crumbling walls, but, consumed by summit fever, I couldn't even be bothered to take a photo. Instead, I rested for 90 seconds, then pulled out on to the road without looking and was almost crushed by a tractor.

Everyone is familiar with the idiom "as easy as riding a bike". But there is certainly a knack to cycling long distance, in contrast to doing a quick lap of the local park. In particular, touring cyclists need to respect the subtle balance between their legs and the bike's gears. With so much ground to cover, we're ultimately trying to reach a sweet point between the energy we exert and the ease of turning our pedals. Under normal circumstances this is relatively easy to achieve, because we're content just ambling from A to B in the most comfortable way. But faced with a ticking clock, for one of the first times in my cycling life, I could feel my legs and the bike pushing closer to breaking point.

Riding deeper into rural Shropshire – a ripple of green, stitched with strands of slate and chalk – I began to encounter more cyclists than I had done anywhere in Britain. Zooming past me on their feather-light bikes, some said hello, but most just enjoyed the thrill of leaving me in their wake. Every time this happened, I pedalled a little faster, egged on by their speedy arrogance. With thirty or so miles on the clock, I was overtaken by a peloton of 20 Chris Hoy types, with twitchy, pear-drop calves and energy gels rattling around in their skin-tight pockets. "Going far?" asked one particularly svelte man, in wrap-around shades and a streamlined helmet.

"Hereford," I lied, not wishing to pique their interest too much, before watching them disappear in a £100k swarm of carbon fibre.

It was nice to tell non-cyclists that I was travelling a very long way under my own steam. At the right time, their awe and praise gave me a much-needed push forward. But some serious male cyclists, especially, could perceive my journey as a personal insult to their own masculinity. That's why I often just picked the nearest major town and tried to give the impression that I was simply an unthreatening grubby eccentric, with panniers full of groceries.

Cycling clubs, too, always made me feel uncomfortable. These Lycra-clad cliques often reeked of locker-room banter and Deep Heat. As a solo rider I couldn't think of anything worse than being out in the countryside with so many other people. The same goes for organised marathons, hikes and triathlons. I could understand how some people would enjoy the camaraderie, but personally I want to be alone, in peace. I fart and wheeze enough already, without having to smell or listen to any more. It was nice to think that my journey was somehow unique.

I yearned for open space. Green was good. Grey was bad. But with lockdown looming, I had no choice but to follow the dreary suburban rhumb line. I pushed on south, grazing the drab outskirts of Shrewsbury. Away to the east, in the direction of Birmingham and its many concrete satellites, a dark smog brooded, but to the west, cotton-wool sheep and polka-dot heifers surfed a wave of mossy pasture, all the way to Wales.

By noon I'd cycled 40 miles, already 20 miles off the pace. Further north, this would have seemed like a hefty half-day return. I should have felt elated, but instead my body was entering another state of panic. As I imagined Cornwall folding away from me on the underside of a giant map, my lips curled over my sharp front teeth and blood ran down my parched throat. How could I keep this up for four days straight?

Somehow, I was still on course to reach Hereford by teatime. If I was really fast, I might even make it to Gloucester and tally up 90 miles by the end of the day. It wouldn't be the 100 miles I really needed, but at least I could remain in the hunt. I pedalled and pedalled, growling through little villages, past dinky post offices and noticeboards advertising pre-pandemic choir practices and cake sales. I resembled a rabid dog, snarling at the air 5 feet ahead of me.

I was starting to feel like Superman, but then, somewhere north-east of Ludlow, I heard the depressingly familiar sound of steel on tarmac. Another puncture, and just as the heavens were starting to open. I had no choice but to push for 3 miles and take shelter in the porch of a church. With a crooked spire and iron gutters clogged with leaves, it creaked and moaned, so menacingly that I immediately yearned for the open road.

In a rush, I whipped off the tyre, but ripped a sliver of my thumbnail away with it, spraying bright-red blood on to the holy tiles. Once again, there was no obvious sign of a puncture. The wheel was clear of thorns and splinters, but somehow the inner tube was still perforated. Heavy rain clattered on the slate roof as a few cars passed slowly by. I tried my best to look as forlorn and despondent as possible but not a single person paused to ask if I was OK.

With a throbbing thumb and slippery hands, I patched the tube and put the wheel back in place. My "rescue pump" was useless and I could barely get the tyre to 30 psi. Clutching the wheel and pump as hard as possible, I forced precious air in, but squirted blood out. I rode gingerly on, awkwardly pedalling with my body weight balanced over the front wheel, so as not to put added pressure on my weakened back tyre.

At some point around 4 p.m. I finally limped into a petrol station and paid 50p to take me back to a bulbous 80 psi. From nowhere, the day had slipped away. The dream of 100 miles had become a reality of just 50, and however much I wanted to keep going, dusk was already setting in. During daylight I would happily push and push until the bike or my body broke down, but I couldn't justify putting myself in even more danger by cycling, sleep deprived, in darkness.

Something had to give, and thankfully rescue came in the form of Alana. She was now just 90 minutes away by car, staying at her parents' house in Stroud. By the time I reached Ludlow, she was waiting for me in a lay-by, with a slab of home-made flapjack and a can of cold beer.

We checked into a cheap hotel and immediately set about organising and prioritising my kit. If I was to stand any chance of reaching Land's End in just three days, then I needed to be as streamlined as possible. That meant ditching all unnecessary weight, and everything deemed non-essential was put into a black bag and thrown into the back of the car. It was time to abandon my tent, old trainers, DSLR, laptop, sleeping bag, roll mat and moka pot. It was also out with the sachets of tomato ketchup I'd been hoarding since Shetland, the roll of emergency toilet paper and all but one change of clothes.

Within an hour, the bike was light enough to pick up. But for every kilo saved, I grew heavier with guilt. I was ashamed that I needed to resort to such drastic measures, and felt angry that I couldn't just finish the trip with everything that I'd started with. "It's either this, or you'll stand no chance," reasoned Alana. And however much it bruised my ego to admit it, she was right.

We enjoyed a few hours of relative normality. We cuddled up on the sofa and watched mindless TV, surrounded by piles of stinking cycling gear. During the adverts she'd turn to look at me and I'd see my scruffy beard reflected in her eyes. I could tell she was desperate to say something – bursting with emotion, but afraid to let it out.

"I'm scared."

"Me too. That's OK. It's normal."

"I just can't handle not knowing what happens next in our lives."

"It won't be like this forever. It can't be."

"How do you know?"

"I just know."

"But we're almost out of money."

"We have enough. Just. I think. When I get paid."

She turned back to the TV and I felt a warm tear fall on to the back of my arm.

"I'm sorry you have to put up with this," I whispered. "I just need to get there, then I promise I'll relax. For a bit."

By 7 a.m. the next morning we were back in the lay-by where we'd met 13 hours before. I was tempted to throw my bike in the car and sneak forward by 20 or 30 miles. But to cheat now would have made all the previous suffering pointless and I knew it would fester in my conscience forever.

When I cycled across the USA in 2016, I had to hitch 10 miles to the nearest town when my seat post snapped somewhere in the Great Plains. Looking back on that 3,707-mile ride, that half an hour still haunts me. This wasn't a world record attempt, or anything more than just one stubborn bloke's bike ride, but I was determined to finish under my own steam.

Alana hugged me tight, as though I was heading off to war, then made me promise to eat well. At home we ate posh foods that I only discovered as an adult, like lentils, avocados, quinoa and brown rice, but on the road my diet was mostly beige and full of delicious MSG. Knowing that my body was burning over 5,000 calories a day, it was far too easy to live on children's party food like biscuits, cakes, sausage rolls and crisps, but we both knew this wasn't doing me any good. Let's just say that while the bike was now feeling lighter, I was still carrying more weight than necessary.

By the time I stopped for breakfast on the south side of Hereford, I'd racked up 27 miles, almost without looking up. Golden sunshine rampaged through the crisp autumn sky and even the city's mangy pigeons took on a tropical iridescence, their blue-grey plumage shimmering like precious tourmaline. With only a gentle westerly breeze, it was almost perfect cycling weather, and at my current pace I could clock up over 100 miles and make up for the previous day's shortfall.

I followed the river Wye, hurrying down tunnels of elm and beech. Where the sun splintered through the gnarled canopy, shards of orange light warmed the lustrous road. Sometimes the route would open up into savannah-like plateaus of green and gold, but I preferred the river – sometimes a trickle of calm, but always urging me forward.

A bushy-tailed grey squirrel skipped from one side of the water to the other across a fallen twig no thicker than a pencil. A cock pheasant crowed from a nearby spinney and when I stopped briefly to catch my breath and inhale an apple, the bluish claw of an American crayfish floated out from a muddy bank the colour of milk chocolate.

Even though it felt like I was racing, I was still travelling at a snail's pace. In these wild corners of Britain, I could zone out, rather than fret over the speedometer whirring in my mind's eye.

A few miles north of Ross-on-Wye a turquoise flash zoomed inches from my nose. A kingfisher, with a mouthful of something meaty and mushy. I slammed on my brakes and scanned the busy undergrowth. Nothing. Then, a few minutes later, I passed a chestnut-brown buzzard sitting silently on an ash branch. Its mustardy talons wrapped tightly around the desiccated bark, but with stocky shoulders and scatty eyeballs, it had the pent-up energy of a jack-in-the-box eager to explode.

I could have cycled along that riverbank forever. The road was quiet, and my legs moved at 14 mph without too much strain. But as I dropped deeper into the Wye Valley, my route grew narrower with every turn of the wheels.

The much wider river Severn was about to appear to the south. I could either turn east, remain in England and reach the south side of the river via Gloucester, or save myself 40 extra miles by entering Wales and somehow crossing the Severn Bridge.

There was no guarantee that the bridge was even open to motorists, let alone cyclists, but backtracking seemed futile, and I crossed the border at Monmouth, a Covid frontier town, more drystone than Trump's wall.

Thankfully, the river Wye had no care for national borders, and it meandered through the earth like a vein on the back of a withered hand. Where the tree-filled valley rose up around it, a riot of reds and golds turned the horizon to flames. The only discernible difference between England and Wales was the tongue-twisting quantity of consonants now busying the region's road signs. Kilgwrrwg, Pwllmeyric and Bryngwyn read like the names of Saturn's moons to my English eye.

Two hours south of Monmouth I finally reached the Severn Bridge and joined the narrow footpath running parallel with the M48. To my right, lorries roared past at 70 mph, but to my left, a chest-high barrier stood between me and a sheer drop of 200 feet. It would have been an unnerving crossing on a calm day, but a fierce icy wind blew in from the west and the roadway swayed slightly from side to side, leaving me drunk from the motion. Towering 450 feet above, the bridge's two steel towers wailed, while hundreds of zigzagged cables whimpered, desperate to snap free. I was too scared to ride, for fear of being blown into the churning water beneath me, so I ran alongside my bike for over a mile and escaped back into England.

The north of Bristol reeked of industry. Hauliers and recycling plants rubbed shoulders with wooden-pallet manufacturers and car-tyre dealers. The potholed road was strewn with oil, paint and shrapnel. Aluminium chimneys belched purple smoke into a sky already thick with noxious gas.

I had little choice but to join the hard shoulder of another busy A-road, running along the southern banks of the river Severn. But just as I set off into a snarling roundabout: POP. A steel rivet the size of a match had skewered my back tyre, leaving me with no option but to limp off, much to the consternation of a procession of disgruntled drivers.

Under normal circumstances, the puncture would have been easy to fix, but the wind now howled so loudly that I couldn't identify where the inner tube was perforated. With my bike in pieces, and the contents of my panniers scattered across the pavement, hundreds of cars crawled past me as though I was invisible.

To make the situation even more bizarre, this had all happened about 20 feet from a lay-by filled with paramedics and police officers. I'd been too consumed in my own setback to realise what was happening. But when I studied the scene a little closer, I could see that a middle-aged man with silver hair sat motionless in the driver's seat of a shiny saloon. He was dead, presumably from a heart attack, suffered in the middle of the busy roundabout. Shards of red tail light specked the black road while a teenage girl sat sobbing on the kerb.

After an hour I gave up trying to fix the puncture, and set off on foot, just as the man was being hauled on to a stretcher. I pushed my bike through the industrialised sprawl of Avonmouth and across the Avonmouth Bridge. Behind me, Bristol throbbed red, green and bright white in the dying gloom of dusk. Beneath me, dozens of sand-trapped yachts and fishing boats longed for the rushing tide to wash their mucky underbellies.

The wind became so fierce that I could barely hear myself think. All I wanted to do was stand in a hot shower and cry. It was hard to imagine my situation getting any more difficult, but then, just as the neon lights of my hotel came into sight, the footpath ended. After 95 miles and 13 hours of cycling, I was finally 500 feet away. On the wrong side of the motorway.

Muckle Flugga Lighthouse: the northernmost point of Britain.

Simon with one of Richard Grains' lobsters.

Cycling south, to warmer climes (in theory, at least).

Stopping for a roadside espresso at the south of Shetland's Mainland.

Fresh eggs, sold from an upcycled microwave.

Wild camping at the Bay of Skaill in Orkney.

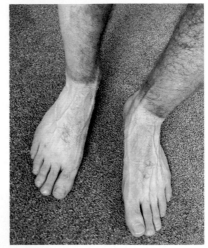

Covered in the grit and
grime of the road.

Navigating through
Orkney's Mainland.

A treacherous path over autumn leaves in the Scottish Highlands.

Starting the day with
strong coffee in the
Lake District.

After 1,307 miles in the saddle,
Simon completes the first leg
of his adventure.

Heavily loaded, taking the
scenic route where possible.

An unexpected detour,
at the start of the second
leg in Cornwall.

With volunteers at the Lyme Regis RNLI station.

At Faithworks Wessex in Bournemouth.

The Yorkshire coastline –
one of the most beautiful
sections of the entire trip.

Heading north in a heatwave,
desperately trying to find shade.

Packed up and ready to leave
at dawn the next day.

Spending the night in a
bivvy bag in the grounds
of Bamburgh Castle.

A moment to savour, crossing back into Scotland.

11 p.m. at Yellowcraig Beach, on the longest day of the year.

Another free night, this time in a
shepherd's hut on Easter Airfield.

Desperate measures to
stay warm and dry.

Almost there. At the top of mainland Scotland.

Back where it all began at Muckle Flugga lighthouse, after 3,427 miles in the saddle.

I'd booked a room at Gordano services because it was the cheapest "in Bristol". But what had seemed like a master stroke was in fact ineptitude. A glitchy Google Maps had directed me to a godforsaken no man's land – a patch of scrub that didn't quite exist. The hotel was impossible to reach on foot, and for half an hour I watched a stream of cars flow past me in a river of noisy light. I wanted to somehow part the waves and cross to the other side, but instead I was left stranded by a grubby bramble bush filled with empty crisp packets and Pepsi bottles filled with urine. As soon as it started to rain, I knew I had no choice but to make a call for help.

"Hey," I said coyly, when Alana answered the phone. "Don't worry, but I'm basically stuck on the side of the M5."

"What?"

"That hotel I booked."

"Yeah…"

"Well, I can't actually get there. I can see it. But it's on the other side of the motorway."

"Oh, for God's sake."

I backtracked to a quieter road and took shelter under a dirty tree decorated with soggy napkins. An hour later, Alana's brother, Matt, arrived with three new inner tubes. By a stroke of luck, not only did he live in Bristol, but he also owned a builders' van plenty big enough for a bicycle.

"I thought travel writing was glamorous?" he asked, with a wry smile.

"I just need this to be over," I shouted, my ears still ringing from the roar of the road.

It was a relief to be rescued, but I was angry that I'd had to cheat such a measly distance. I wanted to reach the end without putting Alana under any more stress, but now I knew she'd be at home, worrying. "I don't know how your sister puts up with this," I said to Matt, before insisting on buying him a beer.

Thankfully, it was much easier to leave the hotel than it had been to arrive, and by 7 a.m. the next morning, I'd done an extra 500-foot loop of the petrol station – to make up for the distance I'd hitchhiked – and was on the A369 to Portishead. The skies had cleared above north Somerset, and the air was hard and wintry. A few clouds of mizzle had blown in overnight and a twinkle of frost still lingered on the shaded flanks of road signs and bollards.

From the south side of the Bristol Channel, I could see Newport and Cardiff blinking awake in south Wales. With 220 miles now left to ride, I'd at least given myself a tiny chance of beating the lockdown. All I had to do was cycle for another 30 hours and climb about 10,000 feet.

A few miles west of Portishead, I stopped to wolf down food. My legs already screamed under the weight of the previous day's miles and my itchy eyes ached for soothing tears. I'd barely slept the night before and only managed to calm myself down with three beers and half a bottle of wine. Somehow, though, I still believed I could make it. After less than 2 minutes' rest, I climbed back on to the bike, only to find that my back tyre was flat again. "Bollocks!" I screamed, before thumping my forehead into the handlebars.

It took me well over an hour to push back to Portishead and then convince the staff at Haiko Cycling that they should prioritise my bike over the dozens that had arrived before me.

"We've not stopped all summer," said manager Ben Sash, carefully inspecting my back tyre while I maniacally paced around the store. "No one predicted such a huge surge in demand, so there's been a break in supply. Part of the reason our servicing has been so busy is because people can't buy new bikes. They're scrabbling around online to buy old stuff. But when it's broken, they bring it to us."

Ben and his colleagues, Jake and Chris, spent half an hour trying to identify the cause of my incessant punctures, only to conclude that a worn back rim *might* be to blame. "I can't even sell you a new wheel," said Ben, as I frantically threw my panniers back on. "We can't get anything in, it's crazy. Millions of bike parts have been held up in China and now that's being felt in Britain. We stock four bike brands. But we can't get anything new in until about April next year. I had to go to eight suppliers just to get one batch of bike pumps."

It was gone 10 a.m. by the time I finally left Portishead, having only moved 4 miles in the right direction. My back tyre was struggling to sit snug in the worn rim, and it now rolled more like a hexagon than a perfect circle. Every revolution resulted in an uncomfortable clunk, sending stabs of pain through my aching buttocks and into my lower back. To make matters even worse, the bike shop had discovered that my chain had stretched from climbing further north and might snap at any point. I also needed new brake pads and gear cables. The sensible thing would have been to stop and get a full service but with time ticking away from me, I had no choice but to limp on south-west, grinding and squeaking into the wind.

For the next 5 hours, I cycled on, head down, through country lanes clogged with red leaves, feeling more unwell with every mile. I hadn't eaten a proper meal for days and was trying to survive solely on sugar, caffeine and alcohol. If I couldn't buy it from a petrol station, then I didn't eat it. This diet saved me a few minutes an hour, but it was playing havoc with my stomach and bladder. I hadn't passed more than a few rabbit-like Malteser poos in over a week and my urine was now as thick as juice and the colour of Tango Orange.

"It's not meant to be like this," I grumbled to myself, wheezing through the bungalowed outskirts of Weston-super-Mare. Only the salty air and the shriek of gulls reminded me that I was anywhere near the sea. When the road climbed into the Mendip Hills, I saw a sign calling it one of "England's most special places". Tidal waves of lichen-scabbed limestone tore through a landscape of a hundred greens. It really was special. But I simply didn't care. All I could see was the finish line.

By 3 p.m. I was racing into Taunton, desperate to reach the other side of town before the school run. But as I sped under the lollipop floodlights of Somerset's county cricket ground and down to the banks of the river Tone, my tyres slipped on soggy leaves, and I slammed to the hard tarmac. For a few seconds, the clouds shape-shifted above me. Was this concussion, I wondered, or just dehydration at ground level? A pair of infant school children rushed toward me, clutching PAW Patrol lunch boxes and football stickers. However, before they could give in to their instinct to help me, they were dragged away by their mother. "Social distancing!" she screamed at their innocent faces.

My palms were grazed and blood spewed from my right knee, but I was too exhausted to feel much pain. Instead, I hobbled to the nearest supermarket and threw random items into a basket, feeling utterly drunk from fatigue. Apples, peanuts, salad tomatoes, grapefruit juice, prunes, a bottle of TCP and 2 litres of water. Anything to make me feel more human.

Before 4 p.m. I was cycling into the setting sun. My bloodied knee now clicked as it pedalled, and I chomped through six apples: cores, pips and stalks, determined to have a proper shit at some point that month.

I joined the towpath of the Bridgwater and Taunton Canal, but what had seemed like a shortcut on the map quickly turned into a gravel track clogged with thick mud. I was too stubborn to turn back and trudged on through pedal-high puddles. At one point, the bank merged with the track and I almost cycled full pelt into the chicken-stock water. Then, a few miles further on, I very nearly clattered into two camouflaged fishermen wrestling a pike into a landing net. I raced on past them, but 50 feet later experienced a pang of guilt and turned back to apologise.

Dressed in green fatigues and black boots, the men looked more special ops than Mortimer and Whitehouse. I'd expected them to be furious, but instead they glowed with a Zen-like calm; a calm that only fishermen seem to possess. "Wherever you're going, it can't be that important," said Ray Jones, as he gently prised a hook from the fish's mouth, then lowered its silver belly into the water.

"You've got to take it slow down here," said his friend of 60 years, Terry Prior.

"We loved lockdown."

"Why?"

"Because we saw so many more people down here on the towpath."

"And that's a good thing?"

"Usually, we get about one an hour, but when it's lockdown we get about twenty or thirty. It's a great chance to have some banter and a laugh, and that's something we've all missed this year. So, take it easy. It might never happen."

After a few short minutes in their company, I continued into the rural no man's land between Taunton and Tiverton. I was torn between slowing down and speeding up. Part of me wanted to sprint to the finish line like Mark Cavendish, but with the journey feeling increasingly like a fool's errand, part of me longed to channel my inner Ray and Terry.

To the south, the brown-green Blackdown Hills tumbled away toward the Jurassic Coast, like gravy-soaked Brussels sprouts bouncing off a Christmas table. To the north, Exmoor was infused with seams of purple heather, something like the amethyst tinge of the Milky Way. I passed cider farms and abattoirs, busy farmers and their dilly-dallying herds.

Most pubs and small shops were already closed for the impending lockdown. In one village I passed a couple unloading two apocalypse-sized carloads of booze and chocolate into a shipping container. If Covid didn't kill them, then cirrhosis of the liver looked nailed on. I crossed the M5 just east of Tiverton Parkway train station and watched a mass of cars flowing south-west, presumably toward their second homes. With duvets and pillows piled high, it could have been an August bank holiday. Instead, the traffic jerked nervously forward.

Devon was easily the hilliest county since Cumbria, and the single-track country road climbed and fell toward the dusky horizon. The vinegary scent of rotting crab apples lingered in the cool air. At the top of brambled summits, I could see lollipop phone masts and twinkling cottages spewing grey smoke. But in their lonely bottoms, the darkness was blinding. Only the brilliant-white cotton tails of rabbits, hopping into the thinned-out hedgerows, hinted at life.

In a stupor, I cycled into the pitch-black of night, eventually throwing in the towel at 9 p.m. I'd managed just over 80 miles and trembled from the adrenaline. Without the puncture and the headwind, I might have managed another 50 miles, but all I could do now was look forward. There seemed no use in dwelling on every hiccup that had thwarted me.

My ill-conceived plan had been to put on all my clothes and get a few hours' sleep in a bus shelter somewhere. I'd only slept for 14 broken hours across five nights; my spine felt crippled and my eyes ached. When I cycled past a B&B offering rooms for £30, I didn't think twice. I locked my bike to a tree and passed out on the soft bed, fully clothed, twitching and constipated; worried, but slightly hopeful, I might soil myself as I slept.

When I woke at 4 a.m., Google Maps suggested I had just 14 hours of cycling ahead of me. If I could somehow dig just a little deeper then I'd reach Land's End by midnight and do it before England went into lockdown. I didn't even bother showering, and my bike was exactly how I'd left it, albeit with a thin layer of ice now dusted across the saddle and handlebars.

For the first couple of hours, I was totally alone, loping along on a broken bike into an icy headwind. Every curtain was drawn, every fire burned out. Even the birds were still asleep. At first, I cycled by head torch, its feeble spotlight illuminating little more than my gloved hands, but at just after 6 a.m. a crisp dawn splintered over the northern reaches of Dartmoor. For a beautiful hour, the sun and moon shared the mauve sky, while a billion stars glinted in the heaven between.

But without proper sleep, my circadian rhythm wasn't just out of tune, it was entirely broken. What trauma was this causing me? I wondered. What hell might unfold when I finally stopped?

With all the ups and downs, I was lucky to average 8 mph, and before the day had really begun, it was already slipping away. In a desperate attempt to shave off 10 miles, I ditched the scenic route at Okehampton and joined the snarling A30. For 15 miles I hugged the hard shoulder as thousands of cars zoomed past me, just inches from my right pannier.

By the time I reached Launceston, exhaust fumes rasped the back of my aching throat.

I diverted on to single-track B-roads, around sunken corners and through muddy farms that echoed with clucks and grunts. These moments were always bittersweet. I hated being slowed down, when I could be racing along. But on the other hand, farms only ever moved at their own unique pace.

Sometime around lunchtime I got caught up in a herd of 100 white and brown-spotted dairy cows as they were being moved inside for the winter. I cycled at a safe distance behind them, but quickly I was surrounded and being washed along in their musty wave.

"You're just going to have to wait," yelled a skinny farmer in overalls and a flat cap as his Border collie trotted beside their marching hooves. "You've certainly picked your moment," he said. "We only do this twice a year. Please just stay where you are. They won't hurt you. If anything, you're doing me a favour."

For half an hour we clip-clopped along at less than walking pace; my new friends chewing their steamy cud and spraying out gallons of raw manure. I was lucky not to be showered in shit, but nevertheless, there was a calming simplicity in their seasonal trudge, a rite of passage as old as ploughing fields or sowing seed. "I normally do this on my bike," said the farmer, as I finally broke free from the scrum. "I've done 1,600 miles just rounding up the cattle this year, but in some years, I can do over 2,500. I love it. And the cows seem to prefer me walking to the quad bike."

By mid-afternoon I'd only managed 40 miles – 40 pathetic miles. The headwind was too fierce and the hills just too steep. Often, I'd have to get off and push. But if a car or tractor passed, I'd pretend that I'd paused by choice, to rummage in my messy panniers. The shame of failure hurt me more than the lactic acid now scalding my veins.

Then, with less than 100 miles left to Land's End, my baggy chain finally fell off. It was now too loose to change gear without sliding free, and with no hope of finding a bike shop I had little choice but to either walk or ride, in one agonising gear.

Somewhere east of Bodmin Moor, dragging my bike up yet another Cornish hill, I finally admitted to myself that the dream of beating lockdown was over. How did I ever think I could miraculously cycle faster? Maybe it had taken 200 sentient eyeballs to remind me that life was best enjoyed at an amble rather than a sprint. Or perhaps I'd finally reached my physical breaking point and by hitting "the wall" my brain was now saving me from myself, before I made another reckless decision.

There no longer seemed any point in tormenting myself with where I was *meant* to be. By only ever obsessing with the next mile, I'd ignored the mile I was already on. For the first time since Shetland, I grew lighter. Emotionally and physically drained but free of excess worry. My brain was too exhausted to fret, so I simply limped along, my mind on standby.

Cornwall no longer appeared in flashes, but as lingering scenes on a gallery wall. A chubby cock pheasant burst out of the undergrowth and landed in the sopping branches of a willow tree. In the soupy half-light of dusk, his aquamarine neck feathers popped out brightly, like a blue iris swimming in a cloudy cataract.

I pushed on, just like I always did. Down tight little lanes littered with thorns, and past iron gates draped in spiders' silken cross-stitch. An hour after dark, I finally checked in to Jamaica Inn, made famous by the 1936 Daphne du Maurier novel, and ate overpriced greasy food until my belly ached. For the first time in months, I finished the day with water instead of beer, and fell into a twitchy, albeit sober, sleep.

————

My body jerked to life at 5 a.m., desperate for exercise. England was now officially in lockdown, and I – like the rest of the nation – was expected to "stay at home". But I wasn't at home, I was in a gimmicky roadside pub filled with tacky faux rum barrels and a pirate-themed menu. The closest train station was 30 miles to the south-east in Plymouth, but Penzance was only 60 miles to the south-west, and Land's End lay less than 10 miles beyond that.

I packed up and set off. Bodmin Moor was a patchwork of heather, peat and granite, trapped under a halo of bright-white cloud. A brown hare raced for a few seconds beside me, then disappeared with a pirouette into a puddled ravine the shade of wilted spinach. With a warm autumn day rising behind me, all I had to do was follow my haggard shadow.

I longed for the Beast of Bodmin Moor, the phantom wild cat purported to live in north-east Cornwall, to leap across my path with a scratch and a growl. Instead, it was just me and the sheep, like always, it seemed. And three hungry buzzards, wheeling and whistling in the sky, urging the road to serve them a tenderised breakfast.

I'd started in Shetland with 14 gears, but I now had just two speeds: sitting or standing. At first, I pined for the sensation of shifting up and down, but slowly, I found a rhythm that worked. By imagining myself in a high intensity spinning class, sprinting the straights and climbing the bumps, I broke the distance down into manageable periods of time, rather than abstract distances. By lunchtime I'd somehow covered 40 miles and celebrated with a Cornish pasty, seasoned by the increasingly salty breeze.

As England narrowed, my focus pulled. I raced through the locked downtowns of Redruth, Camborne and Hayle. The streets had been left to the pigeons. Sweet wrappers and weathered face masks swirled between the windows of empty shops and deserted bus stops.

Under an indigo sky, I finally clapped eyes on St Michael's Mount, the island topped by a medieval castle, off the coast of Penzance. Surrounded by broccoli-like trees and spiky agave, it resembled a wedding cake melting under a hot marquee. To the west, Longrock beach shimmered vanilla caramel, and where the ocean lapped ashore a red setter splashed through the frothy swell. The promenade was busy with people, breathing deeply, exercising for their 1, 2, maybe 3 hours that day.

After all the pain, the sleepless nights and the worry, I knew that I'd finished. "Good for you," shouted a man from his back garden, when he saw my weary face and muddy panniers. "Just go until the road runs out!" And with that, I rode and rode, desperate to fall off the end of the Earth.

West of Penzance, Cornwall felt like a secret world, a maze of twisting lanes and hidden gardens. I wondered if I was going round in circles, but then – finally – I reached Land's End at 4.21 p.m.; an arbitrary crag of land, at an arbitrary moment in time, now covered in parking bays, tacky souvenir shops and doughnut stalls.

It was an abomination, an anticlimax. But for a few proud minutes it was my abomination, my anticlimax. I'd cycled 1,307 miles to reach this silly little place. I couldn't be sure if I had a monkey off my back, or an elephant on my shoulder. I cracked a warm can of fizzed-up beer and looked out to the flat calm Atlantic. Twenty-eight miles away I could just make out the rock-cake dribbles of the Isles of Scilly, bathed in a golden, optimistic light.

I wanted to jump in and swim. I didn't want this to be the end. But for now, at least, this had to be my summit. What might happen next, I didn't really know. It was time to go home, to Alana. Wherever she was, was exactly where I needed to be.

PART TWO:

FOUND

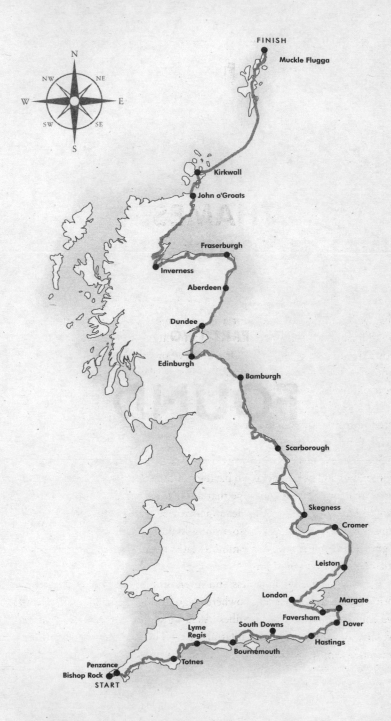

THAMES:
WEIRDO NIGHTWALKER

Just as Britain locked down for a second time, our six-month mortgage holiday came to an end. "You have to start paying again," said the monotone voice on the end of the line. "Or we'll have to start looking into other… options." We knew what this really meant. Defaulting on our less-than-year-old mortgage and having our first home embarrassingly repossessed. For a week, Alana sobbed herself to sleep, while I paced around the flat, deep into the early hours. Most nights I curled up on the sofa, my lungs aching with shame.

We had less than £2,000 between us. Enough to keep us fed through winter, but still nothing close to paying our bills. The only solution would be to rent out the flat and hope that another six months, mortgage-free, would be enough to get our heads above water. On a bright November morning we handed the keys to a smug-looking estate agent with pound signs ringing in her eyes. A few minutes later, two French students wheeled their suitcases into our home.

We were officially homeless; however, unlike the 130,000 evicted British households that had nowhere to go during the pandemic, at least we could fall back on our families. Alana's grandparents had died before we met, but their tumbledown farmhouse – The Red House – in Suffolk remained empty. We packed up the car and drove cross-country, racked with anger and guilt. "This feels like the epitome of white privilege," I said, as we zigzagged into East Anglia. Our savings had all but vanished, but at least we had a leaky roof over our heads.

As the nights drew in, the pandemic's second wave tore through Britain. The daily death count climbed each day, and with no hope of a return to work, I quickly slid back into a depressed and lethargic stupor, unable to sleep at night, then incapable of thinking straight or breathing comfortably during the day. Without the routine of cycling, I had too much time to analyse my physical self. I tuned in to the previously silent rhythms of my body. My laboured inhalations, the gurgles in my stomach, the fluttered palpitations of my heart.

———

No one ever talks about the agonising constipation or the angry anal fissures; they're the least sexy part of cycle touring. But after my frantic push to Land's End, I'd been struck down by both. Each day's 12–14 hours of intense cycling had diverted blood away from my stomach to my quadriceps and calves, leaving me unable to properly digest food. Combine this with a diet of mostly processed carbohydrates, containing hardly any fibre, and I'd been loo-shy for weeks. When I finally started passing rock-hard stools, the toilet bowl was splashed with globules of bright-red blood. Some days the bleeding was so heavy that I had to put a makeshift sanitary towel between my legs and take half a dozen paracetamol to relieve the pain.

I was 99 per cent sure that my ailments were self-inflicted, entirely benign and would eventually pass, but with Sarah having just died of bowel cancer, I became transfixed by the throbbing in my rectum and the startling sight of blood on toilet paper. Just like my hunger for air, and the awareness of each breath, suddenly, I was hyper-conscious of a body part that had previously operated under the radar.

After a few weeks, the bleeding stopped, but the obsession continued. It was impossible to know if I was still in pain, or if my overthinking was now causing a phantom ache, entirely imagined. Alana banned me from googling, but I found it impossible not to catastrophise. Fixated by the image of my intestines growing cancerous, I rattled around the dank, dark house.

Eventually we settled on an endgame: a visit to the local GP, for blood tests and a rectal examination. After that, we agreed, I'd try to put the fear to bed, and a week later I dropped my trousers and curled into a foetal position.

"Considering what you've just put your body through," said the doctor, "it's no surprise that things are struggling to get back to normal. Your blood results, however, show that you're fighting an infection. You're incredibly run-down. You need to rest. Get some quality sleep. Try to stop worrying."

If only it were that easy.

———

Eventually, at some point in January, I stopped feeling a throbbing in my backside and diverted my attention back to my lungs. They'd grown agonisingly tight again. Deflated footballs in a Rottweiler's mouth. The tighter they became, the more I worried. The more I worried, the tighter they became.

"Keep telling yourself that it's temporary," said Alana, as we walked across the frosty beach next to the Sizewell nuclear power stations, a few miles south of Southwold. "It's a panic attack. We know that. You know that. Your body is just in a constant state of panic. You must keep telling yourself that an end will come. I promise it will."

Those hikes became our lifeline. In driving rain, tepid drizzle, frozen snowdrifts and lemon-curd winter sunshine, we trudged to and from the sea, along muddy, gorse-lined pathways, stamped with the prints of badgers, stoats and roe deer. Sometimes, we'd take blankets and a flask of hot tea, and end up at the Sluice, the blustery dunes where Alana's grandparents' ashes had been scattered many years before. "I feel happy here. Safe," she'd tell me. "I don't like it when you're away. Not while our lives are like this."

As night plunged over the North Sea, hundreds of distant wind turbines winked ruby red on the horizon, somewhere between us and Holland. Hunkered down behind the dunes, warmed by our combined heat, our whole world was just four shoulders wide. Without her, I knew, I had no reason left for living.

Back at the house we tried to live on £20 a week. Porridge for breakfast, soups for lunch and lentil curries for dinner. At times it felt like the world's worst yoga retreat. But the more money we saved on food, the more we had left for booze – the one thing that consistently relieved my symptoms. On Friday nights we drove to the local Tesco and unloaded our burdens on the unsuspecting checkout assistant. "Free therapy," we half joked, as our bag for life chimed with discount wine.

Occasionally, our worried parents would send us a few chocolate bars and a £20 note in a shoebox or Jiffy bag "for a treat" – just like when we were cash-strapped students. But we were already embarrassed to be living in The Red House rent-free. And when the boiler broke, we wore thick old coats and fingerless gloves, and warmed our frozen toes beside an open fire. We slept in woolly hats and cuddled hot-water bottles. As we waited for spring to arrive, we took solace in silently, stoically, suffering.

My panic attacks grew from single, tumbling ice flakes, into giant runaway snowballs, picking up physical and emotional weight as they fell. The more I attempted to subdue my state of panic, the more it bubbled up inside me. I felt like a flop, a waster, a teenage stoner again, just without the greasy skin and the hum of Lynx Africa.

I tried adult colouring books, online yoga classes, meditation podcasts, CBD oil, magnesium supplements and a free course of acupuncture. Nothing worked. A hunger for air became my annoying, but familiar, companion, a constant stab in my torso. By March I'd all but given up on sleep. I had half-moon bruises under my blistered eyes, and for the first time in my life, my hair was now more grey than dark brown.

Insomnia, just like my panic attacks, became a self-fulfilling nightmare. The more I tried to sleep, the less likely it became. At night I felt even more wired than during the day. It was as though I was coming down from a three-day amphetamine binge, when the rush of serotonin stops but the jittery convulsions remain.

One midnight I drank a tumbler of cough syrup and some decades-old whisky I found in the kitchen cupboard. It knocked me out for an hour or two, but when I woke, the insomnia was just accompanied by a throbbing headache and a bad case of diarrhoea.

I sat in dark corners of the house and thought long and hard about what Alana's life would be like if I simply walked away, forever. Then, when she fell asleep, I tiptoed out over the creaking floorboards and escaped into the orange light, to walk among the other loners of the night – the foxes, the rats, the badgers. I'd sit on icy benches and watch dawn slowly cut through the winter mist. Alone, on the beach, or in the dunes, I was a weirdo nightwalker without a dog to justify my melancholy.

———

Spring finally arrived. Without it I have no idea what might have happened, or what I might have done. And with a flicker of daffodil yellow and a glint of warm sunshine, my mood slowly improved. For the first time in over a year there was cautious optimism. Old friends began to shake hands again in the street. People in the supermarket stood slightly closer together. The pubs opened, the trees blossomed and one drizzly April morning I marched into the shed and pulled my bike out from behind a pile of logs.

There was oak dust between the spokes and strands of crispy lichen growing around the handlebars. The tyres felt squidgy, the rusty chain growled through the cassette, but the glossy leather saddle smelled familiar, like a pair of summer shorts. I climbed back on for the first time in five months, slippers, pyjamas, dressing gown and a tatty beanie hat.

Aloft in the saddle, a roll of thick tummy fat wedged between my pelvis and ribcage.

For half an hour I lolloped around the village, in and out of cul-de-sacs, across muddy fields and through deep puddles. I was quickly soaked and shivering, but grinning, properly for the first time in months, I knew what I needed to do.

My race to beat lockdown had done more harm than good. Hurried and abrupt, the climax had left a sour taste. I couldn't shake the feeling that I had unfinished business, out there, on my bicycle. Britain's bounceback was only just beginning, and my slide back into anxiety, insomnia and mania could only be stemmed with a therapy that had started to work wonders before. To end now would be like running from the operating table, just as the surgeon was about to stitch me up.

As soon as I could, I'd hit the road for one final ride. I'd start in Scilly, the land of milk and honey I'd spied from Land's End, then return to Cornwall, to ride and ride, until I could breathe, think and sleep again. There were millions of strangers out there, and all of them could help ease my pain.

PLYMOUTH:
A CAVEMAN EXISTENCE

The *Scillonian* pitched from port to starboard: 1,250 tonnes left, 1,250 tonnes right. Up a wave. Down a wave. Stomach here. Stomach there. Even with my eyes firmly shut, the motion made my mouth sweat. "This is a very unique stretch of water," said an annoyingly chipper voice, somewhere out on deck. "This is where the English Channel, the North Atlantic and the Irish Sea meet. If you're going to feel seasick, then this is the place you'll get it."

What had started in Penzance as a pleasure cruise had quickly turned into a confused crossing, tinged with the odour of gullet-fresh vomit. None of mine, thank goodness; it was from the frizzy-haired woman with her head in a bin next to the lower-deck toilets. She huffed and puffed, then groaned a little. I heard chunks slap against a plastic bag, then I made a run for it, holding my breath, all the way to the breeze.

The 28-mile crossing between Cornwall and the Isles of Scilly has turned many a seasoned sailor green. In fact, the *Scillonian* is so infamous for its flat bottom and rocky motion that regulars call it the "Vomit Comet". And this was a good day. Blue skies and only a 20 mph wind. "You can imagine what it's like when it's really lumpy," said a motion-drunk teenage boy clinging to the aft deck with the flecks of a half-digested cream tea on his shoulder.

For an hour we looked out to the horizon, steadying our gaze on the busy white swell. Behind us to the east I could just make out Land's End, its doughnut stalls and car parks. Six months had passed since I'd arrived there, ecstatic that I'd cycled the length of Britain, but overwhelmed by what the winter might bring. That sunny November day felt like a fever dream to me now. But after half a year stuck in the numbed vacuum of lockdown, I knew this was exactly where I was meant to be, and exactly what I was meant to be doing.

I rolled off the *Scillonian* with weak legs and winter-white skin gleaming out from beneath my shorts. After a bleak spring, St Mary's throbbed with summer. Day trippers slurped tall, expensive-looking ice creams. Union Jacks flapped, slapped and rattled in the breeze. A scrum of T-shirt-tanned fishermen lobbed polystyrene boxes of shaved ice, fins, big eyes and claws from one small boat to another.

I wove through a gaggle of silver-haired women wearing poncho towels – the must-haves of the "wild swimming" clique – then rounded a turreted limestone corner into a dinky little square of bougie coffee shops and boutiques selling salmon chinos and boat shoes.

—

Scilly is often lazily compared to the Caribbean, but really, it's more akin to Scotland's Western Isles. The Atlantic archipelago is jet washed by the roaring submarine Gulf Stream, leaving hundreds of tapioca-sand beaches that resemble tropical Windows-95 screen savers. Above the surface, Cornish palms, elm, elder and hawthorn are tumble-dried by the western gales. But in the sheltered crags and cypress-lined allotments, subtropical flowers – like scented narcissi, something like a mini daffodil – flourish all the way through the frost-free winter.

England's westernmost corner made it through the pandemic with just a handful of confirmed cases of Covid-19, making it one of the safest places to be in the world. At Christmas 2020, it was the only Tier-1 region of Britain.

"It might only be twenty-eight miles," said stained-glass artist Oriel Hicks, whom I met on St Mary's, "but that stretch of water was like having a drawbridge between us and the rest of the country. Seeing what was happening elsewhere, I think we all felt very lucky to be down here. We'll never take that for granted again."

Oriel spent the lockdowns redesigning a beach shelter on the Strand, overlooking Town Beach, and with the help of the local community set about turning a drab concrete box into a kaleidoscopic showpiece of hedgehog, puffin and fish illustrations that glinted in the setting sun. "People from across the islands sent me their pictures," said Oriel, as we sheltered in one of the leeward nooks. "Every morning a group of locals sit in here and hide from the wind while drinking coffee. It's become even more popular during the Covid years, because we're all trying to spend lots of time outside. I'm convinced that the sea breeze and our outdoorsy lifestyle have helped keep our infections to a minimum."

Oriel moved to Scilly from Cornwall in her late thirties, attracted by the alternative, arty scene. "I came here for the colours and the light," she told me. "You get a very turquoise sea. There are no rivers, so you get no silt, and the white sand reflects the light back. If you don't mind a quiet life, then this is a great place to be."

Housing prices, however, shot up during the pandemic, making it harder for locals to compete. "People realised that they could work wherever they have access to a computer. This meant that people with money could come over and take the properties that youngsters could have afforded once. It's a shame."

I'd only been back on the road for a few hours, but already my conversations had returned to a common theme. For every person who'd struggled financially during the pandemic, there was another person who came out of it rather well. For every family forced to sell up and downsize, there were others with disposable cash ready to burn.

I left the beach and cycled into the island's interior, a higgledy-piggledy world of sandstone cottages, wildflower meadows and apple orchards. The warm, salty breeze tasted more like Tasmania or South Island, New

Zealand, than anything northern, anything remotely British. I want to live here, I thought; a trite catchphrase uttered by most tourists on their very first day.

These far-flung corners of the country fascinated me the most. Because while the rest of Britain shuddered under the full force of multiple lockdowns, it was hard to imagine how the Scillonian good life changed at all.

Unlike Cornwall, with its second homes and empty holiday rentals, St Mary's looked refreshingly lived-in. Almost every front door was wide open. Not an Airbnb key box in sight. Of course, a few people might have seized the opportunity to relocate, but who could blame them? If I could afford it, I'd probably have done the same.

It didn't take more than half an hour to complete a lap of the 2½-square-mile island. I passed two Land Rovers, a tractor and a quad bike, each with a smile, each with a wave. Back in town, the rush hour was in full flow. A white van and a hatchback politely vied for the same parking space outside the chip shop. A seagull the size of an albatross eyed up the hen party on a picnic bench. They seemed to have their scampi and onion rings safely under lock and key, but for as long as they glugged Prosecco, he had hope.

As the sunlight waned toward the North Atlantic, the surface of the distant sea transformed from a toothpaste blue to a Guinness black, and above St Mary's Harbour, tissue-paper clouds raced toward the horizon like clay pigeons, tumbling away to safety. I pushed my bike along the half-moon promenade, now all but empty, apart from one silent, almost invisible man hunched behind an easel. An entire day had been captured in pencil sketches and watercolour brushstrokes; the crescent beach, a dozen dumpy fishing boats, four upturned Crayola-hued kayaks and Oriel's distant shelter.

"The last year has been challenging," said Stephen Morris, as he dipped a sticky, yellow-brown paintbrush into a mug of dirty water, his horn-rimmed glasses clinging precariously to the end of his nose. "We have an autistic daughter who normally lives in care on the mainland but when the pandemic struck, we decided to bring her home."

"How big a change was that? To your life, and hers?"

"People with autism need routines and habits to follow, so we tried our best to repeat the same activities in two-week cycles. We went for walks and took photos, washed the car and baked cakes. Little ways to give life some rhythm."

"It sounds like a challenge."

"At times, it certainly was. She's thirty-four and my wife and I hadn't cared for her, on our own, for more than a few weeks at a time since she was sixteen. But on the whole it was wonderful to have her back here. She had no comprehension of what was going on around us."

Unlike many people who turned to painting as a form of therapy, Stephen admitted that – just like the musicians Nick and Mary Ann whom I'd stayed with in the Scottish Highlands – the pandemic left him feeling artistically compromised. "I have to have my head in the right place to be able to do this. When I'm stressed – like I have been this past year – I find it hard to find the motivation. That's not an ideal place to be in for a professional artist."

I'd stumbled across a man seemingly entranced by the beauty of his surroundings. But all it took was a quick "how are you?" to remind me that all of us live complex lives, despite what first impressions might suggest.

"The last year has clarified a few things to me," said Stephen. "For example, I think my wife and I might need to move back to the mainland soon, to be closer to our family. I know people who are reaching a point in their lives when they might need medical attention and in the back of my mind, I'm thinking that one day that might be me. People look at Scilly and they think it's idyllic – which it is – but we're not getting any younger."

I checked into a single room, so small I could lay in bed and touch three walls. The Victorian windowpane quivered in the thumping wind, but out to sea, the setting sun bled into the distant clouds, like a scoop of vanilla ice cream thawing under a ladle of hot yellow custard.

Suddenly, I felt alone, stranded. Stephen was right. None of us were getting any younger. Every day, we woke up, closer to the inevitable.

Slightly older, slightly nearer to the grave. Maybe I was a nihilist for thinking this way. But more than ever, life felt like a frustratingly finite journey. All any of us really wanted was to feel like we were in control.

To feel caged and helpless was to feel inhuman.

I drifted in and out of a troubled sleep, wrestled from one windy shore to the next. If I was lucky, I'd stay inert for an hour, then jolt awake for a nervous piss or a massage of my aching jaw bones and temples. In the dead of night, palpitations fluttered in and out of my chest. My legs jerked involuntarily. However much I wanted to, I couldn't simply wander out into the world and feel new again. My year-long hangover still hung heavily on my shoulders like a flak jacket filled with sand.

―――

The next morning, I threw my bike and panniers on to an open-top ferry and took a seat among the purple rinse, destined for St Agnes, the Scillies' southernmost inhabited island. I must have been the youngest passenger by 40 years. "What's your bike made out of?" asked a man with a whistling hearing aid and dentures that swilled in his cheeks.

"Titanium," I replied. "It should make a decent hip one day."

My grandad joke fell on mostly deaf ears. In fact, some of my fellow passengers looked worryingly immobile. One particularly unsteady pensioner with swollen ankles and dangly Pat Butcher earrings took more than 15 minutes to tiptoe on board, while 30, comparatively athletic boomers watched on in polite horror. "That second Covid jab has totally made my balance go," she grumbled, at which point four dozen rolling eyes almost threatened to capsize the boat.

Flanked by a pair of charcoal-backed Manx shearwaters and a fleet of chirping kittiwakes, we set off on the lumpy, bumpy voyage, around lobster buoys and RIBs on anchor. Despite patches of exposed, cappuccino swell, the water beneath us glowed Barbicide blue. We were only at sea for 20 minutes, but the crossing left most of us with damp hair and quivering tummies. Everyone was relieved to step foot on the solid concrete dock.

The island was even quieter than the one we'd left behind. And apart from the people disembarking, there was barely a soul to see. I pushed my bike inland, past a stack of stainless-steel beer kegs, thirty-odd lobster pots and a giant plastic cube filled with agricultural-grade creosote. There were no cars, either. Just a couple of quad bikes, a few battery-powered golf carts and a 1970s Massey Ferguson tractor with a big, toothy claw.

This was a farm island, with floury-sand beaches in place of electric fencing. Livestock nibbled at patches of wild seaweed rather than factory-bought salt licks. I walked past the only pub, the whitewashed Turk's Head, named after the Turkish pirates who arrived in Scilly from the Barbary Coast in the sixteenth century. It seemed poised to do a steady trade in pints of golden Cornish ale, home-made pies and gourmet burgers.

But my budget would only stretch as far as the tiny island shop and lunch consisted of a few cheese and tomato tortilla wraps and a cup of coffee brewed on a drystone wall garlanded in delicate sea pinks. I couldn't find my Swiss army knife, so I resorted to biting off chunks of cheese and spitting them into the edible plate. I then wandered off for a few minutes to admire a big spiky palm tree, the sort you'd find on the Côte d'Azur. The island was silent, apart from the rustle of tree leaves and the hum of a distant mower.

"It's pecking!" shouted a German-accented man, maniacally waving two Nordic poles.

"It's pecking!"

"What?" I yelled back.

"The bird. It's pecking!"

In the space of a few seconds, an opportunist seagull had dive-bombed my picnic, grabbed a tortilla and left a rancid parting gift on my bike's saddle. We watched its silhouette labour off in the direction of Greenland, hauling contraband the size of an LP.

Most things on St Agnes seemed to cost about 30 per cent more than they would on the British mainland, because almost everything must be imported. The weather can cut the archipelago off for days or weeks on end, and the freight charges on some heavy objects, like fresh fruit and vegetables, can be prohibitively expensive.

"We can get one-hundred-mile-per-hour south-westerly winds blowing through here," said Aiden Hicks, a Scillonian in his early thirties whom I'd arranged to meet on his 14-acre smallholding at the centre of the island. "It's the sort of wind you'll want to have at your back as you cycle north."

Aiden greeted me with a cautious fist bump and a broad smile, then introduced me to his three barefooted children, his wife, Grace, and his father, Mike, a silver-bearded widower who now lived in a self-contained outhouse next door. On first impressions, they lived an enchanted life, surrounded by chickens and lambs, wild herbs and old bangers, barnacled fishing boats and bonfires, grazed knees and TCP.

"Many moons ago, this all used to be daffodils," said Mike. "But then we stopped with all that and grew early potatoes. That ended in about the mid-eighties because suddenly it was a worldwide trade, and it wasn't worth our while any more. We went back to growing flowers, but instead of selling them we started extracting their essential oils and blending them into soap products."

These days, the family's biggest income is generated by their 180-tree apple orchard, and their juices, ciders and gins are distributed all over Britain. With great pride, Aiden plucked a bottle of St Agnes scrumpy from their shed-sized distillery and thrust it into my hand. "Something to remember us by."

To be Scillonian is to be self-sufficient. But an idyllic life comes with risk, cost and compromise. "I think we're the only islands in Europe that don't get freight subsidised," said Aiden, as he led me to his pair of beehives, abuzz with thousands of busy drones. "Building materials are the worst. A tonne of aggregate costs £35 to buy, but by the time it lands on the island it will be about £120. You can't rely on any one thing here.

You can't have all your eggs in one basket. You've got to have multiple things on the go, so if one year something doesn't work, you've got other things to fall back on."

"What has this time been like?" I asked. "Considering your history of fending for yourselves, were Scillonians better prepared for the pandemic?"

"All the farmers got together, and we made sure we planted more potatoes, just in case," said Aiden. "If the people who worked on the freight boat all got ill and had to quarantine, then no one knew what might have happened. For as long as we could grow our own vegetables and catch our own fish, we knew this was a good place to be."

But what about the hurdles in life that none of us can truly prepare for? The lumps we might find in the shower, or the mild headaches that become more sinister. "I have a chronic autoimmune condition," said Aiden. "After twelve years, we've still not found out what it is. I also had a brain haemorrhage four years ago. Despite all that, and having to shield for the past year, there has never been a doubt in my mind that I'd rather be here than anywhere else. I was thankful for all the extra time we had as a family. We could go to the beach and go fishing with the kids. In a normal year we'd be too busy."

———

I left Mike and Aiden tinkering with their beehives and cycled west a few leisurely minutes down to Troytown, the farm belonging to Mike's brother, Sam Hicks. It doubled up as a campsite in summer, offering a strip of seaside grass to travellers on a budget. A brisk wind blew in from the Atlantic, just like it always seemed to, but when the gusts dropped for a few minutes, I had just enough time to erect my tent on a slope, partially sheltered behind a drystone wall.

There were better places to camp, sure. Next to the toilets, perhaps, or in the grassy, east-facing bowl out of the wind. But my spot was officially the most south-western camping pitch in Scilly, making me the most south-western camper in Britain. Simple pleasures.

There was, however, one extra pimple of England that I could see 4 miles out to sea: the Bishop Rock Lighthouse, a 160-foot-high beacon on the eddying black horizon. The first iron structure was built there in 1847, before being replaced by the current granite building 11 years later. It marks the eastern end of the North Atlantic shipping route, used by ocean liners in the first half of the twentieth century. This was the most direct line taken by captains competing for the Transatlantic speed record, known as the Blue Riband. Follow the course south-west and you'll eventually bump into Cape Cod, Nantucket and the Empire State Building.

The Bishop, as it's affectionately known, is lovingly personified by many Scillonians. Because long before the advent of satellite weather forecasts, his tabletop crown marked the visible boundary between the fragile islands and the ferocious Atlantic Ocean. If suddenly he fell from view, then it was probably time to fetch a few baskets of dry firewood and pop the kettle on.

I was now almost 1,400 miles from where my journey had begun at Muckle Flugga Lighthouse, right at the top of Shetland. The fact, however, that I could now see the white conical structure clearly from the shoreline filled me with both awe and dread. Because I'd arranged with a local boat charterer, John Peacock, to take me out to see it "if the weather permitted". And right on cue, my phone buzzed. "Meet me at the wharf in 20 mins."

Our voyage started off comfortably enough. John's catamaran chugged westward, using some of the Scillies' uninhabited islands as shelter from the full force of the Atlantic. First, we rounded Annet, a 54-acre dollop of grass and limestone, where half a dozen blackish-brown seals sunbathed with their oily bellies to the sky.

Then we made a beeline for the Western Rocks, a cluster of jagged skerries, infamous for their shipwrecks. Thousands of mariners had lost their lives beneath our bow. Most notably, the wreck of HMS *Association* in 1707 claimed 1,400 sailors in a single night. These days, the islands are popular with scuba divers and ornithologists, but landing a boat was still far too dangerous. "Hidden reefs," said John. "We need to give them a wide berth. We're about to be fully exposed. Make sure you're holding on to something."

As we rounded the last of the islands, the sea state grew from a waist-high froth to green breakers, big enough to swallow a man. Uninterrupted for 3,000 miles, the Atlantic now charged at us. Steaming at full throttle toward the Bishop, we surfed up the onrushing waves, then slapped down the other side. Respite only lasted for a second or two, before the next set came crashing through. "How are you feeling?" asked a steady-legged John, noticing that I'd not uttered a single word for more than 5 minutes.

"Let's just get there and get back," I replied, breaking the illusion of being a rock-hard mariner.

Thank goodness for the boat's two 180-horsepower motors, because without them, I would have sprayed fragments of coffee-hued cheese tortilla all over John and his helm. Forward propulsion at least gave us some modicum of stability, and after 20 minutes of barging our way westward, the lighthouse and a flock of noisy seagulls loomed high above us. "This is the last piece of real estate between us and Nova Scotia," shouted John. "The most remarkable thing about this place is that it's here at all."

The Bishop was only automated in 1992. Before then, teams of three lighthouse keepers used to live and work together for weeks on end, tending to a paraffin lamp. They worked in threes just in case one of them died and left the other to go stir crazy with a corpse. This thought was enough to send a shiver through my spine. It must have taken a very special – or indeed desperate – type of man to live on a battered rock at the edge of Britain, so close, yet so far from his loved ones.

My mouth was beginning to sweat again, but the taste of salty sea air was enough to make me feel reborn, as though lockdown had never happened. I composed myself for long enough to do a quick piece-to-camera on my phone, then we raced, with the wind and waves behind us, back to St Agnes. From here on in, my journey would only ever be heading north.

———

In the blustery dusk, I sat in the porch of my tent, drinking Aiden's tart island cider, and eating yet more cheese and tomato wraps. It was always the way on trips like these. I could only carry so much food, therefore lived off one thing or another until it was all gone. A cycle tour doesn't lend itself to a balanced diet. Buying a loaf of bread means that you only eat sandwiches; 500 g of pasta might feed you for three or four meals in a row, but it was always a struggle to stomach penne and pesto for breakfast.

I wandered around the coastal edge of the farm, stooping to look in rock pools, where baby brown crabs and fidgety shrimps took refuge from the angry might of the sea. As I hopped between slimy boulders, bubbled seaweed fronds popped under my soles like acorns on a hot tarmac road. In a small adjacent field, sheltered from the wind, the milking herd – Shamrock, Sundance, Rose, Honey, Westie, Sunset, Cilla, Humbug and Humble – mooed for their just-weaned calves on the other side of a fence.

Farmer Sam was doing his final rounds before bed. Tall and thin, with wind-burned cheeks and a tussled mop of hair, he emitted the exhausted cheeriness of a man who worked a lot but rested very little. "We have an historic resilience in Scilly," said Sam. "The past year was no different. Everyone stepped up to see us through a tough time. We all grew more produce and stocked up our freezers. Chip in, do your bit and help out. That's pretty much how it goes."

Over several decades, Sam and his family went from only producing milk for St Agnes, to diversifying into ice creams and a campsite. "The farm itself is never going to make us hugely rich, but it is something we can be proud of and that's all any of us can really hope for."

When the pandemic hit, some sections of the community wanted to remain closed indefinitely, despite 10 per cent of the islands' income coming from tourism. "There was naturally a certain degree of tension," said Sam. "This felt like a secure place to be during the pandemic, but when we opened up again, people working in the tourism industry took on a level of extra responsibility for the whole community. Of course, some would have preferred it if there were fewer people, but I feel confident that we did things the right way."

With flakes of emerald silage dusted across his wellington boots and a black eye from a run in with a cricket ball, I immediately warmed to Sam. He radiated a love for Scilly, and clearly didn't take his ocean view for granted. His cows were his pride, joy and livelihood, but with a sideline in tourism, he clearly also took satisfaction in cultivating happy humans, even if they were only in his care for a day or two.

"I was just talking to an A&E consultant from London, camping in the next field. He told me that this holiday is the perfect antidote to a really testing year. I can't fully put into words how much that means." And with that, Sam wandered off into the heavy twilight and left me to ponder the last rusty strands of day disappearing over Bishop Rock.

The night was fitful and uncomfortable. Not through stress, but incompetence, again. What had looked like an innocuous slope when I pitched the tent that morning was in fact a gentle hummock, plenty big enough to pull blood away from any body part that happened to be falling downhill. For hours, I struggled to get comfortable, laying for a few minutes at a time in one semi-flat position, before wriggling into a new one. Perhaps I was still feeling discombobulated by the swirling sea, but the inside of my tent produced a confusing sense of vertigo, like driving through a long road tunnel and losing one's sense of up and down.

I eventually fell asleep but woke up at dawn squished into the tent's bottom right corner, with my face pressed up against the door. For the first 2 hours of the day, I had a zip-shaped indent running between my top lip and left eyelid.

The morning was warmed by a gentle southerly breeze, mild and sunny, but with a tinge of hot Iberian summer. You could practically smell garlic butter and seared scallops in the seasoned air. An almost-tame blackbird skipped around the frame of my resting bike. I threw it some biscuit crumbs from the bottom of my pannier and watched silently as its speckled chest puffed out, contentedly plump with custard cream.

Three days into the second leg of my journey and I was finally, thankfully, starting to find calm. I didn't just see the bird but watched it intently. Its jerky movements, its blinking eyes. My body was sat in Scilly and my mind was there, too.

In my "normal" life I struggled to follow routines and flitted from one task to the other without giving anything my full attention. Smartphones, the internet, social media and rolling 24-hour news were just far too distracting. At home, my default setting was chaos. I would write at a desk covered in mouldy coffee cups and half-read books. I'd drive Alana to fury for not putting my laundered clothes back into their correct drawers. But life on the bike was simpler, mindful. A caveman existence of being and doing. A tidy pannier meant a tidy mind.

The tent almost fitted back into its bag. I pushed most, but never all, of the air out of my mattress. I stacked items on top of each other, in the order of how likely I'd be to need them. I even made the effort to change into fresh socks. But after barely cycling the day before, a shower seemed like overkill. Best of all, though, I'd very nearly finished the now sweaty Cheddar and damp tortillas. What bland, thrifty meal lay around the next corner? I wondered, as I jumped on the first boat off the island and set my sights on another idyll, St Martin's.

———

We skidded over glassy shallows, sandy-bottomed blue, interrupted only by flashing glints of platinum fish skin. Even with 20 knots of breeze, the hot sun seared my exposed skin. There was barely a cloud in the azure sky. As we slowed into Higher Town Bay, a fingernail beach with a single yacht moored in its shoulder-deep cuticle, a man jogged across the sand, struggling to hoist a blue, green and yellow kite above his waist. Two young boys under droopy sunhats watched on, before losing interest and wandering off toward a woman sitting on a plaid blanket surrounded by crudités, baguettes and ramekins of blitzed-up mush.

St Martin's was perfection, but a sinister beast grumbled out to sea. "Wind and rain," said the man who lashed the boat to the dock and helped me lob my bike and panniers ashore. "Lots of it. Less than a day away they're saying." I brushed it off at first and climbed up the concrete track to the bakery at the summit of the squat sandstone island. But then another warning came, this time delivered on the warm scent of fresh pasties.

"Could be with us for a while," said the woman behind the counter. "Mad rush to get on and off."

I was racked with fidgety panic. Scilly now threatened to become more like a prison than a paradise. My ticket back to Penzance was booked for the following day, at exactly the same time an Atlantic storm the size of Ireland was set to make landfall.

The prognosis from Isles of Scilly Travel – the company that manages boat and plane transport to and from Cornwall – didn't fill me with optimism. If the sea was rough, but not too rough, then the *Scillonian* would run as scheduled. But be warned, it wouldn't be for the faint of heart or weak of stomach. The Vomit Comet would be rendered a Puke Nuke.

Alternatively, if the crossing was ultimately deemed too dangerous, then I might be able to fly. However, none of the planes had room for a bicycle. The only option, therefore, would be to cut my visit short by 24 hours and escape before the storm hit. I liked Scilly, but I couldn't risk being stranded there indefinitely. It would send a shock wave through my plans.

I now had just 3 hours to explore St Martin's before taking the ferry back to St Mary's to then catch the *Scillonian* to Penzance. And instead of cycling around aimlessly, I wanted to find one final story, to illustrate how new arrivals to the islands might have fared during challenging and unprecedented times.

Just beyond the tiny cricket pitch, which had kayaks at square leg and fishing nets at long on, I found it. Holly Robbins and James Faulconbridge bought the island vineyard, the most south-western in Britain, at the start of 2020, before 99 per cent of the planet had ever heard of Covid-19. There couldn't have been a worse time to take on a new business, let alone one at the edge of a country about to endure three national lockdowns. Nonetheless, they welcomed me into their 5 acres of south-facing grapevines with exhausted smiles and a dogged outlook. "The past year was tough," said Holly, as a few silken strands of silvering hair glinted in her hazel ponytail. "But in some ways, it helped us out a little bit. We've come out the other side and things are finally looking up."

The couple must have been in their mid-thirties and – just like me – wore worry and work around their eyes, cheeks and lips. "The past year has taught me that if there's something you really want to do, then you should just do it. If you don't, then you could end up kicking yourself for the rest of your life."

In a good year, they'll expect to produce 3,000 bottles of wine, but if a bad one comes along, they might only manage 500. As a fallback, they hoped that vineyard tours and a self-catering shepherd's hut would provide them with a year-round income. But pursuing their dream didn't look entirely straightforward. They were living in a Mongolian yurt, with a double bed, a desk and a wood-burning stove. A seemingly idyllic, boho lifestyle under calm blue skies, but no doubt a drag during heavy wind and rain.

"A lot of our friends and family thought we were mad, leaping into the unknown. But we feel incredibly lucky to have this opportunity. No regrets. If you don't gamble in life, then sometimes you might miss out on finding something even better."

I cycled off into a fuzzy heat mirage, my shoulders feeling lighter from their optimism, my right pannier now a litre heavier with dry white wine. The island was busy with tourists, dawdling like tourists always do. Young families, laden with buckets, spades, bags of fudge and foil windmills that whirred as they walked. Pensioners with panting dogs, Thermos flasks and sandwiches in Tupperware. Cash-rich forty-somethings wearing Serengeti-ready walking boots, baseball caps with UV protective neck covers and those ridiculous trousers that can be zipped off at the knee. Trousers that are only ever unzipped once, before the owners realise that:

- You need a PhD in textiles and the patience of a Shaolin monk in order to connect them back together.
- You could save a significant chunk of your precious life by simply removing the trousers entirely and replacing them with a conventional pair of shorts.

St Martin's was a third the size of St Mary's and only a fraction bigger than St Agnes. Once I'd climbed to the island's summit – home to the shop, a community centre, an old red phone box and a few cottages – all I could do was freewheel down the other side and wait at the jetty for my lunchtime ferry back to St Mary's. For half an hour I sunbathed with my eyes closed, safe in the knowledge that I'd soon hear the chug of an outboard engine.

They were sounds that never came.

"Are you expecting the 1.30?" asked a topless, barrel-like man, walking on the beach.

"Yes. But it's now 1.40."

"That's it, over there," he said, pointing toward a white shape, skipping across the waves.

The ferry had departed. Right on time. From a different dock. And was now travelling at full tilt toward St Mary's and the *Scillonian*, which was already busy taking on freight ahead of its 4 p.m. crossing back to Penzance. Now, without me.

I sprinted to an upmarket hotel, where people in fedoras and designer sunglasses sat calmly feasting on gourmet burgers, lobster tails and Aperol spritzes, and explained my predicament to the receptionist. "The ferries leave from different docks, depending on the tides," she said. "That's the last one until this evening."

I paced around the grounds of the hotel, infecting the holiday mood with bad vibes. I felt suffocated, forced to survive on a quarter of the oxygen my body was used to, like being waterboarded or squeezed into a wardrobe.

I was stuck. An idiot. An amateur. My epic journey had ground to an embarrassing halt, after just two days and barely 10 miles of leisurely cycling.

After an hour, a lifeline came. An expensive one. But a lifeline all the same. "I've just found out that we have a guest getting a private RIB to catch the *Scillonian* back to Cornwall," said the receptionist. "She said she'll share it with you, if you pay half."

Thirty pounds for a 5-minute transfer. Enough to feed me for a week.

PORTLAND:
HIS FATHERLY LOVE

Sailing downwind, the crossing to Cornwall felt positively Mediterranean. There were still no signs of the storm that was hurtling across the Atlantic, and the *Scillonian* buzzed with the sound of relieved chatter; the smug tone that comes from swerving a bullet.

We docked just before 7 p.m. and waited patiently for our turns to disembark. Social distancing restrictions seemed even more farcical at times like these. Strangers could sit on a ferry, shoulder to shoulder, mouth to mouth, for 3 hours, but were then asked to separate themselves by 2 m when it was time to waddle off.

Nevertheless, it was a relief to be back on the Cornish mainland. I could now ride for as far as I wanted, without being interrupted by the weather. But the afternoon's stress had created a new cycle of panic in my body. My snatched breaths had already made my windpipe sting and my throat felt like it was bleeding. My intercostal muscles ached, as though I'd done 500 press-ups. I'd been clenching my jaw so tight that the patch of flesh just inside my earlobes was now gnarled and knotted.

I also didn't have anywhere to sleep. There wasn't a room in Penzance for less than £200 and the nearest campsite with an available pitch was 7 miles in the wrong direction. Heavy rain and 70 mph winds were expected to make landfall in the early hours. Even an illegal "wild camp" somewhere would, no doubt, leave me soaked and exhausted. I bought a portion of chips, and then fired off a few desperate messages to people on Airbnb.

Only one replied: a single room in a nearby terraced house for £50, which seemed extortionate. But it was either that or the piss-splashed bus stop next to the bowling green. And that was already occupied by two frisky pigeons.

The owner wasn't there when I arrived, and I let myself in via a combination key box. The house stank of stale cannabis smoke and unemptied bins, the familiar scent of student digs. There were three fixed-speed bikes in the corner of the living room and a dozen dirty plates in the kitchen sink. Halfway through my first shower in three days the plug between my feet belched out a sticky, fetid hairball.

The bedroom was clean enough, or at least the sheets looked and smelled fresh. Alana would hate this, I thought, as I inspected under the bed. No old tissues, empty bowls of cereal or used condoms, thank goodness. Just carpet. Wonderful, normal, carpet. I locked the door and leaned my bags against it. If I needed the loo in the night, I'd just go in one of my water bottles and disinfect it later. Is this fun? I wondered. Was I living the dream or enduring a nightmare?

There were slams and bumps in the night. Doors closing, kettles brewing, rollies being smoked in the dank alley beneath my window. But nothing more haunting than the thumping wind and rain, which built to a crescendo, until it was finally time to drag myself out of bed. I tiptoed through the house and emerged on to the street. It had become a wind tunnel. A kerb-high stream of water flowed between the wheels of parked cars. A few slate tiles had been ripped clean from their roofs and now lay in hundreds of mosaic pieces, scattered across the greasy cobbles. I locked the door behind me and posted the key back through the letter box. There was no turning back.

The storm was more ferocious than anything I'd ever encountered before. Angrier than the headwinds I'd faced in the Great Plains of Iowa and Montana. Louder than the bone-dry gales that rumbled, unabated, across Tajikistan and Uzbekistan. Wetter than the fizzing sheets of monsoon rain that lashed into the parched Bay of Bengal. Colder than the frozen squalls that whipped across the north Pacific in winter.

I made it as far as the harbour, where grizzly men in tangerine overalls were already tucking in to their lunches in the cosy cabs of their bashed-up vans. Cigarette smoke twisted out of postbox chinks in rain-lashed windows. Skips filled with scrap metal, old lawnmowers and broken boats rattled around like giant tambourines. Over the harbour walls, the sea curled and crashed into the promenade. "What the hell am I doing?" I grumbled, as I took shelter in a rotten nook behind a public toilet stinking of urine and disinfectant.

The previous month had been the sunniest on record in Britain, bringing dry but crisp weather to the final few weeks of a nationwide lockdown. Now, however, the jet stream had shifted unseasonably north, and some parts of the country had seen a month's worth of rain in less than 24 hours. I made a cautious attempt to set off through the town centre, but the sideways rain was so fierce I was thrown from my bike just outside the train station. With a grazed palm and a dented sense of belief, I reluctantly threw in the towel and took refuge in the nearest bike shop.

"Where are you headed?" asked the resident bike mechanic, Steve, a silver-haired, moustachioed road cyclist in turned-up jean shorts, a greasy T-shirt and Vans skating shoes.

"North. I guess. Everywhere is north from here."

"You don't really know?"

"Not really. The south coast first, then maybe London. Scotland if I can make it."

"Shit, man. That's heavy."

"Do you think?"

"Yeah, big time. Do you know how far that is?"

"Not exactly, no. 2,000 miles, maybe? But I don't want to give it too much thought or I'll freak myself out!"

"In this weather, even worse. You'd better give me your bike and I'll make sure it's up to the job."

For the rest of the morning, I sat in Steve's warm workshop drinking thick black coffee, buzzing off his friendly vibe. As the rain slapped against the windowed frontage, the scent of caffeine and chain oil made it harder and harder to leave.

"How much do I owe you?" I asked, worrying I was starting to outstay my welcome.

"Don't worry, man. Consider it a gift. From one cyclist to another."

He agreed to take the bottle of Scillonian white wine as payment. "Very communist," I joked. "A cashless society." I then bundled out on to the soggy streets of Penzance, confused whether I should stay or go.

The weather forecast was grim. Solid rain for as far as the Met Office could predict, and all of it was making landfall in Penzance. It was cold, too. Barely 10°C. The only element I had slightly in my favour was the wind. It was currently whipping in as an 80 mph southerly but was expected to round to a 60 mph south-westerly overnight. In theory, at least, I could wait another day and have it perfectly at my back. I looked to the heavens, felt heavy rain drops clatter into my eyeballs and took shelter in a bus stop rattling with beer cans and Pringles tubes.

Throughout my journey around the country, I'd been shocked by the amount of litter that clogged up our parks, ditches and hedgerows. Blustery Penzance was certainly no different. The storm had picked up wheelie bins and tossed them around town. Hundreds of soggy crisp packets and chocolate-bar wrappers fluttered down the high street.

Closed international borders had triggered a British holiday boom, attracting even more people than usual to the south-west of England. Some locals working in the tourism sector were, unsurprisingly, thrilled at the prospect of grounded Britons and their furloughed spending money. On the flip side, however, the county's bins were now filling up much faster than normal, and all along Penzance Promenade, dozens of brilliant-white camper vans seemed bedded in for much longer than a Polaroid and a stick of rock.

Before I trudged off in search of a place to stay, I met up with Rachel Yates, a community engagement officer from Plastic Free Penzance, a campaign group set up by the charity Surfers Against Sewage. "There is definitely a correlation between tourism and plastic pollution," said Rachel, as heavy rain sploshed against her beanie hat and down her waterproof jacket. "It isn't anyone's fault as such, it just shows that we are using and buying too much single-use packaging and systems can't cope. It has a lot to do with the UK's waste-management systems not being uniform."

What might be recycled in Yorkshire or Greater London isn't necessarily recycled in Cornwall or Devon. This means that people put things in the wrong bins, and extra waste ends up strewn across Britain's streets and beaches. "As a coastal location, plastic pollution is ever present," said Rachel. "Every time you go down to the beach for a walk there will be something that needs collecting. We see it every day here."

Besides beach cleans and demonstrations, Plastic Free Penzance aims to stem the flow of single-use plastic at source, by encouraging local schools, cafés and businesses to ditch plastic, long before it enters the supply chain.

There are now more than 800 plastic-free communities across Britain, each attempting to banish litter from their beaches and green spaces. The challenge they face, however, is enormous. Every single day 32 million plastic drinks bottles are bought and sold around the country and each and every minute more than 100,000 pieces of plastic packaging are carried out of the nation's supermarkets. The pandemic saw our dependence upon single-use plastics increase even further. Latex gloves, face masks and visors will surely fill our drains, lakes and oceans for hundreds of years.

"At first there was a lot less plastic pollution," said Rachel, "because people weren't out and about so much, but then we saw a lot of gloves and masks and more plastic bags turning up in people's online shops. But once the initial knee-jerk had passed, it was encouraging to see how ingrained the whole plastic-free ethos had become. All of the local businesses began to push back and say, 'do we really need this?'"

———

Later that afternoon, I checked into a cheap B&B, emptied my panniers across the bed and asked myself the very same question. Do I really need this? I'd never been a stickler for weight saving, but suddenly every gram mattered. The next stage of my journey intimidated me more than any other, and with Rachel's words still ringing in my head, I set about reorganising my small but complicated life.

Dry clothes at the top of the bed, wet ones at the bottom. Moka pot, Swiss army knife and DSLR on the floor next to the door. Evening clothes folded and draped over the radiator. Soaking cagoule hanging on the shoulders of a desk chair. All perishables: six slightly damp teabags, two ketchup sachets, nine loose ibuprofen tablets, three cereal bars, five bruised apples, half a loaf of mouldy brown bread and a quarter of a chocolate-chip cookie.

Spread out in landscape, my life was a haphazard Picasso painting. It was also startling to see how much single-use plastic I was carrying. Three old Diet Coke bottles. Umpteen sweet wrappers. Supermarket sandwich packages and the elastic bands that manufacturers tie around inner tubes.

I fell asleep fretting about what the next day might bring. I had no idea where I'd spend the night, or how far I might ride. Every campsite on my route had demanded a three-night minimum stay, and most of them required guests to book an entire pitch, big enough for several cars, a couple of caravans and a dozen screaming kids. They also charged close to £100 per night for the privilege, while all I really needed was £5-worth of flattish grass. It was a relief to be back on the open road, but I worried that all the spontaneous thrill of my adventure would be replaced by forward planning.

The morning brought yet more driving rain, but at least it lashed in from the west as a tailwind. I certainly couldn't afford to linger for another night and knew I had to take advantage of the conditions while they lasted. I was packed up by 7.30 a.m. and flying, wind-assisted, out of Penzance, past scowling children trudging toward school.

No one in their right mind would go out in such horrendous conditions. The B-road sandwiched between St Michael's Mount and the busy A394 was so engulfed by water that I had to unclip from my pedals and splay out my legs just to keep my feet dry.

I should have diverted inland, but I'd developed a weird obsession with following the coast of Britain. In my mind's eye, I enjoyed tracing the squiggly contours of the map, even if that meant entering an unpredictable relationship with Poseidon.

As waves crashed in, unabated, from the Atlantic, green water shook the earth beneath my wheels. Even though I could see them coming, I flinched every time. Somewhere near Marazion, I saw an old man and his even more ancient Jack Russell put a slipper and paw outside their bungalow, only to take one look at each other and retreat straight back inside. All along the seafront between Prussia Cove and Porthleven, scraggly-haired surfers huddled in the fronts of VW camper vans as their waxy boards rattled above them.

I was moving fast, 13 miles inside the first hour. I should have been happy, but cold and wet I descend into a damp and lonely fug. Why am I doing this? I wondered. What am I trying to prove? Alana was in Bristol, meeting her newborn nephew for the very first time, a giant moment in all their lives. I could practically hear her cooing from 200 miles away. Was this journey of mine so important that I'd forgo all those shared moments? Did my selfishness know no bounds?

A decade and a half of adventure had meant many sacrifices. Missed weddings, family parties and christenings. But where would I eventually draw the line? Where was the balance to be struck? If we were to have a family one day, could I honestly tear myself away from Alana, and our children, to fling myself up a mountain or descend a raging river, for little more than my ego?

One moment, my journey seemed like the most important thing in the world, as though the universe was spinning on its axis around me. But then I'd catch my pathetic reflection in a drizzly windowpane and feel like a deluded loser. David Brent on a bicycle.

Instead of following the quiet coastal roads around the Lizard Peninsula, I joined the A394 at Helston and hugged the shoulder all the way to Penryn. It wasn't clever, and it certainly wasn't pretty, but it was my only option. The ferry I'd intended to take from Falmouth to St Mawes had been cancelled due to the weather. This left me with a 2-hour slog north, before I could eventually turn north-east again.

———

Cornwall was, without a doubt in my mind, the most overrated of English counties – or Duchy, if you're that way inclined. I'm sure that most visitors had no idea why they were actually there.

Sure, the landscapes were gnarled and pretty. *Poldark* one minute, *The Wind in the Willows* the next. But by the time I reached Truro, somewhere around lunchtime, I must have passed 50,000 sour-faced tourists stuck in cars packed with duvets, suitcases and bags of charcoal.

The people who had escaped their cars weren't much happier. A pair of sullen pensioners licked their luxury ice creams so agonisingly slowly they'd clearly cashed in a pension in order to afford them. A young family of four stood outside a café with their arms folded and brows furrowed, looking as though they'd been served pubic hair paninis for lunch. It was impossible to discern if anyone, anywhere, was having any fun whatsoever. Or if they were simply enduring the ordeal because they were too embarrassed to admit that they should have stayed at home and saved a couple of grand.

Thankfully, by the time I reached St Austell, 54 miles east of Penzance, I had an offer of a place to stay in a hamlet just north of Looe and a 13-mile scenic route that could get me there. But I'd already climbed more than 3,000 feet that day and had another 2,000 ahead of me. One of the toughest days of my entire trip had come when my legs were their least prepared.

All I could do was creep forward. Up a hill. Down a hill. Up a hill. Down. Throwing bananas and biscuits into my mouth, chipping into the miles, one pedal in front of another. In some places, the route became so muddy and narrow that it was hard to determine if I was on a road, a footpath or a bridleway. However, unlike the bleak landscapes I'd cycled through six months before, the hedgerows were now alive with white, purple and pink blossom. Bursting with spring, they emitted a minty, sugary dust that tasted of humbugs.

I have zero interest in Strava, PBs, or macho chest-beating. I don't see myself as a cyclist. I've never read a cycling magazine or bought a pair of those pointless cycling socks. I'm just a bloke with a bicycle, who likes going on big journeys. But on days like these I studied the ascent reading on my bicycle computer intently. Every time it jumped up, I was a few feet closer to a cold pint and a packet of salty crisps. Stress and panic weren't options, either. My lungs could barely keep up.

Once you have a reasonable base level of fitness, cycling 100 miles on the flat is relatively easy. But ascent can be deadly. And Cornwall was a killer. At the bottom of great hills, the whole world seemed to loom above me.

In the Scottish Highlands I always tried to keep the highest gear in reserve. It was nice to know it was there, but I resisted using it. Something like a smoker giving up cigarettes, but still carrying a pack of Marlboro in their top pocket, to remind them they have the willpower to persevere. In Cornwall, however, I'd already chain-smoked my gearset and had nothing left. With my bike and panniers fully loaded, it felt as though I was dragging an anchor. On a particularly mountainous stretch just east of Par, a blustery village with a small sandy beach and a penchant for static caravans, I had no option left but to push.

The rain eased off occasionally, allowing the tailwind to blow-dry my sopping back and calves. But then it would pour down again, even heavier than before, and leave me with squelching shoes and road grit in the folds behind my knees. After 67 miles and 4,938 feet of climbing, I finally grumbled into Pelynt, a small village with a shop, a campsite and a sports and social club.

My legs hadn't quite reached the painful tender stage that I knew would leave me shambling around the next morning, but my hands were already seizing up from tightly gripping the gear levers on the dozens of steep descents. Exhausted and forlorn, I pushed my bike into the waterlogged campsite at Hall Barton Organic Farm, the only place that had agreed to let me pitch my tent for a single night. There wasn't a soul to be found, just the sound of a few cows mooing in a distant field. I checked my phone and found a text: "It's too wet to camp. Take the shepherd's hut. No charge. We will be back soon. Just feeding the animals."

By the time I'd showered, eaten half a kilo of pasta and pesto and spread my sodden clothes across the hut's electric heater, the farmers, Jenny and Giles, were back in their Aga-warm kitchen and welcoming me in for a drink. They were much younger than I'd envisaged, early forties at a push, and were farmer-fit with rosy cheeks and barely an ounce of fat between them.

Jenny was still in her muddy waterproof trousers, and had steam rising off her thermal sweater. Giles, meanwhile, resembled a messy-haired nutty professor, as he crouched over a 25-litre bucket, funnelling home-brewed beer into a row of recycled bottles. The aroma of fresh hops kissed my nostrils, then curled away into distant pantries, stores and tack rooms. "Works out about a pound a pint," said Giles, as he poured me a glass, taking extra care not to include the inch of pollen-hued sediment that had settled at the bottom of the bottle. "It should taste a bit like Tribute, the ale they brew down the road in St Austell."

The couple clearly adored their farm and the hard but rewarding lifestyle it afforded them. "We've always felt very lucky," said Jenny. "We're grateful for the life we lead, working with animals, surrounded by fields, often with a view of the sea. Not much changed for us, really. We worked seven days a week and caught up on all the things we never had time for."

Farming became one of the pandemic's few boom industries. In 2020, British milk sales grew by 10 per cent, while an increased appetite for organic food helped supermarkets enjoy their highest sector growth since December 2016. During the first national lockdown, worldwide Google searches for "local food" reached an all-time high. In Britain, the search term "veg boxes" increased sixfold. "Obviously, people were stuck at home, unable to go to restaurants," said Jenny. "Disposable income was spent on things like food boxes. I also think people became more aware of boosting their immune systems and looking after themselves."

At the height of lockdown, mainstream supermarkets struggled to keep up with demand, giving farms like Hall Barton Organic a rare opportunity to take up the slack. In the first two months alone, more than 500 British veg-box providers delivered 3.5 million boxes, more than double their usual sales. Jenny and Giles sold all their organic beef and lamb to Riverford Organic Farmers, based in nearby Totnes.

"Demand just kept going up," said Giles. "We simply couldn't produce any more."

I liked the couple a lot. Generous and genuine, they didn't beat around the bush or mince their words. As a journalist, I'd met hundreds of people to the contrary, and it was always refreshing to meet characters who kept me guessing. We sat and chatted for almost an hour before Jenny dropped a bombshell. Neither of them had been, or probably would be, vaccinated against Covid-19.

By this point in the pandemic, vaccinations had been available to Britons for six months, and Giles and Jenny would have been eligible for two doses. In contrast, Alana and I were still waiting for a text from the NHS, and we were eager to roll up our sleeves and get it done. For us, vaccination meant freedom, and for me, in particular, it symbolised getting my old life back. A life of travel, of new people and places. Because without those things I was nothing.

"For me, there's not enough information out there about potential problems later in life," said Jenny. "Nobody knows. They're using humans as guinea pigs. You've seen our lifestyle; we don't mix with big groups of people. We are only ever on the farm. I sanitise my hands and wear a mask when I go to a shop. I take the most sensible precautions, but I don't know what's in that vaccine and I don't want it in my body, basically."

If I'd read her words on Facebook or Twitter, I'd have probably assumed that Jenny also believed the Earth was flat. But in person, and not on a shouty social media platform, her concerns were measured, sincere and entirely valid. It was unfair to crudely lump the couple into the "anti-vaxxer" crowd. They weren't vociferously against the vaccine and weren't critical of people who chose to take it, they just didn't fancy it themselves. And I found it impossible not to respect that.

We shook hands and I made a run for the shepherd's hut seemingly floating away on the far side of a quagmire. For the rest of the night, I listened to the heavy rain crashing against the corrugated tin roof. No tech. No phone. The time to think, a moment to breathe.

To have one's beliefs challenged and refreshed was, surely, one of life's greatest privileges. Stuck at home, behind a smartphone and laptop for months on end, my echo chamber had only ever become more echoey. But back out on the road again, not knowing who or what might appear next, my opinions and convictions were being challenged. Travel, I was reminded, was only ever a force for good.

Dawn broke to the sound of two dozen rooks shrieking in the branches above me. The rain had abated slightly, but the sky was black like ink. I was tempted to wait it out, drink a gallon of tea and let the mumbling tones of a wind-up radio warm my body and mind. But I knew I had to push on. Or, at least, I *felt* like I had to.

Restlessness was an affliction, and it smacked hardest on journeys like these. The more I moved, the more I *needed* to move. However, it was unclear if I was racing to the next place out of necessity, or simply feeding my addiction to adrenaline, a moreish drug, just like any other.

As teenagers, my friends and I were too young – and too skint – to drink legally in pubs. Instead, we spent our weekends hiking from one Cotswolds village to the next, smoking joints in the awnings of far-flung cricket pavilions and necking cheap spirits in bus shelters. We'd climb tall summer trees and skin up in their canopies. Scramble over barbed-wire fences and watch diamanté dawns sprinkle fairy dust across undulating wintry fields.

Some journeys would take us hours – a bench with an epic view, a stately home with a weak fence to crawl under. Reaching our target would feel like a monumental success, but then the restlessness would bubble up in us again and another adventure would always unfold. Movement felt good. But to be still was to stagnate. From then on, my lust for motion would seldom be sated.

———

Reluctantly, I left Pelynt and crept east, plunging into steep valleys of faultless bluebells, now swimming up to their necks in virgin pools. At the tops of treeless hills, I had enough signal to stream music, but in the lonely, forested hollows my world fell eerily silent. Just the cracks of distant twigs and the occasional frog-like ribbit of a woodcock.

Away from the main roads, the traffic and the busy beaches, Cornwall was a different world entirely – a bucolic dream of sleepy farmsteads, forgotten cottages and meadows in brilliant flower. There was a simple but thrilling joy in not knowing what might appear around the next corner. A bleating lamb on the wrong side of a fence. A tractor with a spilled load. Men wearing tweed flat caps and plus fours, with 12-bore shotguns broken over their shoulders.

Nevertheless, by mid-morning, I'd taken so many wrong turns that I was caked in mud and famished again, so I diverted away from the scenic route and ducked into an American-themed diner just off the A38. It seemed like a splendid idea at first, but the place was so starkly juxtaposed to my green and drizzly norm that I was soon feeling nauseous from Americana.

Photos of Bon Jovi, Elvis and Michael Jackson filled every patch of wall space where there wasn't already a Harley-Davidson bumper sticker, an oversized bottle top, or a Midwest licence plate. The soundtrack jumped from Tina Turner and Journey to Bruce Springsteen and Mötley Crüe. In fact, the diner was so authentically American that the coffee looked and tasted just like diarrhoea.

Most words on the menu were fused together with an "n" instead of the word "and", like mac "n" cheese and fish "n" chips. The veggie breakfast was decent enough, beige, crispy and calorific, but when it was time to leave, the waitress insisted that I used the clunky "order 'n' pay" QR code, despite having already taken my order with a good old-fashioned pad and pen. We shared a protracted look of mutual contempt and then I departed without leaving an American-sized tip. There's only so many times you can ask for salt "n" pepper before you feel like you're being ignored.

I crossed the river Tamar at Plymouth and was well into Devon by the time I tired of humming "Simply the Best" and started on "Born to Run". Then, with 30 miles under my belt, something truly remarkable happened: the clouds parted, and the sun came out. Suddenly, I was cycling through a steamy rainforest mottled with puddles of warm light. Beetles and dragonflies vaulted through the thick air and a heron resembling a pterodactyl flew across my path with a silvery morsel clamped tightly in its beak.

Britain was practically photosynthesising before my very eyes. And with a full belly and a drying back, Devon's hills seemed flatter than the ones behind me. Everything was swell with the world. I was cycling through the exposition of a technicolour Disney film. But then, a few miles south-east of Plympton:

POP.

SLAP.

KERB.

HEDGE.

The 45-mm steel bolt that held my seat post in place had – for some mysterious reason – decided to shoot out of its forever home. It ricocheted off a fence post with the force of an air-rifle pellet and disappeared into the lush undergrowth. It was a miracle I didn't swerve into an oncoming lorry. I was even luckier that the bolt didn't bounce off the bike's frame and make a beeline for my scrotum.

This was another freak event that I couldn't have militated against. But with my arse now slumped to the height of the bike's top tube, there was no way I could travel far without a proper fix. A rational man would have cycled back to Plymouth, found a bike shop and sucked up the 12 extra miles. What I did, however, was stubbornly ride on east, with my knees akimbo, looking like a clown on a kid's tricycle.

There wasn't a single bike shop between me and Exeter, but within half an hour I'd found the second-best thing: a busy pub, the Foxhound in Brixton, and a pair of friendly builders with a fresh reel of gaffer tape. It took just half a dozen wraps to fasten the seat post back in place, and I was left so cock-a-hoop with the result that I bought them a pair of frosty lagers to say thank you.

The temptation to pull up a bar stool and drink with them for the rest of the afternoon was so strong that I didn't dare sit down. If I had done, there's a fair chance my trip would have ended there and then. I'd have spent all my money on beer and scampi fries, and might now be labouring, cash in hand, on a building site in west Devon.

All I wanted to do was race to Totnes and sink a beer with an old friend, but by the time I'd reached Ermington, a small village 6 miles east of Brixton, my saddle had already sunk by a few painful inches. It would have been foolhardy to continue, even by my low standards, so I diverted north to South Brent, where an amateur bike mechanic had kindly offered to take a look.

Bob's Bike Shed was a shrine to all things round and rollable. A dozen shiny racing rims, a faultless Triumph motorbike. With its polished alloys and liquorice-black tyres, I didn't dare touch it with my grubby road hands. On every patch of vacant floor, there were lawnmowers, prams, hydraulic jacks and pressure washers, each in a different stage of repair.

On the back wall, a cornucopia of spanners, screwdrivers, ratchets, Allen keys and drill bits hung ready to fix any conceivable problem with a bike, garden machine or spaceship.

"Get the panniers off," said Bob, a slim, bald-headed man with fit calves and chunky black glasses. "I'll do my best, but I can already tell that this isn't going to be easy."

After 30 years as a firefighter, Bob converted a van into a mobile bicycle repair shop and began fixing up broken bikes, either on the roadside or back at his shed surgery. "I wouldn't want to say that I've done well out of the pandemic," said Bob, "because I think that's a crass attitude to have. But from a mental-health point of view, it has been great for me to be able to keep working and to know that I'm helping people get back out on the road."

Bob and his wife lived in a modern house, with ceiling-high windows and a perfect emerald lawn. With a cup of tea in one hand and a spanner in the other, this was clearly a man who had earned every second of his retirement. He was now perfectly content tinkering around with spokes and gear cables, rather than dragging bodies out of burning buildings.

"I worry most, however, about my daughter," said Bob, as he threw my bike into a vice.

"How come?"

"She's a twenty-six-year-old theatre producer living in London. Everything just came crashing down around her."

"Tell me about it."

"I really believe that the past year and a half has been robbed from her, from all of us."

"You sound pissed off."

"There seemed to be a total lack of planning from the people in charge. In the fire service we had contingency plans for all kinds of scenarios. We used to train for all sorts of crazy things, like planes landing on shopping centres in the middle of towns."

"Planes crashing into shopping centres?"

"Of course. We planned for everything. But this government did nothing and I feel angry. A quarter of a million people have died in this country. Was that necessary? I don't think so."

It took Bob less than an hour to fix something that would have taken me a week. Not only was he a skilled mechanic, but he spoke with rage and sincerity. I found it hard to drag myself away.

My job seemed too easy at times like these. I could knock on any door in Britain and nosily ask, "So, how have the past couple of years been for you?" and receive infinite unique responses. Journalists used to travel to war zones and natural disasters to document acute moments in history, but Covid-19 – with all its societal, cultural and economic permutations – had impacted on every single person, in myriad different ways.

The afternoon grew warm and hazy. Fluffy cumulus clouds cast football pitch-sized shadows across a breadbasket of wheat, rye and barley. Hedgerows of hawthorn, bramble, elder and dogwood echoed with the chirp of invisible birds. My legs screamed with lactic acid, but at least I was now moving downhill. I had 3,500 feet on the computer from the morning, and barely strained a muscle all the way to Dartington, just north of Totnes.

I found Jack at the bustling community centre, sitting on a grass bank eating pizza with his partner, Joanna, and their two toddlers, Ted and Frida. Jack, Joe and I were inseparable as restless teenagers, and grew into young men together accompanied by a soundtrack of Dilated Peoples, Jurassic 5 and Roots Manuva. When Joe died, I instinctively called Jack first to break the news, because they were brothers to me, the brothers I never had.

When I look back on the tragic events of my teenage years, I remember their pain, just as much as I do my own. For our adolescent brains, the loss of our friends' lives, so young, was impossible to digest. And now that Joe had gone, too, being with Jack felt more like an instinct than a choice.

We shook hands, then hugged nervously. He still radiated the same calming scent. A blend of soil and leather, hot bread and nag champa. Jack was cycle touring long before try-hards like me jumped on the bandwagon. In fact, he discovered my first adult bike at the back of a shed on Joanna's parents' farm; a 1970s Claud Butler racer, with a turquoise steel frame, drop handlebars and a squidgy foam saddle that had been nibbled by mice.

In our early twenties we used to strap FM radios to our rucksacks and cycle out to the coast, listening to *Test Match Special*. A few years later, he took me on my first ever overseas cycling adventure, an ill-fated week in Normandy where it rained constantly.

We sank a quick beer, loaded up our bikes with snacks and offspring, and headed for their house in Totnes along the banks of the river Dart. With pizza cheeks, muddy feet and big helmets that made their heads wobble like field mushrooms, the children were almost too cute to comprehend. We stopped to say hello to a family of ducks, then waved at a man in a bright-blue kayak. After all the racing around, my journey had been slowed to the gentle pace of a child's pure and unpredictable intrigue.

While Jack and Joanna put the kids to sleep, I squeezed my tent between an apple tree and a Wendy house filled with toys. I was out of the wind for the first time in days and hearing new sounds again. The buzz of a bumblebee, the goat-like scream of a seagull, the iambic mumble of a children's story escaping from a chink in an upstairs window.

As soon as we could, Jack and I absconded to a pub to chew a year's worth of fat. Neither of us enjoyed phone calls, so we had plenty to get through. Ever since his death, we'd both been dreaming about Joe. Mine were more abstract slide shows of sounds and smells: the strum of an out-of-tune guitar, the fizzy pop of Diet Coke, the acerbic scent of cheap teenage hash. But Jack's dreams had proper, weirder storylines. "The other day I had one in which he turned up at my house on a ride-on lawnmower," Jack said, laughing into his pint. "He'd driven it all the way from Oxford."

The thing that still hurt us the most about Joe's death was that we never got the chance to give him a proper send-off. His passing was swept up in the chaos and confusion of the pandemic's first wave. At his funeral we were too scared to shake hands or hug. I'll never forget the loneliness of that wet April morning, surrounded by distant friends, our salty tears diluted by cold rain.

"I hadn't seen Joe for a while, so it didn't hit me immediately in the same way as if it was someone much closer, but it has been bubbling beneath the surface," said Jack. "Grief is something that seems to linger. I think about him most when I'm cycling or gardening. Something physical like this allows you to really go into yourself. I suspect it has been the same for you on this trip, with loads of time on the bike."

Less than six months after Joe died, Jack's father passed away after a five-year battle with Parkinson's. "He got his diagnosis at the same time Ted was born," said Jack. "I think what hurts the most is that we didn't really get the chance to share that experience together to the fullest, because his mental health wasn't great. It still doesn't really feel like they've gone. I kind of have to remind myself that they have."

Jack was clearly still grieving. Not in an intense torrent of tears, but in a state of deep and measured thought that, he conceded, could last a lifetime. "It just seems so unfair. Joe was so young, but my dad was also only in his early seventies. He spent his whole life looking after himself, eating well and keeping fit, and then something like Parkinson's [a disease that affects 1 in 500 people] comes along by fluke."

I'd seldom spoken about grief to anyone in my life, let alone with one of my oldest friends. It felt uncomfortably serious to plumb such depths, instead of joshing about football, embarrassing states of inebriation or ex-girlfriends. But it helped. Miraculously, and unsurprisingly, it helped. Moreover, to hear someone else say the same words that had been rattling around my mind for months made the burden less personal, less heavy.

Jack squared the inevitability of death with the unbridled joy of starting a new family. "Me and Joe talked a lot about how having young children to provide for gave our lives so much more purpose. That's perhaps the most heartbreaking thing about Joe's death, because I knew just how much he wanted to provide."

We certainly couldn't drink like we used to, and I woke early the next morning with a thudding four-pint hangover. Just outside the tent an attention-seeking blackbird chirped and chimed; an alarm clock I couldn't quite reach. I unzipped the awning and pillowed my head on a deflated kids'-size rugby ball. The new day smelled of creosoted fence posts and tasted of unbrushed teeth coated in India pale ale. I looked up to a heavy sky, so dense and tense it threatened to pop at the pointed beak of a passing bird.

Jack was pottering around on the other side of French windows, drinking tea and pouring out bowls of cereal for the pyjamaed children, already stacking bricks and slamming spoons on the dining-room table. On the TV in the background, a scary garish creature looked down the barrel of the screen with bulbous wild eyes. I got halfway through bundling my stuff into bags, then joined them, now on the sofa filled with books. "You know what, mate," I said, as Ted climbed on to my knee for a story. "Would you mind if I crashed another night?"

My eyes ached on their stalks, but the warmth of the house felt soothing, healing. To have dragged myself away early would have been like abandoning a course of antibiotics, just as they were starting to work. For just 24 hours more, I needed to be around Jack. His spirit. His friendship. His fatherly love.

WIGHT:
I KNEW I WOULD
SUFFER

I left early the next morning, my lungs and panniers feeling lighter. It seemed crazy to be hauling around kit that I barely used: a stove, a cooking pot, a DSLR and tripod. All told, I managed to jettison a surplus 8 kg under Jack and Joanna's staircase. I'm sure they weren't particularly glad of the extra clutter, but my bike now felt streamlined and efficient. I also had a reason to return to Totnes someday soon.

There was little need to plan for every hurdle and mishap any more. Spring was sliding into summer and Britain was feeling more normal than I could remember. On the first leg of my journey – much of which I spent in rural Scotland – there was no guarantee of finding a petrol station, let alone a bike shop. But now, if I needed new inner tubes, I could simply divert to the nearest small town. When I was hungry or thirsty, I could easily find food and water.

If I'd been really switched on, I might have posted boxes of stuff to different corners of the country, then rearranged my kit on the hoof. A thin bivvy for the south of England, then a heavy down sleeping bag for the Scottish Highlands. Flip-flops, a baseball cap, factor 50 sun cream and a spare shirt for the south. Old trainers, insect repellent, waterproof gloves and a warm jumper for the north.

I stopped in Newton Abbot for a quick breakfast – four rubbery poached eggs, lashings of brown sauce and six slices of toast – then followed the puddled banks of the river Teign toward Teignmouth. The water was bright and glassy but hummed of rotting fish – enough to make my eyes squint and my nostrils shudder.

Above me, the sky was bolder and bluer than it had been for months, and with hot sun frying my sweaty face, I wound through dinky riverside hamlets; all thatched cottages and walled gardens. When the road climbed up, I could peek inside. Hexagonal flagstones, boxed hedges and greenhouses bursting with foliage. The British middle-class dream.

Soon I was in the seaside town of Dawlish, where the scent of fresh pasties mixed with the salty sea. Families walked in happy scrums, clutching ice creams with tall flakes and clouds of pink candyfloss. A pair of buttoned-up old ladies shimmied past me, pushing yappy chihuahuas in prams designed for newborn babies. Their thick Devonshire accents were hard to decode, but their smiles needed little translating.

There was a sense of entitlement in the air, but not in an arrogant or conceited way. People just seemed proud to be exercising their basic human rights again; to be out, biting chunks from the breeze, hearing their flip-flopped feet clop on hard tarmac. Living their lives, with the ones they loved.

My route was flat and easy for a while, with just the occasional dog turd or bollard to swerve. Ahead of me, England's south coast curved and curled away, in splotches of yellow, grey and blue. The beaches excited me; the cliffs filled me with dread. On the cinnamon sands of Dawlish Warren, a handful of camouflaged fishermen cast out fluorescent lures the size of cats, from rods the height of houses. In the shallows, a black Labrador struggled with a great hunk of barnacled jetsam. Out at sea, half a dozen empty cruise ships floated in spooky stasis, patiently awaiting a return to business.

I was relieved to reach Starcross, the small village 10 miles south of Exeter, and discover that the ferry across the river Exe was operating as normal. I was the only passenger, on an open deck buffeted by cool wind, yet the deckhand insisted I wear a face mask. This seemed overzealous, but without his help I'd have had to cycle an extra 11 miles in the wrong direction, and I begrudgingly swallowed my pride for the chance to rest and breathe.

It turned out to be a worthwhile concession, because as soon as I rolled into Exmouth, the road climbed again, so steeply that I spent the majority of the next 2 hours pushing. By the time I'd reached the east side of Sidmouth, I'd hauled my bike up more than 2,000 feet and had left a trail of sweat and dirty sun cream in my tracks.

Mercifully, the asphalt eventually levelled out, before plummeting sharply into the swanky outskirts of Lyme Regis. With my gears gripped tightly and my cycling shoes unclipped, I descended rapidly into town, hoping not to clatter into a Porsche or Range Rover.

I'd spent more than a month setting up a meeting with the town's Royal National Lifeboat Institution (RNLI) crew, in the hope of finding out about how the pandemic had impacted on their work. The loose plan was to link up with a few volunteers and have a relaxed chat over a cup of tea. Instead, I arrived to find the town's main beach abuzz with sirens and flashing lights. Hundreds of people had jumped up from their buckets and spades and were now pondering silently, but nervously, out to sea like in the movie *Jaws*.

One of the station's crew, Maria Barbashina – a blonde-haired Russian artist in her late thirties – cut me off on an electric scooter and told me to follow her. "We've got to be quick," she said. "This might be a drill, but it could also be the real thing!"

It all felt very dramatic, weaving through holidaymakers while trying not to be decapitated by retractable dog leads. If I'm honest, I found it impossible not to be riled up with bloodlust. A splintered ankle, perhaps? An eyeball skewered with a harpoon?

We skidded into the station to find a support crew readying a tangerine RIB, and a rescue team dashing from one peg to another, pulling on canary-yellow drysuits, bright-red life jackets and brilliant-white helmets.

They then jumped into the boat, crashed into the calm shallows and zoomed out toward the frothy sea.

"Some people went fossil hunting on that beach over there," said crew member Andy Butterfield, pointing to a strip of custardy sand, at the base of a greyish-black cliff. "But the tide has come in and now they're trapped."

I was underwhelmed. More than 20 volunteers had been scrambled from home or work in the space of just 7 frantic minutes. A helicopter was also now on its way from south Wales at a cost of goodness knows how many thousands of pounds. Nevertheless, the tide was certainly racing in, and I suppose the amateur palaeontologists had been left with no other option but to call 999. Any of us would have done the same.

It had already been a busy year for RNLI crews all over Britain. Closed borders had resulted in more domestic holidays, and in the summer of 2020 alone, they'd saved 140 lives, a 32 per cent increase on the previous year.

"It became very busy, very quickly," said Andy.

"I bet."

"People just do silly things. Pushing boats off their moorings, swimming and jumping."

"And more so this year?"

"The more people you have out and about, the more likely it is that people will become cut off by the tide. A lot of people also hadn't been out on their boats for many months, so obviously mistakes happen."

We could hear the helicopter rumbling over the steep cliffs, but where the coast curved inland, it made it impossible to see the beach beneath. "If we're quick, we might be able to get a bit closer, to see what happens," said Seb Cope, the station's moustachioed press officer. I thought this would entail another cycle or run through town. But instead, we jumped into Seb's car, a racing-green 1970s Austin Healey Sprite, complete with a red soft-top and shiny alloy trim.

The streets of Lyme Regis became our very own Monte Carlo. The car was so low to the ground that golden retrievers resembled woolly mammoths.

By the time we reached a car park on the east side of town, I was dizzy from motion. My knees were also almost horizontal to my shoulders, leaving me with little choice but to disembark via an ungainly deathroll.

We got there just in time to see the helicopter drop a fluorescent man on to the beach, hoist the pair of embarrassed tourists to a nearby football field, then chug off back to Wales.

"All of this for two people on a walk?" I snorted.

"You have no idea how often this sort of thing happens."

"And what happens now?"

"I'll have to write a press release about this later."

Back at the station, the mood was chirpy and relieved. This was clearly a tight-knit community that took pride in protecting townsfolk and visitors alike. Moreover, there were another 237 lifeboat stations just like it dotted all around Britain and Ireland, making an average of 24 rescues between them every single day. At a moment in history when we were told to keep our distance from one another, the RNLI was clearly bringing people much closer together.

"Ever since I started volunteering here, I've never felt like there's something I can't achieve," said Petrina Muscroft, one of the station's shore crew. "It has given me so much confidence to do things that I wouldn't have done. It's a family. Everyone has got your back and the past couple of years have taught me to appreciate the community that I'm in. It's so easy to take things for granted, but you need to seize the day and support anyone you can."

———

Maria kindly offered me her spare room for the night, so I followed her back to her house for a shower and a bottle of red wine. She lived with her eight-year-old daughter, Clara, a quiet and impeccably mannered girl with a school textbook constantly clasped in her hands.

The night had turned dark and damp, so we sat beside a wood burner glowing hot orange. Soft rain tickled the skylights above us. Through a porthole over the kitchen sink, we could see grey waves crashing against the shivering town.

Maria had grown up in St Petersburg in the 1980s and 90s but sailed into Portsmouth in 2004 while working as a deckhand on a replica Viking longship. She soon discovered Lyme Regis and decided that she preferred its narrow, cobbled streets to the sweeping boulevards of the Russia she'd left behind.

"I can't say I ever felt threatened there, but it certainly felt acutely safer here," she told me, before dropping another log into the fire.

"Do you think you'll ever go back?"

"It's hard to say, but it is certainly easier for me to be an artist here because I think art feels more appreciated."

"You've certainly built an enviable life for yourself down here, it seems."

"I wanted to make sure that my life was productive and enjoyable, and not just constantly working toward some goal ten years in the future."

Nearly two decades after arriving, Maria still had no regrets. Her experience of living in Britain during the pandemic, however, made her think more about her early years in the Soviet Union.

"All the panic buying, and the greed of some people here was so alien to me. I grew up in a country where the economy collapsed. It was normal for supermarket shelves to be bare, but we survived through a culture of sharing things and being resourceful. At times in the crisis, I thought people were just pathetic and entitled."

Sometime around 10 p.m., my eyes grew drunk and droopy, and I sloped off to bed at the back of the house. I envied Maria. She'd had the confidence and zeal to up sticks and make a new home in an alien place. But from empty beginnings, her house now radiated benevolence and it smelled, wonderfully, of wet clay, acrylic paints and herbal teas.

Early the next morning, Maria plied me with toast, boiled eggs and strong coffee, and released me back into the wild. A summer haze fizzed above the town's wet blue cobbles. Out at sea, a pair of fishing boats still blinked brothel red on the sinewed grey horizon.

The climb out of town was as tough as any stretch I'd faced before. Doorstop-steep with barely a switchback to rest. All I could do was sit in and grit it out. One pedal in front of the other, my greasy palms squeaking on the handlebars.

By the time I reached Bridport for a second breakfast, the sun had burned through the last of the cloud and the temperature was already nudging 30°C. My plan was to reach Bournemouth by the end of the day, but the thick heat made my calves cramp and my brain throb. I wasn't getting enough sleep or putting enough salt or water into my body. I paused in the hot shade of a centuries-old oak tree, but passed out and headbutted the trunk as I crumpled toward the earth.

Some seconds or minutes later, I woke up with a frottage of acorns, leaves and bark etched into my neck and jaw, and the tender beginnings of a black eye. The experience left me feeling shell-shocked and shivery. Lying there, alone, I was overcome with shame. "Why can't I do this?" I growled to myself.

On a map, my adventure was simple; I could trace the route with a single finger. But in the flesh, every skipped meal, unexpected hill and extra degree of heat had real-life consequences. I wasn't superhuman, like I liked to believe. I was a 34-year-old man, no longer in my prime. Was this journey a new beginning? Or a massive cry for help?

Either way, I now found myself – unexpectedly – at a crossroads. I could choose to ignore my throbbing eye socket and brush it off as a freak mishap, or I could feel, embrace and learn from its pain.

If I was honest with myself, all the bike rides, the hikes, the sailing and the paragliding was a front, a mask. Deep down, in the annals of my subconscious, perhaps I was trying to live some extra life, for the young men and women who hadn't made it as far as I had. Dave, Tim, Emma, Joshua, Joe and Sarah. What adventures might they have gone on? I wondered. What faraway lands might they have explored, before regaling their friends in the pub.

I brushed dust from my hair, then hit the road. Dorset had grown so intensely hot that it threatened to explode. City-sized clouds now hovered over the seam between land and sea. Nothing could get in or out. I was cycling around the rim of a simmering saucepan covered tight with impermeable cling film.

The coast looked prim and comely from afar, coffee-brown, with pockets of dark red and bright blue. But I didn't have the energy to divert from the flattish green headland or have the inclination to join the tourist scrums of Weymouth or Swanage. Instead, I reminded myself to "ride the day" – to move a few miles per hour slower than I knew I could, to preserve energy for the future. However much it annoyed me to admit it, my journey was a marathon, not a sprint. A tale of tortoise, not hare.

By the time I reached the muddy wetlands west of Poole, flashes of white lightning detonated in the heavens above. Minutes later, a few spots of cold rain splashed my seared neck. Then, a flock of Egyptian geese sprang from a spinney of static reeds. I crossed into Sandbanks, a grotesque teardrop of fenced-off wealth, just as the sky erupted into a monsoon of rattle and fizz. Within 5 minutes I was as wet as I'd ever be.

In 2005, it was reported that the 0.4-square-mile peninsula had the fourth highest land value in the world, after London, Manhattan and Tokyo. By 2018 its "Millionaires' Row" of 13 mansions had a combined value of £93 million. Then, in 2020, as most of the world's economies fell into recession – and I couldn't even pay the mortgage on my £250,000 apartment – one Sandbanks estate agent enjoyed its best year on record, doubling its turnover.

If they weren't all cocooned behind giant iron gates and monitored by Big Brother, I might have been tempted to stage a dirty protest on one of the immaculate driveways. Instead, I wove through the nose-to-tail Range Rovers and Ferraris of the day trippers that had come to take a look, and escaped to Bournemouth as quickly as my legs could manage.

After the unashamed gluttony of Sandbanks, the town felt ragged and raw. A man about my age, with no front teeth and his right hand in plaster, argued with an emaciated woman about cigarettes, or the lack of them. Another man, old enough to be my grandfather, slept in a puddled doorway snuggling a haggard mongrel with silver whiskers and bleeding paws. Beside them, someone had left a bag of doughnuts, cakes, crisps and fizzy drinks. Poor food for poor people.

I was only playing at homelessness. A middle-class hopscotch from one spare room or lawn to the next. Alana and I felt cheated by the pandemic, but we were still some of the most privileged people on the planet. Educated, confident, wealthy, white. We had friends and family to fall back on if we really needed them. This, however, was homelessness by necessity. No one to help, nowhere to run.

In Britain, rough sleepers are six times more likely to attend A&E. In Dorset, the mortality rate for homeless people is higher than anywhere else in England and Wales. In 2019, the charity Shelter reported that at least 459 people were living on the streets of Bournemouth, plus a further 287 and 150 in nearby Poole and Christchurch, respectively. When the pandemic struck in 2020, the government, working with a network of local authorities, attempted to house everyone who needed it.

Remarkably, it took an infectious disease that threatened the rich and poor, indiscriminately, for us to remember the often silent and invisible subculture living on the grubby fringes of mainstream society.

"Everyone came in and was put in temporary accommodation," said Alistair Doxat-Purser, chief executive of Faithworks Wessex, whom I met outside Bournemouth's St Michael's Church, a place of worship that also now doubled up as a workshop where homeless people could make and sell items. "We're now working to make sure that people are helped to stay off the street. But it's about more than just putting a roof over people's heads, it's about empowering them. Just like any of us, these people have hopes and aspirations. This place gives them the self-confidence to make things with their own hands. The boost to a person's self-esteem can be quite incredible. Come on in and have a look around."

If I'm honest, I was reluctant to enter the church. I only ever set foot in them for the weddings and funerals I couldn't wriggle my way out of. I'd hated every moment of the cold and tedious Sunday schools my parents sent me to just before puberty. Then when my teenage friends died, I lost all hope in an afterlife. How could God be so pernicious? To me, churches were wretched places that reeked of tears.

This church, however, felt different. A vestry had been filled with all manner of vices, bandsaws, planers and drills. Instead of the fusty dampness I expected, the grand building emitted the scent of warm sawdust, nicotine and instant coffee.

"When you're in a spiral, you can't see the wood for the trees," said one of the workshop's newest recruits, Daniel. He used to own a successful business selling commercial vehicles but was ruined by the 2008 financial crash. Later that year he broke up with his partner of 11 years and his life began to unfurl.

"I was like a ship at sea without a sail."

"And a mooring, no doubt."

"I pressed a big red button and became heavily addicted to drink and drugs. I experienced a lot of violence against me and now suffer from post-traumatic stress disorder. Twelve years later, here I am, just climbing up the ladder again."

Of the dozen or so men in the room, Daniel fascinated me the most. He was older than me by about 10 or 15 years, but his story felt oddly familiar. It could have easily been mine. I'd been lucky to judder into adulthood, relatively unscathed, but I could certainly empathise with how a few spliffs, or cans of beer, might quickly move you from a friend's sofa to a betting-shop doorway.

Daniel spoke in crisp metaphors that left me hanging on his every word. "Without a safety net it's very easy to fall into the lion's pit. It can be very hard to climb a mountain." He was now more thankful than most, for the simple things in life. Food in his belly. A warm bed out of the wind. "When you've experienced that level of deprivation, it's impossible not to be humbled."

Just like me, Daniel's pre-existing mental health conditions had been compounded by the pandemic, but with the support of Faithworks he was now hoping to reintegrate himself into society.

"We're social creatures, but not being able to socialise affected me the most."

"Me too. I couldn't handle it. I never want to go back to those days."

"I'm now ready to get into a cycle that is positive, rather than one that is negative."

"How easy will that be?"

"This is a springboard. A lot of people just pay lip service to the homeless community, but these people are actually putting their faith into action."

I spent the night in a cheap hotel popular with tradesmen and lorry drivers. It boasted creaking floorboards, mildewed bathtubs and carpet stains that predated decimalisation, but at least we had the luxury of running water, central heating and shelter from the rain.

My sleep was worrisome, remorseful. I jumped from one fuzzy dream to another. I too had an addictive nature, so easily steered off track. It was currently sated by coffee, work and exercise but might have easily turned to drink and drugs.

———

The morning broke, sharp and cloudless. I'd been back on the road for a week already and my body was desperate to move. Bournemouth's streets were all but empty, apart from a few faceless figures cossetted in doorways, soon to be swept away. I felt guilty but relieved to leave, desperate to cleanse myself with green. Within an hour I was on the western edge of the New Forest, crunching over sundried earth, through channels of wild garlic and oceans of wood anemones; soft, white and yellow, like poached quails' eggs.

Successive national lockdowns created pent-up demand for long walks and domestic holidays, but an increase in footfall also placed added strain on Britain's fragile natural habitats. The New Forest, in particular, had struggled with overtourism. Its proximity to Bournemouth, Southampton, Portsmouth and Salisbury meant that people not only came to wander, but also to fly drones, camp illegally and spark up barbecues and campfires.

For years, local authorities had been calling on nearby retailers to remove disposable barbecues from sale, but in the first five months of 2021 alone, fire crews responded to a staggering 427 blazes in the park. A fire in 2018 still smouldered in local memories. It decimated 86 acres and turned Hampshire's skyline a hot, menacing red.

Moving at the gentle pace of a bicycle allowed me to focus on the precious details that would have otherwise whirred past, unnoticed, in a car. A fox moth caterpillar, with long dark hairs on the sides and a short orange Mohawk on top. More than 2,600 species of beetle live in the New Forest, and most of them seemed to be flying over, or crawling across, the warm asphalt. Many were matt black like coal, but some glowed an incomprehensible greenish mauve, a colour so magnificent, that only Mother Nature could have imagined it.

What struck me the most, however, was just how flat and savannah-like the "forest" was. Sure, there were pockets of trees, but it seemed more like an oversized city park than an expansive wilderness. There were ponies nibbling at grass, just a few feet from a discarded McDonald's. Cars parked on the soft verges, despite signs politely asking people not to. I saw spaniels chasing hares, then a man flick a red-tipped cigarillo from his car to the gorse. But what if the forest was left to its own devices? What wonder could unfold, without humans and their selfish ways?

Professor Russell Wynn, director of Wild New Forest, met me in one of the central car parks. Tall, tanned and Lycra-clad, he jumped off his bike and I followed him along a sandy track the colour and consistency of mustard powder.

Russell spent 2020's first national lockdown studying the local wildlife, to see how the flora and fauna might react. "If you take all the recreational pressure away, what does the wildlife do?" he asked, as we watched a pair of long-beaked curlews noisily mobbing a hobby falcon, in a desperate bid to protect their newly hatched chicks. "With no people around, we found that some of our most endangered breeding birds began to move into new areas."

Forestry England quickly began using the data to guide seasonal closures of selected car parks. In essence, staging bogus lockdowns.

"So, Covid was bad for us, but good for animals?"

"The evidence we collected showed that reducing human footfall in specific areas makes a difference. Lockdown was a once-in-a-lifetime opportunity to document how animals respond to being on their own."

I cherished these fleeting encounters. Meeting busy people fascinated by their surroundings. I took comfort in knowing that the world was filled with passionate souls, desperate to work out problems. Not only for the human race, but also all those sentient creatures without a voice.

"If you look toward that car park over there," said Russell, pointing at a distant patch of scrub, shadowed by flaky birch trees. "When that was closed, it was one of the few places where curlews managed to raise chicks through to fledgling stage. It was no coincidence that this happened in an area that was unusually quiet."

A local farmer, Andrew Parry-Norton, had kindly offered to put me up that night. But by the time I reached him on the north-east side of the park, the afternoon was hot like boiling broth. The sky could have belonged to Oman, Algeria or Zimbabwe. I limped into a muddy stable yard with sweat leaking from my helmet and every patch of exposed skin dusted in road grime.

After a cold shower, I joined Andrew and his wife, Sarah, on their early evening rounds. Chickens mingled with geese and peacocks. Fat piglets paddled in cool mud. The air tasted of warm hay and smelled – strangely wonderfully – of cow urine. The nostalgic scent of childhood walks.

The New Forest was declared a royal forest by William the Conqueror in 1079 and features in the Domesday Book. It remains one of the largest tracts of unenclosed heathland left in southern England and Andrew, a "commoner", possessed an 800-year-old right to graze his livestock there. Lambs in spring. Cows and horses in summer. Pannage pigs in the autumn, to hoover up all the acorns and chestnuts.

In the twenty-first century, however, the relationship between people and animals weighed heavily on his shoulders. On a busy day, he could share the same land with more than 80,000 visitors. "It's not particularly helpful that the New Forest is called a national park," he told me, throwing a few handfuls of layers' pellets at the hens. "I think a nature reserve would be more apt terminology. I love sharing this place with other people, but at the same time this is like my back garden. The problem is that most people are so far removed from livestock these days. They go to a supermarket and grab a piece of meat in a plastic bag that looks nothing like what it came from. When people come here and feed the ponies or walk their dogs in a field of cows and calves, it raises emotions."

With broad shoulders and thick forearms, Andrew had the build of a prop forward but the demeanour of a friendly giant. "Every inch of ground is precious to me," he said softly, before tussling the curly perm of a three quarter-tonne bull with testicles the size of bowling balls. Beside it, Andrew became a dwarf. "I want to make sure that the farm I hand over to my son is better than the one it is today. I've planted forests that I'll never see. But he will."

Impassioned and erudite, Andrew and Sarah were so much more than farmers. They were custodians, defenders of the land and the creatures that used it. They were also warm and enthusiastic hosts with an unwavering instinct to fatten up their house guests.

Later that evening we were joined by some of their farming neighbours, Rick and Anita Manley. "Asset rich, but cash poor, like many farmers," said Rick, a forthright and friendly man with a taste for red wine and holding court. "Sometimes, farming can feel like living in Buckingham Palace, but without having a tenner in your pocket."

As we tucked into plates piled high with acorn-rich pork, roast potatoes, steamed greens and a bowl of salty brittle crackling, I was eager to find out how the pandemic had impacted on their lives. "People went crazy for eggs," said Anita. "It was mad for a while."

But then things calmed down. The drawn-out process of rearing livestock meant that their daily routines didn't change all too much. It did, however, leave them feeling more valued. "I think we were placed on a pedestal for a few months," said Rick. "I wouldn't dream of comparing us to someone who works in the NHS, but because we were providing an essential service, I think people started to better appreciate what farmers really do."

And what of their mental health? I wondered. It was a sombre statistic to consider, but between one and two farmers a week committed suicide in Britain.

"There's a preconceived idea that farmers are tough and indestructible," said Andrew. "They like to live up to that image. But sometimes that's not always for the good. I know of several farmers that have had problems and they can accumulate very quickly because it can be a lonely job at times. A sad case recently involved a local farmer who lost his father to cancer. He struggled to cope with the farm and it rapidly went downhill. It ended up with Trading Standards taking his stock away and the farm being sold. It's a slippery slope when things start to go wrong."

By the time I'd scoffed second helpings of pork, a big bowl of rhubarb crumble and necked half a dozen pints of golden-brown ale, our conversation had meandered from Brexit and farming subsidies to Southampton FC and the horsemeat scandal. Honest, fervent chatter that nourished the soul.

But with my eyelids drooping and my speech slurring, I excused myself at 10 p.m. and crept off to the spare room. Laughter and chinking bottles soothed me to sleep. But I knew I would suffer.

DOVER:
SERENDIPITY, FATE, LUCK

I barely slept. Instead, I spent most of the night lying in a strange bed waiting for light, wondering how early I could get up and leave without being rude. The farmhouse was warm and homely, with low ceilings and creaking floorboards, but it wasn't my space, it wasn't my home. I found it impossible to slow the pace of my whirring brain. I counted to 100, then started again. Over and over. A futile waste of time.

As the alcohol wore off, a headache set in. The food in my stomach pressed heavily on my diaphragm and my lungs fought for room. I'd been here before. Many times before. Overeating, overdrinking, overthinking. I slid into a state of fidgety panic. Clammy palms, gassy bowels. Closed eyes, open eyes. Duvet on, duvet off. Entirely self-inflicted.

This charade played out until the sky turned mauve and the first cockerel crowed. I then crept downstairs to find Andrew, up with the lark as farmers do, and reassured him that I'd slept like a log. We drank strong coffees and chatted some more. Strung out and sleepless, it felt like the dying embers of an all-night party, when someone reluctantly turns off the Bluetooth speaker and silence floods the void.

It was set to be another hot day. Crisp, unrelenting heat, not the sort of heat you want to face having not slept. Nevertheless, I filled my water bottles, thanked Andrew for his hospitality, and set off. Away, away. Back to the lonely road.

An hour later I was in Southampton, feeling dreadful. Eyes aching, lungs wheezing. A petrol car filled with diesel. Having lived with, and studied, my anxiety disorder for a decade, this was turning into a classic case of the physical feeding the psychological.

The worse my physical symptoms became, the more I worried about them. But the more I worried about them, the worse the symptoms became. Quickly, I lost track of the initial cause and its subsequent effect. What had started out as a full stomach and a sleepless hangover, quickly became a befuddled mental state. Put very simply, this is how a barely noticeable shortness of breath could escalate into a malignant panic attack, capable of tainting a day, a week or a month.

I should have thrown in the towel and checked into a hotel. At the very least I might have paused in the shade for an hour or two. But I stubbornly kept going. Not resting, just self-medicating with sugar and caffeine. Enough to get to the next pit stop, to upload smug social-media posts, depicting a joyous, enviable #bikelife.

"Amazing day down here," I lied.

I diverted north-east, away from the south coast, and made a beeline for the strip of agriculture sandwiched between Portsmouth and Basingstoke. I was nervous to leave the seaside route that had served me so well, but up there, away from the grey suburban splodge, I could ride on single-track roads in a wired daze. Few people. Few eyes.

The world quickly grew pastoral and affluent. Polka-dot cows munched golden hay. Trust funders in jodhpurs led thoroughbreds over immaculate polo lawns, while all manner of hanger-on watched. The Kensington set with wicker picnic baskets and gold-trim gilets. The stable girls with Kardashian thighs and dimpled smiles. Old men in tatty wax jackets. Dopey springer spaniels with burdock seeds matted in their tails.

By the time I reached Petworth, a small red-brick town north of Chichester, I was crashing. The heat had sucked out any life I had left, and I slumped into a café for food and shade. I must have drifted off to sleep, with my head in my hands. I came round to a plate of hot chips radiating vinegar into my stinging nostrils.

My vague plan had been to reach Worthing or Brighton by the end of the day, find a cheap hotel and maybe pop a sleeping tablet with a whisky or two. But this would have meant another 30 miles under a blazing sun, and I had no idea if my legs could take it.

Lost and alone, I returned to my comfort blanket: mindlessly scrolling through social-media notifications on my phone. Most of them were from bots: "Great job. DM for collab. 50% off Ray Bans." A couple were from strangers finding vicarious joy in my suffering. But another, from a real, wonderful human, popped up, sending a spark of energy through my tired eyes.

"Si. If you're in the South Downs you should come and stay with us. We're living on a farm for a few months. Loads of room to crash. Call us. Ads and Emms."

From my lowest ebb grew a giant spring. Adam and Emma were two of my oldest and dearest friends, and as luck would have it, they were now less than 10 miles away to the east. A blur of green raced past me. Tractors, lorries, cars and bikes. Sedated but elated, the road carried me to their familiar arms like a moving walkway in an airport.

Adam and I grew up with Joe, Jack and a dozen or more tight-knit friends, united by the tedium of an adolescence in the countryside. He'd met his wife and soulmate, Emma, while working as a musician in the French Alps a decade before, and ever since, the pair had emitted a warm and positive aura that could only ever serve to lift one's spirits.

Serendipity, fate, luck. Whatever it was that put me there, in their path, I will forever be thankful. Within 90 seconds of our hard embrace, cold beer washed down my parched throat and tears of relief ached behind my tired eyes.

The first leg of my adventure hadn't just been socially distant, but almost always alone. During those first 1,307 miles, I'd toiled on the open road with barely a fist bump, scarcely a friendly smile. Since leaving Scilly, though, I'd already met dozens of new people and had hundreds of conversations.

The greatest joy of journalism is meeting new people and learning about their lives, but this requires you to be "on" all the time. As such, I'd quickly reached a point at which I wasn't just physically exhausted from cycling, but weary from over-socialisation. Adam and Emma, however, reminded me of what it felt like to be at ease. Suddenly, there was no urge to fill dead airtime with words.

Barefooted, sharing in-jokes, listening to the same songs we'd heard countless times, we stole forkfuls of curry off each other's plates and retold stories we'd heard umpteen times before. I laughed and smiled. Louder and more broadly than I had done in months, maybe even years. Friends, true friends.

But friends at a crossroads in their lives. Having decided to start a family at the end of 2018, they'd struggled to conceive naturally and were now almost three years into fertility treatment. I'd already heard murmurs within our friendship group but hadn't wanted to pry over Zoom or FaceTime. It was neither my place, nor my business. Now, however, we were back together again, rubbing shoulders, sharing the same glorious oxygen.

"It has become an annoying taboo," said Emma. "But it's crazy, because it's so common. It's so strange, even when my mum asks me about IVF, she whispers it down the phone. I'm like, Mum: it's not a fucking swear word!"

We giggled together, in the same way we had done for years. Nevertheless, when they spoke about their less-than-romantic sexual habits, the rigmarole of daily testing and the intricacies of NHS red tape, they grew thoughtful and solemn, in a manner I hardly recognised.

"The thing that we, and probably a lot of our friendship group, take for granted is our age," said Adam.

"Mate, I'm older than you."

"We're all in our early thirties now, but hardly any of us had babies young."

"How does that impact IVF?"

"No one seems to know this, but the NHS cut-off age for IVF is thirty-five. We only get one shot at this. And then if we get successful, that's us done."

"Forever?"

"If we wanted to have two children, we'd have to pay. Some people will reach a point in their lives where they have to make a choice between getting a mortgage or starting a family."

They were both slightly embarrassed to admit that the pandemic, and its subsequent lockdowns, had provided an unexpected chance to reset. They'd been at risk of becoming overworked and under rested. Adam would return home from gigs in the early hours, then Emma would leave for work not long after. "For the first time in our lives, we were forced to press pause," said Adam. "Personally, I went on a massive journey of discovery in terms of my mental health. But together, I think it really solidified what we wanted out of life."

"What if you don't manage to have a child?" I asked, somewhat bluntly. Perhaps in a way that only a close friend really could. "Have you considered that?"

"Honestly," said Emma, "this has already been so much of a mission of a journey that I haven't even looked that far ahead yet. Just getting pregnant is enough of a challenge right now. I've done hundreds of pregnancy tests so far. If one actually comes back positive one day, I can't even fully comprehend how I might actually feel."

There was a commune vibe to the farm, dotted with friends, and friends of friends, living in shacks and outbuildings, vans and tents. Later, a handful of us descended on a field of pure, luscious spring, to watch the sun dip beneath a hieroglyphed sky of semicolon stars, comma clouds and hyphen contrails. A greyhound, a terrier and a cockapoo hurtled from one distant fence to another in a cyclone of yaps and yelps. Mayflies danced majestically above us while their horsefly cousins chewed on the meaty flesh behind our knees.

As a travel writer who thrived on people being interested in my work, I felt oddly embarrassed to talk about my journey. It seemed far too flashy and grandiose to describe it out loud. On the flip side, to quickly gloss over a cycling trip of such magnitude risked coming across as arrogant and blasé. "I'm just trying to see how far I can get," I said. "Catch up with a few old friends along the way and lose a bit of lockdown weight."

I never wanted to let on that the trip was anything more than just a mindless joyride. To admit to anything else would be to surrender to my many morbid insecurities. It felt safer to keep them bottled up, preserved for a later date, to be reassembled when I had the tools to work on them properly.

It was tempting to drink and drink, chat with Ads and Emms into the early hours and fall asleep on their sofa. But I held back. I digested, I rested. I excused myself early, put my phone on aeroplane mode and read until my eyelids grew heavy.

Usually, a sleepless night would leave my circadian rhythm so jangled that it would resist sleep the next. But that night I don't even remember placing my head on the lumpy pillow. Tranquilised by exhaustion, warmed by love, I blinked, and the next thing I saw was dawn.

At times, insomnia felt like a crippling ailment, a malevolent illness. But at others I flaunted it as a weird superpower, a chance to exert prowess over others. People who stayed up late and got up early were successful and proficient, while those who slept long were slackers, weak and inefficient.

Nights like these, however, curled up on a futon surrounded by amplifiers, microphones and computer screens busy with waveform, reminded me that sleep was a fuel, just like water and food. They proved that I *could* sleep. My only problem was that a lot of the time, I didn't really *want* to.

I was back on the road by 8 a.m. and zigzagging into Brighton by 10. In contrast to the hypnotic swirl of the Downs, the city was an eyesore, clogged with heavy traffic and chip-crazed seagulls. I moved through as quickly as possible without clattering into anyone grey or infirm, then joined the coastal path that sneaked under tall chalk cliffs all the way to Seaford.

Famished, I stopped for lunch in the first place I could find: a Second World War-themed café, with Union Jacks and model Spitfires dangling from the ceiling. "Your Country Needs You" and "Dig for Victory" posters filled every patch of wall that wasn't already taken up by a faceless mannequin in army fatigues. The omelette and chips were palatable enough, but rather than evoking a Blitz spirit, the greasy establishment seemed more English Defence League than Vera Lynn.

I sat outside drinking tea. A woman with a backpack rattled loose change in a Starbucks cup. Meanwhile, two policemen cajoled a homeless man from a bench. His crime? Silently supping a can of lager in the sunshine.

Seaford was the first place in Britain where instinct told me to lock my bike to a drainpipe when I nipped to the loo. Nonetheless, if I'd been destitute and desperate, then I too would have had a crack at its shiny frame. It was, however, so heavy and cumbersome that no one on Earth had the knack to move it without falling flat on their face. At least this way, it saved the blushes, and the bruises, of all parties.

South-east of the town, the English Channel lapped flat-calm. Distant ships fizzed into a European haze. A pair of skylarks skipped along glassy pebbles as a three-legged Rottweiler gave fruitless chase. At first, the cycle path was flat and gentle, but then wound up and around Cuckmere Haven, under two dozen paragliders riding invisible thermals that bubbled up like lava lamps.

I cycled past the first of hundreds of Second-World-War concrete defences, then popped out in the small town of Polegate. Waiting for me was a blonde-haired, blue-eyed father of three, wearing a fluorescent-pink cycling jersey and Lycra shorts. "This feels a lot like a blind date," I said, "but you must be Adam?"

Adam had contacted me on Twitter when he found out I was heading his way. Long before the pandemic hit, he was diagnosed with multiple sclerosis, an incurable disease that will slowly degrade his brain and nervous system. "It affects my mobility," he said, as we rode beside the shimmering sea. "But when it started getting worse, I began using my bike as my main form of transport. It became a simple joy, but it was also incredibly important for both my physical and mental well-being."

MS, Adam explained, wouldn't define him. "With a chronic disease I think it's important to stay positive and cycling feels like I'm taking some form of control."

"But there's no cure?"

"I eat clean and healthily. I sleep well and do breathing work."

"And it helps?"

"I think so. I feel like it's better to do something than nothing at all."

I wouldn't be so patronising as to call Adam an "inspiration". But it was hard not to be impressed by his eagerness to crack on with life, despite the less-than-rosy narrative unfolding ahead of him. Rather than descending into self-pity, he'd decided to put his faith in tried-and-tested remedies that were either cheap or free: a healthy diet and plenty of sleep and exercise. In a strange way, I figured, perhaps an illness without a cure was easier to come to terms with. And for the time being, at least, Adam could still cycle on an electric bike and play golf with the help of a buggy.

"I have no idea how I'd cope with something like MS," I confessed. "The idea of losing my mobility, my freedom. It seems like a predicament worse than death."

"I suspect you'd just get on with it, like I and everyone else have to."

"You seem to be incredibly positive."

"A degenerative disease teaches you to live in the moment and to savour what you have right now. It's a waste of energy getting too far ahead of yourself."

We followed the coast road between Eastbourne and Bexhill. It snaked in waves of salt and chalk, carrying us up, then throwing us down. Burly men with pink chests ate teacakes in the awnings of their Neapolitan beach huts. Tufts of seakale and samphire wilted in the hot breeze. Loved-up couples mooched, arm in arm, through inch-high shallows that reflected the fluffy clouds above.

These shared interludes were a privilege. A chance to experience the shape of someone else's shoes for a short while, but we eventually made it to Hastings and said our goodbyes. Adam returned to his wife and daughters, while I found a cheap hotel and a cold shower.

It was always a relief to end the day on my own terms. I loved cycle touring and the thrills and spills that came with it, but to reach a satisfying conclusion, with 70 miles under my belt, made me feel like I was in control. Like I was winning.

I ventured out in search of dinner and a beer. It was a Friday night and Hastings seemed edgy, almost fraying at the seams. The smoking areas of pubs looked like they might combust at any moment. I sat on a wall and quietly ate a sandwich. Maybe I was imagining the fractious vibe. Perhaps it was all in my head.

But then, the stocky owner of a fish and chip shop rushed out from behind his counter and chased two giggling men down the street. "Come on, then!" he screamed, as he tightened his fists like a boxer. They turned and fronted up, about to trade blows. But then they saw the size of his biceps, and their grins drained from their ashen cheeks.

From what I could gather, the two men had made a lurid remark toward one of his female staff and were now about to be battered like sausages. A crowd gathered, baying for blood. But after a few minutes, just out of earshot, they nodded meekly and skulked off in silence. The giant returned to the shop and plunged more chips into hot oil.

Half a million tourists visit Hastings each year, to see its Old Town, castle and the battlefield of 1066 fame. But they were of little interest to me. I had nothing to gain, only my teeth to lose. I took the hint and slept.

Six hours later, at 3.38 a.m., I was enjoying a rare and tranquil night in a bedroom overlooking the town centre. I might have lain prone for days, if it wasn't for the 30-man brawl that had kicked off under golden street lights beneath me. One group of men in ripped shirts threw drunken punches at another. A bin was thrown, a pint glass smashed. A woman with a broken stiletto tumbled to the floor while a few onlookers wolf-whistled and chanted football songs. It was by far the worst version of *West Side Story* I'd ever seen.

I recorded most of it on my phone, just in case someone got seriously hurt, but after half an hour, things calmed down and the crowd stumbled off in search of processed meats. I, meanwhile, was wide awake. There was no getting back to sleep. So, I packed up and rode out through the war zone.

The 1066 Battle of Hastings was fought between the Norman French and the Anglo-Saxon English, but this 2021 re-enactment played out exclusively among apes and Neanderthals.

———

I headed east along National Cycle Route 2, through the village of Cliff End, then Rye. Just like following the banks of a river, seaside riding seemed like a master stroke, a twist of fate to celebrate. Flat and gentle, there was plenty to keep me entertained. Cocoa-chested wheatears skipped beside my wheels, almost getting caught up in the spokes. Ringed plovers, avocets and redshanks whistled and squawked on the marshes between land and sea.

By 7 a.m. I was rounding Camber Sands, a stretch of fortified dunes. A few early dog walkers savoured the calm before the weekend crowds arrived. I stopped at a café for scrambled eggs, grilled tomatoes and a glass of orange juice. It was the most nutritious thing I'd eaten in days.

The path meandered inland, through gated fields flooded with daisies. Spring lambs bounced around on elasticated limbs. Their doting mothers watched on, pretending they'd not seen it all before. Rapeseed, cow parsley and broad beans were in full flower, sending pockets of floral joy up and away on the wind. Under candyfloss clouds and a SLUSH PUPPiE-blue sky, the morning was bliss. I tried to simply ride and breathe. Restfully, meditatively, restoratively.

But change was afoot. After cruising at 13 mph for most of the morning, the road climbed steeply toward Folkestone. For more than an hour I ground through the gears. Up, up, up, stopping every few minutes for rest and water.

I'd been dreading this stretch. In my mind's eye it was overpopulated and covered in concrete, and at first, this turned out to be a rather accurate imagining. Folkestone was a hot splodge choked with traffic. But then, as I burst out the other side, soaked in sweat and gasping for air, emerald pasture rolled away across brilliant-white cliffs. The white cliffs of Dover, no less. The site of a million shed tears. Of countless welcomes and goodbyes.

I'd never visited this corner of Britain before. I suspect I'd taken it for granted, like many millennials. But as I cycled on, beside giant concrete acoustic mirrors – used in the Second World War to concentrate the sound of approaching planes – I was left punch-drunk by history.

I imagined a Messerschmitt roaring over me, so close I could see the wide eyes of the pilot within. The long grass might have parted in its wake. Perhaps a few Dad's Army types would have waved a pitchfork in its direction.

I could see all the way to France, a fuzzy apparition on the horizon. But instead of looking out, my gaze jumped inward, to my grandparents' council house. Suddenly, I could smell crusts of thick white bread toasting under a gas grill and the sound of my nan, singing through her dentures. "There'll be bluebirds over," she'd start, "the white cliffs of Dover. Tomorrow, just you wait and see..." At which point she'd forget the next verse and hum the rest, tip-tapping along with her knitting needles. For all I know, there are no other lyrics. With the wind in my eyes, I now did the same. Crooning those first 15 words, over and over. Up into Dover and out the other side.

In a strange way it became a mantra. A distraction from the baking asphalt that throbbed beneath me and the miles I still had left to complete. A green and pleasant land, I could have cycled that stretch of coast forever.

Sometime in the late afternoon, the road dropped back down to the seaside, and it finally dawned on me that I'd now crossed over into Kent: the south-eastern extreme of my journey around Britain. This meant that the country was levelling out at last; for a few hundred miles, at least. Because, very crudely: west equals hilly; east equals flat.

This wasn't the home stretch by any means, but it was a relief to know that the toughest days – at least in terms of gradient – were behind me.

———

In Deal, I'd arranged to meet Faye Smith, a woman I'd read about in the national press, in the hope of learning how to move on from the lingering stain of grief. Her alcoholic ex-husband had taken his own life in 2011, then exactly two years later, to the day, her 12-year-old daughter drowned in the bath from a suspected seizure.

Despite all this pain and tragedy, she found love again, and got engaged to a man from her church in Sheffield. But when that relationship broke down, too, and then her beloved father died shortly after, her life finally came crashing down. "Everything collapsed, like a Jenga tower," she told me, as we ordered gin and tonics from a busy seaside pub. Dressed in a cotton print dress and a green cardigan, with bright-red lipstick and rosy cheeks, she throbbed with colour. I felt scruffy and dirty beside her.

Like me, she suffered panic attacks, insomnia and nightmares. She became overwhelmed with resentment and anger. At the start of 2020 she took the bold decision to relocate to the Kent coast, 250 miles from home.

"Why here?" I asked. "You could have gone anywhere in the world."

"I needed a fresh start, next to the sea, and Deal's Christ Church therapeutic trauma recovery team had agreed to support me for six months."

"They were your only hope?"

"They had to do what seemed impossible. To put Humpty Dumpty back together again."

But just two weeks after arriving: lockdown. "I had no friends or my bereaved mum to turn to. I was stuck in my tiny, rented flat in a scary pandemic, with few possessions, no Wi-Fi, no TV, no gym, no swimming. Some thought I would go home, but I was determined to stay, and we made it work against all the odds."

Faye was clearly a superpower. A remarkable spirit with an incomprehensible tolerance for adversity. Moreover, she still had a son to support and protect.

"My children were two and six when we separated and then ten and fourteen when he died. This massively impacted on their mental health. But when my daughter died, too – exactly two years after my ex-husband – I had to be there, to protect my son more than ever, because without me he had no one."

Having been obsessed with death for my entire adult life, Faye's story walloped me in the sternum like a cricket ball. I couldn't quite fathom how she'd found the energy to continue. How could she enjoy life with such injustice hanging over her?

"It certainly gives you perspective. But you can have post-traumatic growth."

"What do you mean?"

"Good things can come out of shit. You can make manure out of it and make other things grow."

"And what of God?" I asked, gingerly. "Surely, you don't have any faith left after all of this?"

"It's all I have!" she said, her gentle voice cracking for the first time. "If I didn't believe that heaven existed then I'd probably have topped myself by now! I must believe that my daughter, and all those that I've lost and loved, are up there, waiting for me. Without that eternal hope, I have nothing."

I cycled into the wind, my blood sugar rising and falling in dizzying spikes, my mind consumed with death and finalities once again. How could life be so tragic, so desperately unfair? If God existed, how could he be so wicked? What reason could there be for taking such a young life? In my mind there was none, but in Faye's, I accepted, there had to be.

The evening whizzed by in a blur of deep thought. A greasy burger for dinner, a cheap hotel as shelter, a TV that mumbled but didn't speak. I looked at myself in the full-length mirror and barely recognised the reflection. Physically present but psychologically distant, as though coming round from a general anaesthetic.

My meeting with Faye had left me with a hangover that made my skin tingle, but now threatened to become a rash. I was tempted to drink, to erase the unrelenting memories of Joe, Sarah and my teenage friends, but instead I vowed to stay sober. I read, I wrote, I stretched. I repacked my panniers and washed my filthy socks in the bathroom sink. I called Alana to tell her I loved and missed her. I texted my dad to tell him I was OK.

The next morning, I followed the east coast of Kent, through Ramsgate and then into Margate. Glossy magazines, newspaper travel sections and lifestyle websites had been going giddy for this seaside town for a decade. The Turner Contemporary art gallery opened its doors in 2011. The sculptor Antony Gormley plonked one of his cast-iron human sculptures in its north facing shallows in 2017. The artist Tracey Emin set up a home and studio there in 2020.

I had high hopes, but I'm afraid the Margate I found was just another dreary seaside town, an asphalt jungle, crumbling to rubble. In normal times I'd receive at least one press release a week telling me how the town was "bouncing back". If you believed the hype and PR spin, then Margate was England's answer to San Francisco or Porto.

But you can't just whack a few double-decker buses on the seafront and hope it becomes the next Coney Island. The much bigger problem facing Margate, it seemed, was working out how an influx of hipsters might positively impact on its full-time residents, many of whom, I assumed, had little interest in session pale ales, smashed avocados and flat whites.

Statistics compiled by the Consumer Data Research Centre put Margate's life expectancy at 73, the lowest in the county and almost eight years below the national average. Drug users, in particular, are three times more likely to die from a heroin or morphine overdose in this region of Kent than anywhere else. For every ironic moustache and copy of *Wallpaper* magazine I saw, there was a tired soul, probably surviving on state benefits, with barely enough food to fill their stomachs.

I turned west, in the direction of Whitstable. Ahead of me, the horizon sprawled out in sumptuous greens and vivid blues. Money, freedom, opportunity. Behind me, Arlington House, Margate's tallest tower block, blazed dusty brown in the sidelight of mid-morning. From a distance, the town seemed like less of a go-to enclave and more like a neglected ghetto.

By lunchtime, the early summer sun was so fierce that the back of my neck was hot to the touch. The cracked earth hadn't seen a proper storm for weeks and sprinklers threw water into the air like rain in rewind. Hundreds of acres of hops and strawberries sweated under polythene tunnels. The Garden of England tasted of tangy Belgian fruit beer and drummed to the beat of a million busy bees.

My plan was to cycle all day and lay up in Gillingham, giving me a straight run at London the next morning. But when social media threw me a lifeline of yet more familiar faces – Chris Hacche, an old housemate from university, and his partner, Charlotte Appleton – I diverted to Faversham and threw in the towel.

We hadn't spoken for more than a decade, since waving goodbye to each other on a golden-sand beach in Vietnam. They now had had two young sons and looked tired but wonderfully content. "Life is very different since we last saw you, but I wouldn't change anything," said Charlotte, as she opened a bottle of cold white wine.

I missed those warm days of cheap rum, bottomless cigarettes and light hangovers, but I too wouldn't have changed a thing. Sure, we were different now. More serious, more adult. But to chase the past would have seemed tragic. "I work in recruitment," said Chris, before raising his eyebrows. "It doesn't set the world alight, but it pays the bills and helps give us a nice life."

Their sons were staying the night at their grandparents' house nearby, so we spent the late afternoon drinking cold pints over Faversham's hot cobbles. Unlike most British town centres that had succumbed to the gaudy frontages of Costa, Betfred and Subway, the streets reeked of history. You could almost hear the clip-clop of Roman armies shuffling through, and the crackle and pop of the gunpowder factories that once lined the banks of the Swale, the muddy tidal channel that separates mainland Kent from the Isle of Sheppey.

As the sun dripped away, we followed the soft banks of Faversham Creek, the silted home of itinerant narrowboaters and reed warblers. Grasshoppers, beetles and dragonflies skipped between the summer-crisped leaves of purple sea lavender and yellow horned poppies. In the middle distance, redshanks, skylarks and marsh harriers pecked and scuffed at a bank of burnished sand.

It was a relief to get back to the house for dinner. Having barely walked for weeks, my hamstrings ached, like they might snap at the knee. Sleepy and half-drunk, I took a shower before bed. I looked at myself naked in the mirror. I was sunburned from head to ankle, my skin mottled in patches of pink and white.

I set off early the next morning, a bank holiday Monday, ideal for an assault on the capital. Sittingbourne, Rainham and Chatham whirred beneath me, grey and nondescript, but mercifully quiet. "This was never going to be pretty," I mumbled, as I approached Gravesend and clapped eyes on south-east London's industrialised navel of shipping containers, cranes, distribution centres, sewage works and refineries.

I'd been here before. Almost five years ago to the day, at the end of a 135-day expedition spent sailing and cycling from China to London for the BBC World Service. Looking back, the person who completed that journey was a ghost to me now. Insecure, irritable and with something to prove. I'd embarked on that mostly wretched project for recognition.

Travel for all the wrong reasons. Half a decade on, however, and I felt more solid, less hollow. Morosely cynical and jaded, sure, but much more comfortable in my own skin.

I cycled west, along the southern banks of the Thames. Hard and black, the water hummed of sulphur and rotten fish, something like those stink bombs that children used to let off in playgrounds. All along the route, almost all signs of the natural world had been drowned in a trillion litres of malignant concrete. Even the hardiest brambles were dying back.

———

Before calling it a day, I diverted to Deptford to visit The Bike Project, a charity that donates more than 150 bicycles to refugees and asylum seekers every week. Under a grimy railway arch that rumbled every 30 seconds, mechanics in beanie hats and face masks were busy upcycling rusted wrecks. The whole operation bounced along to the beat of foot pumps and spanners.

Unable to work, asylum seekers are forced to survive on just £37.75 a week, in a city where the average weekly wage is more than £500. "These bikes change people's lives," said The Bike Project's founder and CEO, Jem Stein, a stubbled man in a grey hoodie. "Bicycles allow people to travel to schools and hospitals, but they also give them access to exercise."

"You're preaching to the converted!"

"This is about not just physical fitness but also mental well-being."

Since 2013, the charity had given away more than 8,000 bikes to people from countries such as Syria, Eritrea and Albania. "Not only does having a bike save people about £20 a week in transport costs, but it also gives them a way to access the services they need. We also try to encourage refugee women to cycle for the first time via our Pedal Power project and we're linking asylum seekers up with cycling 'buddies' across the city."

Jem was keen for me to meet one of the project's first beneficiaries, a man from Guinea-Bissau who wished to remain anonymous for fear of somehow damaging his 14-year appeal for British residency. "If this project hadn't existed, I don't know what might have happened to me," he said, fixing a new brake cable to an old Peugeot three-speed.

"Do you know when your case might be resolved?"

"After fourteen years I'm still struggling. I've been dealing with so many psychological issues. I worry about my family, my dad and my kids back home."

"How did you get here?"

"I was in prison in my country, I managed to escape, then my brother took me to the Senegal border and then I walked for twenty-five kilometres. From there I got a taxi into Gambia, then from Gambia I got a flight to the UK."

Perhaps he was nervous to talk to me, but the man looked pained; tortured by a feeling of being stranded. He could neither work in Britain, nor return to the country where he was born. "If things get better in my country I'd prefer to go back, rather than staying in this situation. I feel like I'm being squeezed and squeezed."

Fixing old bikes was the only thing that kept the man going. But when the pandemic hit and the workshop closed, he grew doubly lost. "My bike helped me so much during lockdown. It gave me a reason to get out of my house."

Our bikes had been lifelines. Without them, who knows what might have happened to us. These simple contraptions had given us hope in the darkest of hours; a way to move, a reason to live.

To me, the humble bicycle was everything that Jem and the man had described. But perhaps more than anything, it was one of life's greatest levellers, with little care for race or status. As I cycled north through the multicultural wonder of London – Peckham, Whitechapel, Spitalfields and Shoreditch, I shared the road with the capital's rich, poor, white, brown, black, citizen and stateless.

Wheels whirring, brakes squeaking, we weren't doctors, barmaids, cleaners or journalists. We were cyclists.

HUMBER:
THE HARIBO RING

Finally, after 60 miles under an unrelenting sun, I made it to the place where I'd spend the next couple of nights. A 70-foot-long steel canal boat on the Regent's Canal, the pride and joy of one of my best friends, George Godson. I found the spare key in the greasy engine bay and climbed in. The galley thermometer displayed 53°C: the textbook temperature of a medium rare steak.

By midnight it was just about cool enough to sleep, but by 8 a.m. the next morning, blood was boiling in my veins, so I escaped to London Fields to doze in the shade of a flaky old plane tree, with a trunk as crooked as a giraffe's back leg. The park throbbed to the beat of filthy dubstep. Hash smoke wafted up from the south. Skunk blew in from the north. If this had been Los Angeles or New York, then the city's fire hydrants would have been busted long before. Instead, Londoners wilted stubbornly. Dog paws sizzled on the frying-pan pavements. Human forearms dangled from chinks in high-rise apartment windows.

After much-needed visits to a launderette and a barber, I was joined on the boat by travel journalist Andrew Purvis and his wife, Naomi. Andrew had handed me my first ever commission as a travel writer and without his support and encouragement I might never have enjoyed so many brushes with death. I certainly wouldn't have had quite so much fun.

Andrew and I were kindred spirits. I considered him a mentor, a confidant in a sometimes fiercely cut-throat industry. "You're utterly bonkers," he said, his stock response to most of my hare-brained ideas. "But this story needs to be told. It's current, it's important. Keep pushing on."

A normal catch-up would have resulted in a late-night curry and half a dozen pints. Often, I'd end up on their sofa, cocooned in a sleeping bag beneath a Masai spear. This night, however, we enjoyed a quiet pizza in Broadway Market and I downed a glass of water for every beer. "Please just be careful," said Naomi, offering a motherly dose of candour as we hugged goodbye. "Alana needs you back in one piece."

———

I set off early the next morning. The canal was warm and brown, like forgotten coffee. A moorhen perched on a nest of twigs, white feathers, sweet wrappers and plastic straws. Ducklings tittered in the shadows of hoary nettles. I joined a wave of expensive haircuts jogging in the direction of the City, then turned north to Stratford, Wanstead and Epping Forest. Green, glorious green.

I found another fellow travel hack, Oliver Smith, waiting to give me an escort into Essex. He was a serious cyclist, at least much more serious than me. His bike was svelte and light, with scarcely a surplus gram. He could clean and jerk it to shoulder height without straining a muscle. Mine, meanwhile, looked and felt embarrassingly cumbersome. Heavy and fat, with two dirty trainers and a 3-litre water bottle hanging from its rear.

Oliver was the first person to commission a story from me when I dreamed up the crazy idea of cycling around pandemic Britain. Without an editor like him, willing to publish my articles, I would never have survived. In normal times, we spoke almost daily via email, but he was now enjoying six months' paternity leave following the birth of his first child.

"I'm not for one moment suggesting I've worked it all out, after just a couple of months of being a father," he said, as we rode through a tunnel of golden cypress trees. "But it is certainly the most incredible thing that's ever happened to me. Watching my daughter change, every single day, is just fascinating. Family really is the most important thing we have."

Like most journalists, I could tell that Oliver was slightly wary of drifting into clichés and superlatives, but his pure and wholesome grin was worth the weight of a thousand words. "She also sleeps a lot," he said. "So, I've been managing to get out and cycle every day, and there's plenty of time for reading. After thirteen years of almost constant work, I didn't realise just how much I needed a rest."

Travel writers are like ships in the night. I could count on one hand the number I'd spoken to properly in person, and while I had his undivided attention, I was eager to mine Oliver for insight. Not only was he a razor-sharp and opinionated journalist of a similar age, but he'd also managed to find a balance between a normal home life and the addictive allure of overseas travel.

"If you want to start a family of your own one day, only you and your partner can really work out how that might look and feel."

"That's what I find so confusing."

"As an editor, I'm chained to my desk most of the time, but I know that many others have struggled."

"But we *need* travel, don't we? It's not just a job."

"One thing I'd stand by is that having some time apart from each other is healthy for a relationship. Working out just how much time is the hard bit."

Before I met Alana, I was hopelessly hooked to my work. In a normal year I was travelling to over 30 countries and filing 50 or 60 stories. I didn't earn a great deal, travel writers seldom do, but it was worth it for the perks alone. In 2016 I made about £15,000 from journalism, but calculated that all the complimentary first-class plane tickets, business-class lounges, chauffeur-driven cars, Michelin-starred restaurants and glitzy accommodation would have cost around half a million pounds.

Travel was the most moreish drug I'd ever tried. I'd been to over 100 countries, to the Namib Desert, Svalbard, the Australian outback, St Helena and the Atacama. These were the places that had kept me awake at night as a teenager. Better still, to then see my name in print afterward symbolised the "success" I'd always craved. The catch? I'd done it all alone.

"I can't quite work out if I'm just exhausted from it all or feeling weirdly broody," I told Oliver, as we whizzed over Chelmsford's baking streets.

"You are reaching *that* age," he laughed.

"My biggest fear used to be not doing enough with my life. But now I'm petrified of dying alone in an airport hotel somewhere."

"Clutching a passport filled with stamps."

"I don't want to be one of those loners who have no one to call when they step off a plane at Heathrow. I've been there and it wasn't nice."

We reached Maldon, on the banks of the river Blackwater, and made light work of fish, chips and three rounds of lagers. We couldn't agree on whose afternoon would prove to be more sluggish, but begrudgingly we went our separate ways: Oliver back to Epping, and me in the direction of Suffolk.

———

Alcohol and cycling simply don't mix. I didn't feel particularly inebriated or in anyway a hazard to other road users, but my spine now slumped, heavy in the saddle. Thank goodness the route was flat, and I had a tailwind that pushed me all the way to Colchester.

I was tempted to try and push on even further, to Leiston and The Red House. My first Covid-19 jab was booked in for the next day and I was eager to roll up my sleeve and move on with my life. But while the air was still and the rooms were cheap, it made sense to hunker down and rest my legs.

"I miss you," I said to Alana, when we spoke before bed, my voice quivering with nerves.

"Are you OK?" she asked. "You sound shifty. Anxious."

"Fine, just tired. I'm a bit hung-over from lunch, to be honest. I can't wait to see you tomorrow."

"I love you."

The next day's route between Colchester and Ipswich was so flat and unexciting I barely remember it. Either that, or I was so consumed by daydreams that I rode on autopilot. Before I really knew it, I'd reached the vaccination centre at Leiston and was standing in a queue.

"You look terrified," said the nurse, when it was finally my turn.

"I'm OK. I don't mind needles. I've just got a lot on my mind."

With a trickle of warm blood running down my arm, I rode through town, under street lights that had once illuminated my gloomiest nights. I passed the benches where I'd whiled away countless manic hours, and the shop windows that had gathered dust in the darkest days and nights of winter.

A few minutes later, I arrived at The Red House to a noisy hero's welcome. Alana's parents, Ruth and Tim, her Auntie Anna-Jane and her partner, Rob, whooped enthusiastically, as though I'd completed the Tour de France. "Alana's on her way," said Tim, dressed in his usual get-up of baggy jeans, Crocs and a skateboarding T-shirt. "She's not far away now. Go and have a bath. She'll be here soon."

I soaked like a pig in mud, pondering the same pollen-dusted windows that had once resembled prison bars. Warm sunshine tore through the panes and kissed my naked skin, but I needed Alana to burst through the bathroom door and bury her face into mine. This was our lockdown cell and I felt lost without my fellow inmate.

I waited and waited, hot hope becoming tepid irritation, my skin turning white and wrinkly. After more than an hour, I finally got out. I was so incensed at having been ignored that I ran toward the kitchen, pumped for a fight.

"She's had a crash," said Rob, causing my throat to grow tight and lumpy. My mind whirred catastrophically, jumping from one terrible outcome to the next. I held my breath and bit my bottom lip. Not again. Please, not again.

"She's fine. Just a bit shaken up. Ruth and Tim have gone off to find her."

A mother on the school run had thwacked into the back of her car, at a roundabout somewhere near Cambridge. The rear window had been smashed into thousands of pieces but thankfully the tow bar had borne most of the impact.

For 3 tortuous hours, I paced around the house and garden, flitting between fury and guilt. In my mind, I wrote her a long and impassioned dressing-down. How could *she* be so stupid? What would *we* have done if she'd been injured, or worse?

But then, when she finally arrived, with bloodshot eyes and tiny fragments of glass glinting on her trembling shoulders, I couldn't say a word. I just threw my arms around her, never wanting to let her go again.

———

We spent the evening in the garden, laughing, talking and listening to music, then early the next morning I sneaked out to the local supermarket and filled a rucksack with all her favourite sweets.

"Why are you wearing such nice clothes?" Alana asked, when I woke her up. "You smell… weirdly nice, for a change."

"I was thinking that we should go for a walk," I said. "Maybe the Sluice? I've packed a bag already."

It's hard to cajole someone into moving quickly when they have no idea why they're being hurried along. Nevertheless, I coaxed Alana down Sizewell beach with squares of dark chocolate and the promise of a pub lunch and a bottle of wine. "The way to Alana's heart is via her stomach," her parents had told me, on the very first day I'd met them. Their words had echoed in my ears ever since.

"You're being so weird," she said, when I told her to sit down in the dunes and dig her heels into the sand where her grandparents' ashes had been laid to rest. The same place where we'd snuggled together on those dark lockdown nights.

"Close your eyes, and don't open them until I say you can."

On a flat-topped stone, about the size of a dinner plate, I arranged two chipped wine glasses, a few party poppers and a bottle of warm champagne. I then pulled a tiny box from my pocket, took out the Haribo ring I'd hidden inside the night before and knelt awkwardly on both knees.

For a few lonely seconds, I paused in the swirling silence. Grass rattling, the North Sea hissing. A courting male snipe drummed its tail feathers against the wind. Hidden in the hummock of the undulating earth, we were the only souls for miles.

"You can open them now," I said, my voice shaking.

"What the fuck," she blurted out, impulsively, before her cheeks flushed ruddy.

"I was wondering if you'd like to get married," I said, embarrassed by the triteness of my words. "To me. I was wondering if you'd like to get married, to me. I've had so much time to think, and I know that this is what I really want. I want to be with you, forever. To start a family, to have dogs and chickens and... children, I think. I know the last couple of years have been tough, but if we can get through that, we can get through anything. I honestly can't imagine my life without you."

I don't remember Alana actually saying "yes" but for some reason we grabbed the champagne and ran into the sea. It might sound like a ridiculous romcom, but the water was so painfully cold that we merely plunged our heads under the surface and ran straight back out.

Wet and shivering, we popped a few stones on the cairn that marked her grandparents' lives and made a break for the local pub. Barefooted, guzzling fizzy bubbles straight from the bottle, we passed a mob of ramblers with Nordic poles and a twitcher in camouflage.

"Are you two OK?" he asked, alarmed by our wet clothes and drunken smiles.

"Smashing," said Alana, before taking another glug of booze. "Just happy."

The next morning, we packed up our bikes and hit the road. Alana, my fiancée, would now join me for the next two hundred or so miles north. It was another hot day, with hardly a cloud in the sky, and even with the sea breeze, we were quickly hot and bothered, plagued by swarms of flies.

Having spent three weeks on my own, I'd been worried that having Alana on board might put me on edge. Instead, she cycled faster than I could and took on the stress of navigating. "It's about time we stopped for some food and liquids," she'd tell me, almost on the hour. "You've not got long left now, so you need to start looking after yourself better."

Suffolk hummed of sweaty pigs, awaiting their turn at the abattoir. The route was mostly flat and agricultural, with barely a rise and fall. Where possible, we followed the coastal tracks – along a route of sand and seaweed. It was so quiet and private that by the time we rolled into Lowestoft, we'd mapped out our next 50 years together. It was exciting, but oddly mischievous, to finally say the words out loud.

Two children, hopefully. A girl and a boy.

A chocolate Labrador and a golden retriever.

A shed at the bottom of the garden where I could write.

A room where Alana could practise yoga and which she could fill with exorbitantly priced candles.

"How the hell did my aspirations become so middle class?" I joked. "A few years ago, this was my idea of a living hell, but something weird has happened to me. Last week I was daydreaming about a new kitchen, for God's sake!"

We bought lunch on the outskirts of Lowestoft, then diverted to Ness Point, the easternmost extreme of the British Isles. "It's just a signpost, in a car park," said Alana, when I started to eulogise about its geographical significance. Nonetheless, she patiently humoured her future husband and took a photo of him standing proudly by the muddy sea. "You're such a nerd."

Following Suffolk's pancake-flat coastline, we bickered occasionally, like most couples do. Mostly about where and when we should next eat, or if I had or hadn't farted. "It's just the muck on the fields," I'd lie. "That's just what the countryside smells like!"

But most of the time we simply cycled in contented silence, feeling little need to fill the dead air with more than our silly sounds and catchphrases.

———

We crossed the river Waveney and cycled into Norfolk, a county that so often becomes the brunt of the joke. Jimmy Carr, Jeremy Clarkson and Al Murray have all had a pop in recent years, labelling it a backwater filled with uneducated and incestuous people.

As a travel writer, I'd hate to be quite so harsh. And on first impressions, we discovered a verdant land that rustled with wheat and splendour. But as we rode into "Great" Yarmouth, I must admit that I was, once again, left feeling oddly bereaved for the sorry state of the British seaside.

The town suffocated under a weight of neon-lit dereliction, so kitsch and gaudy it resembled a Black-Sea sanatorium that had been abandoned in the fallout of a nuclear catastrophe. Only a few mongrels and a handful of stubborn pensioners had been left behind, to live on until the toffee apples ran out.

We cycled past a compound labelled "Joyland", which looked about as joyless as an exercise yard in a maximum-security prison. The nearby Britannia Pier Theatre would soon welcome Roy Chubby Brown, Jim Davidson and Jimmy Carr, no less. No doubt with a regionally tweaked set list.

As we pushed north, past the eerie foundations of bulldozed holiday parks, it was impossible to determine what might become of these relics. Dark tourism, perhaps – were they Britain's answer to Fukushima, Chernobyl and the Soviet Union's abandoned fairgrounds? Or apocalypse film sets – surely primed for a post-pandemic boom. Whatever the outcome, it seemed hard to reconcile with the notion of a nationwide "housing crisis" – so much of the country could simply be refurbished.

After the urban dribble came an emerald lawn. The Norfolk Broads, criss-crossed with canals and marshes. Yellow-and-black swallowtail butterflies fluttered lazily around cottony reeds. A kestrel hovered high above them in a gravity-defying pause.

We rested in the shade of the Horsey Windpump, a National Trust site popular among baby boomers in hiking boots and crampons. Norfolk is, of course, one of the flattest counties in Britain, but who am I to assume that they weren't training for a mountain trekking expedition in the Maldives.

The afternoon was flat, hot and long, and it was gone 6 p.m. by the time we made it to Cromer and checked into a creaking old hotel overlooking the town's Victorian pier. This was the sort of establishment that seemed to delight in not having changed a single thing for centuries. I suspect the owners had only recently adopted electricity and still hankered for the stench of seal-blubber candles.

We tiptoed across the chandeliered landing, half expecting the floorboards to give way and send us crashing into the kitchen. Our "sea view" room was mostly held together with Sellotape and butchers' twine and looked out to a padlocked balcony that had been taken over by a flock of a pigeons. They loved nothing more than to procreate rampantly in their own corrosive faeces.

While I battled with the shower, Alana looked under the two single beds, in the drawers and behind the TV. "There's semen all over the teabags," she revealed, when I emerged a few minutes later. My natural reaction was to get angry, to chastise her for being so uptight. But she was right, our room was the pits. It was hard to work out if it had been cleaned this side of the millennium. And whatever the milky ectoplasm really was, it was more than enough to put a person off their morning brew.

Dinner options were limited to supermarket meal deals or two plates of scampi and chips for a tenner in the pub across the road. We settled on the latter, but spent most of the evening squabbling about the quality of the hotel and the lack of fresh vegetables in my diet.

On reflection, I'd mis-sold the trip to Alana as a "cycling holiday" when really it was a frantic push from A to B, just like it had been on all the other days without her. I found it hard to stop and rest. I always felt like I had to be somewhere else.

"Please can we actually pause to look at something today?" she asked in a sleepy daze, when I woke her at first light, crashing around the room like a boisterous drill sergeant. "And I want proper food," she told me. "Not just fried things! These are the only days I've had off work for months and it feels like all you want to do is piss in hedges and eat chips."

Having not earned proper money for so long, I was set firmly in my frugal pandemic ways. I still had my back to the wall. I found it hard to part with the few precious pounds I now had in my bank account. Alana, meanwhile, was insistent that we'd worked so hard that we now needed to reward ourselves, even just a little.

Wells-next-the-Sea must have seen us coming. The town was doing a roaring trade in bougie snacks, rounded up to the nearest tenner. The streets were all but paved in gold. We bought a punnet of strawberries and a bag of cherries, then dangled our feet over the harbour wall. They were, without doubt, the most delicious things to grace my chapped lips in months. I couldn't, of course, bring myself to admit this to Alana. Instead, as the expensive red juice sloshed around the insides of my cheeks, I wondered what auntie or uncle we might now need to cull from our list of wedding guests.

Buzzing with vitamin C, we escaped the bustling town and followed the coast road running beside Holkham beach, a long eyebrow of vanilla sand bordered by Corsican pine trees and multicoloured huts. It was, however, so windy we could barely hear each other shout. After just a couple of miles, we gave up and retreated to the hushed countryside, where a cricket match was playing out on a mole-hilled field surrounded by a crowd of freshly shorn sheep.

I could have stopped and ogled the scene for hours but swiftly remembered that there were two of us now, and there always would be. As we cycled along together – through lavender fields and beneath the mighty oaks of the Queen's Sandringham Estate – I noticed that we were breathing in unison.

By the time we reached Long Sutton, a small market town in the south of Lincolnshire, we were thirsty and desperate for cold showers. We found a pub with a room and drank warm white wine from teacups while listening to our favourite playlist. We'd cycled 144 miles together across two broiling days. Alana's nose was pink and freckly, and as we sat and looked at each other across plates of steamed broccoli, I could see heavy tears building in the creases of her sunburned eyelids.

"Everything felt…"

"Normal?"

"Yeah. Again."

"I promise that our lives will be better now. They have to be."

"Please just get this finished in one piece."

The next morning, Tim arrived to take Alana home. "Do you think this a respectable way for your daughter's husband to make a living?" I asked, as we lobbed her things into the car.

"You're alright," he said, reassuringly, before giving us a moment of privacy to say goodbye.

After a long hug and a dozen kisses, they watched me cycle off north, waving and laughing together in the same way they had done for 30 years. It was a relief to leave her with a man who loved her just as much as I did. But without her company, every turn of the pedals soon felt like wading through quicksand.

I couldn't remember the last time the sky was anything but a hot and heavy blue, and within an hour I was soaked in sweat and ruminating deeply. Alone with my thoughts again, I worried what fatherly advice Tim might be imparting in my absence. If I was in his shoes, would I be so supportive of a suitor who disappeared so frequently?

With my lungs starting to breathe into my shoulders, I pulled in to a lay-by, eager to press pause before my symptoms could escalate further. Hiding behind a bush, away from any nosey drivers, I placed one hand on my chest, the other on my diaphragm and closed my eyes.

Eight breaths in.

Hold.

Two, three, four.

Eight breaths out.

Hold.

Repeat.

It must have taken me 10 or 15 minutes, but through a combination of positive thinking and repetitive motions, my lungs softened again. And although she was now driving away from me in the opposite direction, Alana was still with me, talking me through it, every step of the way.

Thankfully, the terrain was flat. As I pushed deeper into southern Lincolnshire, the highest natural contours were the mounds of fine red topsoil piled high around sun-crisped potato plants. With its water towers, seed hoppers and corrugated iron hangars, the landscape reminded me of the American Midwest, and the vast agricultural plains that stretch from the eastern foot of the Rocky Mountains, all the way to the shores of the Great Lakes.

By late morning I'd made it to Boston, a market town with a 266-foot church – St Botolph's – and the small port from where emigrants set off for the east coast of the United States in the early seventeenth century. These days, however, Boston, Lincolnshire, is better known for migration in the opposite direction. After Poland and nine other new countries joined the European Union in 2004, its immigrant population grew by 460 per cent within a decade.

I'd tried hard not to taint my trip by constantly viewing Britain through the blurry prism of Brexit. I, like many Britons, felt fatigued by the subject and was now eager to crack on with my life, for better or worse. In Boston, however, it was impossible not to. The town was at the apex of the national debate. In fact, when I used to produce news programmes in the early years of the 2010s, a few vox-pops from Boston trumped anything we might source from a major city or a member of the Cabinet or Opposition.

In the 2016 referendum, Boston recorded the largest Brexit vote in the country, with more than three quarters of the electorate voting leave. The following year, perhaps unsurprisingly, Lincolnshire Police recorded 256 racist or xenophobic hate crimes, a 21 per cent increase on the previous year.

I rested in the shade of a coffee shop and eavesdropped on a gammon-faced man pontificating tabloid headlines verbatim. It was hard to determine if he did or didn't support the latest controversial actions of the Home Secretary. I'm not sure if he really knew either, but he certainly wanted his voice heard all the same.

Soon, however, it was too much to bear, and I set off on my journey once again. The high street buzzed with people, but on the edge of town, just before leaving, I discovered a cultural melting pot like no other.

Tourists visiting Britain should give all the costly attractions a wide berth and simply attend one of the greatest displays of British culture for free: the humble car boot sale. Staggeringly, £1.5 billion-worth of loose change is exchanged at them each year. You might have thought that VHS, cassettes and laserdisc had been rendered obsolete. Or that no one in their right mind would buy a bucket-load of random wires covered in concrete. Think again.

Britons, and Poles, it would seem, love the intoxicating thrill of a bargain so much that they will part with their hard-earned cash for almost anything. I stood for more than 10 minutes, spellbound by the plots and subplots playing out in real time. A balding man with grey jogging bottoms hoisted up to his armpits inspected a dilapidated Henry Hoover with the crazed eyes of Gollum. There were enough Zimmer frames to kit out the entire cast of *The Best Exotic Marigold Hotel*, and their stunt doubles. A middle-aged woman with wrap-around shades and socks and sandals barged through a small crowd and hoisted up a pirated *Jurassic Park* DVD as though she'd just unearthed the Watergate tapes. I found it hard to tear myself away, but the road beckoned and a meeting loomed.

I'd arranged to call in on John Nuttall, aka the "donkey man" of Skegness beach, and I found him under a fierce orange sun, shirt off, with Armani shades and a "made in England" tattoo inscribed around his belly button. His family had been looking after donkeys for more than a century. But then the pandemic came along, and his business collapsed.

"I thought that was it for us," said John, as excited children waited for rides on his hairy colleagues, Alfie, Pedro and Noddy.

"Forever?"

"We were in lockdown, but we still had seventy donkeys to keep feeding."

"And you're still here."

"It wasn't the season we should have had, but we pulled through with grants and donations. It was amazing how much the local community got behind us."

After a stop-start year, things were finally looking up. The "lockdown effect" had caused so much pent-up demand for fun in the great outdoors that he was struggling to keep up. "I've never seen it so busy. But the last year has really taught me to never take things for granted. I've lost four friends due to Covid. I feel lucky to be here on the coast, surrounded by fresh air."

I'd heard this sentiment time and time again. A clean breeze and space to breathe was now a priceless commodity, worth more than the consumer trappings of pre-pandemic life. I was happiest on my bike, my mind and lungs distracted by new places and cool oxygen. John felt similar. To work outside, often in inclement North-Sea conditions, was rarely a chore but a privilege. "I'm outside for ninety per cent of my life," said John. "People would pay a lot of money for that sort of lifestyle."

At £3 a ride, John and his human and equine staff worked hard for their keep. But coins aside, it was the sight of young faces with broad smiles that brought him the greatest joy. That, and the belief that he was doing his ancestors' legacy justice. "I had a lot of time to look through old photo albums this past year," said John. "My dad left them when he died. It was amazing how they kept this going through the war. Some of them couldn't go overseas, so they worked their donkeys on the beach. I thought that if they can get through a war, then I can certainly get through a pandemic."

John was a grafter, and time was money, so we shook hands and I rode off to find a hotel for the night. The reception was normal enough, but my room resembled an 80s porn set, decorated in five different shades of green, a velour bedspread and a bank of flashing LEDs above the mantlepiece. I was in two minds whether to ask for a refund, or at the very least a seasickness tablet.

TYNE:
CALM, NOT PANIC

Britain is incapable of dealing with hot weather. It arrives at some point every summer, yet our star's presence in the sky surprises us like a supernova. Even the very sniff of a heatwave will leave the nation's feeble train tracks quivering. You'd think we would enjoy a respite from the incessant 12°C and drizzle that sets in for the other 355 days. Wrong. Because to complain about the sky above is as British as beans on toast.

"It's too bloody hot," I heard the next morning from a teenager slumped outside a petrol station on the western edge of Skegness. With a can of cold fizzy pop pressed against his pink cheeks, he was doing a grand impression of a downed pilot in the Sahel.

Nevertheless, his was also the first properly northern accent I'd heard since leaving Manchester some seven months before. It felt like a moment to cherish. There was a smooth and wondrous cadence to his adolescent lilt. If southerners had jabbed at English like staccato trombones, then he sounded more like a legato oboe. "Haaaavvveee-you-got-any-Calippooooooooos?" he warbled to the man behind the counter.

Rather than stubbornly follow the coast, which was rapidly clogging with day trippers craving a sea breeze, I diverted through the steamy Lincolnshire Wolds, an Area of Outstanding Natural Beauty that – unlike some places I'd seen – immediately lived up to its reputation. Rippling away, on waves of grassy green, clay red and oilseed yellow, the chequered land was living and breathing. I had seldom clapped eyes on anywhere quite so luscious and pure. Even the jungles of Borneo and Costa Rica didn't pulse with life in quite this way.

They were also the quietest roads I'd cycled on since Scilly. It was a travesty, but also a privilege, that I had them almost entirely to myself. "Hidden gem" is one of the most hackneyed phrases in travel writing, but nowhere in Britain deserved the moniker quite like Lincolnshire.

With just 386 people per square mile, Lincolnshire is one of Britain's most sparsely populated counties. A lack of people has done wonders for the local wildlife. The narrow chalk streams that criss-cross the former home of poet Alfred, Lord Tennyson, are some of the cleanest in Europe. So clean, in fact, that the local otter population has grown, year on year, since the 1980s.

"Otters are a keystone species," said Stewart West, a local naturalist, whom I met beside the meandering banks of the river Bain. "This river is filled with invasive American crayfish, but the otters keep their numbers down."

"And without them?"

"Without them, the crayfish would eat all the eggs of the young chub and trout."

"So, they're not just cute, they're helpful."

"Sometimes otters get a bad rep from fishermen, but there's a lot of data that proves the rivers are healthier because of them."

Stewart was a passionate advocate for the countryside and the way it can have a positive impact on our mental health. Without it, he admitted, he would have struggled to get through the pandemic's lockdowns.

"This place, and the past year, has definitely slowed me down a lot," said Stewart, a teacher from 9 to 5.

"I can see how it could do that."

"I'm leaving work half an hour earlier and getting out to do things. It has made me think about perhaps giving up teaching to take people out on canoeing trips."

"That's huge."

"In a strange way, the UK wildlife tourism industry could benefit from the pandemic in the long term, because a lot of people, like me, have had a chance to think about new careers."

Otters are shy creatures, and unsurprisingly we didn't see one. Even their poo was hard to find, despite Stewart's best efforts to pick up and smell as many doppelganger turds as possible. But we did see a water vole scurrying from one crumbled bank to another. And as a swarm of iridescent dragonflies gambolled above the rippling rapids, a herd of Lincoln Red cows waded in for a drink beside nine palm-sized ducklings.

We didn't encounter another human for more than 2 glorious hours, and after a couple of cold beers in the local pub, I pitched my tent at the edge of a farmer's garden. He was, somewhat ironically, away on a life-affirming cycling trip of his own, but his wife, Lizzie, and their giant lurcher, Margot, gave me a warm welcome all the same.

Stewart had introduced us, and they were more than happy to let me shower and charge up my gadgets. I know that more intrepid adventurers would have "wild camped" anywhere, regardless of the laws preventing it in England, but it felt courteous to ask, rather than skulk around a private forest on my own. And they were only too keen to help a weary traveller. I drifted into a deep sleep under a weeping willow, calmed by the gentle trickle of the river Bain. Stewart was right, this land had the power to not only soothe but also heal.

Dawn broke with a chirp and a crow, so I packed up quietly and joined the silent road. I'd set myself the challenge of reaching Scarborough by the end of the day, but this was an ambitious task, and almost 100 miles lay ahead of me. I probably didn't need to embark upon such a long and no doubt arduous journey, but while the weather was set fair, and I had almost 20 hours of daylight, it seemed like the right thing to do. Wind and rain would inevitably return at some point in the future. This was like putting miles in the bank for the slow days around the corner.

I was feeling at peace, both physically and psychologically – more so than at any point before. I was sleeping longer, thinking more clearly and breathing – unconsciously – into the pit of my navel. By simply turning the pedals, over and over again, my body had fallen into a rhythm that induced calm, not panic. It was also a huge relief to know that Alana and I would be getting married. Perhaps without really knowing it, I'd been carrying the burden of the proposal with me, not only around Britain, but as excess luggage for years.

But 100 miles are never easy, and by the time I reached the Humber, 35 miles to the north, my calves twitched with lactic acid and zaps of electric pain jolted through my lower back. I had little choice but to limp into Yorkshire, wondering if I'd pushed myself too hard.

———

At 4,626 feet long, the Humber Bridge is the longest suspension bridge in Britain. From the walkway, I could see north as far as the North York Moors and east to the North Sea, where a fleet of snub-nosed fishing boats steamed in toward Grimsby.

This was so much more than just a walkway. I was treading a cold and lonely path. Bouquets of plastic flowers had been lashed to the rusted handrails, their cloth petals ripped and gnarled by the wind. Steel towers squealed and whimpered high above me. The air felt hard and stony.

More than 200 people are believed to have committed suicide on the Humber Bridge since it opened in 1981. In spring 2021 alone – toward the end of England's third national lockdown – six people died there in the space of just 31 days. I passed a stubbled man with a walkie-talkie and a high-vis jacket. "If I see anyone looking suspicious, I call it in immediately," he told me. "There's always a chance we can save someone's life." It was a relief to reach the other side. The Humber Bridge isn't a place for tourism or pretty pictures, it's a living, creaking memorial.

To travel is to learn. We cannot simply experience the world in 2D, on screens in the palms of our hands. And to see, hear and feel a place, in the flesh, is – to me – the greatest privilege in life. If I'd read about suicides on the Humber Bridge in a national newspaper, I might have skimmed the headline, without as much as a passing thought. Two hundred mothers, fathers, sons and daughters, ignored in the flick of a wrist.

But to taste that place, the brackish breeze and the bitterness of its rust, to hear the shriek of seagulls and the rumble of lorries. It felt like one of the most profound moments, not only of this trip, but of any trip that had come before it.

I'd teetered on the edge of mania and despair myself, but to have stood over a precipice, staring into a dark abyss, believing that to jump was my only option? I found it impossible to comprehend just how lost and lonely those people must have felt.

———

Exercising for 14 or 15 hours a day is not normal. You can, however, fool yourself into believing that it is. There was always a temptation to ride and ride, and to push my body to the brink of failure. In my mind, this was the man I was meant to be. An intrepid, fearless adventurer, oozing with testosterone, and with a high threshold for pain. Rest was for sissies. Eating was cheating.

There's no room in all those gnarly TV adventure programmes to show people doing boring things like eating or sleeping properly. The most you might see is a grimaced glug of product-placed single malt next to a campfire. Sustenance nearly always comes in the shape of fresh meat sliced with a machete. Proper adventurers sleep in hammocks, then somehow have the capacity to abseil into spewing volcanoes. Once upon a time that was me, but the reality of my "adventure travel" was becoming more sobering, more civilian.

It annoyed me to admit it, but rest and proper food allowed my body to recalibrate. Just half an hour off the bike had given my legs and lower back a chance to reset. Moreover, an apple, a pear and three bananas, instead of a protein shake and a dextrose-laden cereal bar, made my muscles purr, like a sports car filled with super unleaded. I zoomed through Hull, feeling as though I'd spent the afternoon lazing around a posh hotel spa.

Unlike the gentrified boroughs of north-east London, the outskirts of north-east Hull were mostly abandoned and derelict. I cycled through the cool shadows of the British Extracting Company silo, a red-brick, cathedral-like structure that was built in 1919 but has stood empty and unused since the 1970s.

Similar nearby buildings have been razed in recent years, but Grade II listed status with Historic England has kept the former linseed and cottonseed storage unit intact. It struck me as one of those industrial blights on the British skyline, which probably should be demolished or redeveloped, if only the money existed to do it. These days it's the sort of place where YouTubers go to film themselves climbing up rickety staircases. Less David Cameron's Northern Powerhouse and more Boris Johnson's "House of Horrors".

———

Somewhere west of Hornsea, I hit the sweet spot between rest, calorie intake, hydration and just the right amount of caffeine. In my mind I called it "Beast Mode", but I'd be embarrassed to actually say those words out loud. It sounded far too much like an inspirational poster you'd find in a grunt-filled gym.

It is, however, a remarkable physical state, that only very occasionally kicks in. I'd experienced it for the first time when cycling across the USA in 2016, when I had to claw back 450 miles in just three days, while "wild camping" and pulling a trailer up and over the Appalachian Mountains.

For the first time since then, my body now felt machine-like; sucking in oxygen, expelling carbon dioxide and roaring forward at 15 mph. As I flew north, with 120 bpm house music ticking like a metronome in my ears, I could almost feel my adrenal gland pulsing out raw bursts of energy. It was no wonder that people could become as addicted to exercise as they might hard drugs. I was experiencing an endorphin rush akin to dancing on ecstasy, albeit without the sore jaw or shrunken penis.

I finally made it to Scarborough at just after 5 p.m. I had 95 miles on the clock, but instead of feeling exhausted, I was wired. I had no appetite, and my heavily dilated pupils almost filled the whites of my bloodshot eyes. There was only one way to bring myself down: alcohol, so I necked four or maybe five pints in the closest pub then crashed into a nearby hotel. I don't recall much of what happened next. But I woke up at some point in the early hours of the next morning with a pounding headache and the TV blaring out an episode of *Dr. Pimple Popper* – a surprisingly satisfying, albeit nauseating, show about warts, blackheads and boils being relieved of their gooey insides.

The next day I decided to rest. The adrenal gland that had once resembled a chubby grape had all but shrivelled to the size of a raisin and I found it hard to pull myself out of bed, especially while a Test match was in full flow. It wasn't until the early evening that I finally ventured out for a walk around Scarborough, a town under siege from tens of thousands of seagulls.

Within 50 feet of leaving the hotel, I had their sour shit in my hair, mouth and ears. Every car, noticeboard and window ledge had been covered in their corrosive filth. The Grand Hotel – once a beacon for all things prim and proper – had been all but ransacked. I'd visited cleaner seabird colonies in the North Atlantic.

By the time I made it down to Scarborough's South Bay Beach I resembled a painter and decorator without overalls. But the air, thank goodness, was fresh and pure. Dozens of ankle-high sandcastles awaited the encroaching tide. A few women in their early twenties persevered, doggedly, with a game of pissed-up Frisbee. As dusk engulfed the half-moon cove, the promenade jerked to life with flashing lights and spinning wheels.

A middle-aged man wearing large earphones waltzed across the warm sand with a metal detector. Its search coil floated just an inch above the earth, and when it picked up the scent of a coin or ring pull, it whirred and whined like a 1920s theremin. Instinct, journalistic curiosity and my general proclivity to be a downright nosey bastard sent me marching toward him.

"Excuse me, mate," I shouted, startling him from his trance. "What are you looking for?"

"Anything!" he yelled back, with an accent that hinted at London. "You'd be amazed by what gets left on this beach."

David Rahaman, it quickly transpired, was more than just a hobby detectorist. This was his lifeline.

"Due to the pandemic, I lost my job. I was sat at home all last year becoming stressed and depressed, so I decided I'd had enough."

"No benefits?"

"I couldn't get jobseeker's allowance because when my wife died of cancer in 2017, I didn't pay enough National Insurance."

"This is your passion."

"It's my therapy. Metal detecting helps focus my mind. It's an amazing way to feel grounded. It brings all the various pieces together and gives me a single focus."

"And makes you a living, too?"

"If I can hit twenty beaches a month then I'll be looking at bringing in somewhere between £600 and £800, all in pound, 50p, 20p, 10p, 5p, 2p and 1p coins. They're all on this beach!"

I was awestruck. Not only by David's resilience, but also by his ingenuity. He had clearly sunk to a desperate place, but when his wife died, "God bless her soul", he told me, he had turned to a passion that could keep both his mind and body busy.

"I'm heading off on a big adventure. I'm planning to travel all around the coast of the country. Best of all I won't be sat at home doing sweet FA like I was last year, watching episode after episode of *Star Trek*."

I couldn't help myself but ask, "What's the most expensive thing you've ever found?"

"I knew you were going to ask me that. I was down on Brighton beach, and I saw something glint in the sun. It was a stack of coins, with a gold wedding ring on top and a Rolex watch wrapped around it. I waited with it for half an hour to see if someone would come back, and then handed it in to the police. Six months later it still hadn't been claimed, so they gave it to me. Either that person had Alzheimer's and forgot about it or they left it there and committed suicide. I sold that watch for £3,500."

I could so easily be "a David" one day, I thought, as I climbed out of Scarborough early the next morning. Sure, we can plan and dream, but none of us quite know how our lives will play out. There will, inevitably, be bumps and potholes in the road. Most of the time we'll swerve around them, but occasionally we will fall in. The only thing we can really control is the way we react afterward. Do we pine for what we had before? Or do we clamber out, just like David had done, and crack on with life as quickly, and as positively, as possible?

I tried to remind myself of this sentiment when the cable connecting my gear shifter to the Rohloff hub snapped, about a mile south of the Danby Beacon, right in the heart of the North York Moors. Somehow, I'd managed to break the unbreakable, and in the worst possible place. It had barely rained for over a month and the moors were now more Martian than Earth-like. The boulder-strewn cycle path would have been a challenge on a mountain bike, but on a touring bike designed for the road, I could barely ride a few feet without having to jump off and walk.

As if that wasn't already bad enough, my bike was now stuck in one agonising gear and the nearest town was Middlesbrough, some 20 miles to the north. I had no option but to push up every hill, then freewheel down the other side. I quickly went from moving at a satisfying 12 mph to an infuriating 3 mph.

Thank goodness for mobile phones, because while I trudged along, I could ring ahead. Exasperatingly, however, every bike shop in Middlesbrough was either fully booked or closed for the weekend. The only place willing to fit me in – albeit the next day – was a Halfords in Hartlepool, another 13 miles to the north-east.

It became the toughest, slowest and hottest afternoon of the entire trip. Some of the hills had triangular signs at their bases, warning of 25 per cent gradients. Without the breeze from cycling, I poured with sweat. When I occasionally jumped into the saddle, my sodden shorts squished and squealed against the leather.

By the time I made it to the outskirts of Middlesbrough, some 4 hours later than planned, I felt so dehydrated that I bought a 2-litre bottle of water and necked the whole thing in one go. Only later did I find out that this could have led to a potentially deadly state of overhydration but at the time, even 2 litres barely quenched my thirst.

I zigzagged through the city, then took a moment to rest in the shadow of Middlesbrough FC's 35,000 all-seater Riverside Stadium. I'd been there once before, for an FA Cup fifth-round match against Oxford United. On that bitter February day, my dad and I had cheered and shivered together, and warmed our hands on hot pies and cups of steaming Bovril. Of all the thousands of matches we'd seen Oxford play over the years, that one remains etched in my mind. Because on the final whistle I decided to drive the length of England to visit a young woman I'd only just met. Her name was Alana, and in the early hours of the next morning I confessed that I loved her.

———

The empty stadium rattled with ghosts, so I continued north toward the river Tees, through a gritty wasteland of old salt-, steel- and ironworks. These places both fascinated and terrified me. Spooky and ignored, the road was lined with beaten-up shipping containers and abandoned lorry tyres. Chemical refineries belched out sulphury, off-white plumes. A jumpy vixen with three doe-eyed cubs appeared briefly, then vanished in a puff of ginger under a clapboard fence. I was about to cross the river and grind on to Hartlepool, but when I passed a lay-by filled with three parked cars and four men tinkering with expensive cameras, my fingers gripped the brakes without even asking my brain for permission.

Paul, Harry, Geoff and Dave were the members of a Teesside WhatsApp group that shared information about bird sightings in the region. A peregrine falcon had nested in one of the nooks of the Middlesbrough Transporter Bridge and her fluffy fledglings were taking their first nervous flights – to a nearby warehouse, and to adulthood.

I'd never been made to feel so immediately at ease by a group of strangers before. Within 30 seconds of stopping, I'd been offered a coffee, a chocolate bar and a beer. The men waxed lyrical about birds of prey – their markings, their diets, their sounds – then paused mid-sentence to snap at black wisps in mid-flight. Their telephoto lenses were so powerful that a black spot could be blown up to reveal the unique motifs of a bird's wing or the taut sinew in its talons.

Peregrine falcons are the fastest animals on Earth. They can dive at more than 200 mph, three times the speed of a cheetah. No wonder the men were in awe. Some people spend their life savings on a two-week African safari, but there we were, in a worn-out corner of northern England, in the company of the planet's foremost apex predator.

Without the birds, and their twitcher community, the men admitted they'd feel lost. "You've got to have a hobby, man. Birding and photography have kept me sane," said Paul, a grey-stubbled man with a youthful smile, wearing head-to-toe hunting fatigues. "It has kept me out and about and meeting like-minded people."

"Did you struggle with the lockdowns?"

"Massively. I'm used to spending a lot of my life outdoors and I found myself climbing up the walls."

Even at the peak of the pandemic, they ventured out to photograph albatrosses, spotted flycatchers and black-necked grebes. At a time when international borders were closed, there must have been a certain magic in welcoming feathered tourists from overseas. "One policeman gave a few of us a bit of a talking to," laughed Paul. "But we just wanted to go out and check on the local birds. We love sharing this with other people, like you. Some birding communities can be like secret clubs, but we don't see it that way. This is our lifeline."

As I cycled north, the squeal of peregrines grew fainter, but within half an hour Paul had already tagged me in a photo on Twitter. A bright-eyed female, with a pigeon in its grasp. I must have missed the kill by just a few minutes, but I took comfort in knowing that – if only on social media – I was now part of a niche community, in a corner of Britain I may never physically visit again.

———

I suspect that no man had ever been quite so happy to reach Hartlepool. But after 69 miles in the saddle – 30 of which I'd completed in a single gear – I checked into an £18-a-night guest house and stretched my aching legs to an overture of screeching tyres and blaring sirens.

Force of habit always compelled me to book the cheapest possible accommodation. The way I saw it, there was no point in wasting money on a place that I'd only be in for 8, hopefully unconscious, hours. This room, however, was particularly dingy, even by my standards. The toilet didn't have a seat. The shower didn't have a curtain. The TV didn't have a remote. Two of the three pillows didn't have cases. The underside of the bed sheet was splattered with blood, or at best tikka masala.

A mangy old crow landed on the window ledge, took one look, turned up its beak and flew off. The window looked out to an alley-cum-rubbish tip that rustled from beneath. I counted no fewer than three used condoms, eight surgical face masks and a pair of ice skates. It was unclear if the items were somehow related.

I slept for as long as I could, then set up camp outside the Halfords until it opened. The initial triage was far from encouraging. The first mechanic perused, tutted and hummed, then decided it couldn't be fixed. The cabling was far too specialist and his expertise only stretched as far as bolting stabilisers on to children's bikes.

This meant that I had to wait another 2 agonising hours for the more experienced mechanic to arrive. Time I spent weighing up the potential options and outcomes:

- Hope that he had the skills, tools and confidence to try and fix it.
- Abort the whole trip in Hartlepool and get the train home.
- Attempt to cycle to John o'Groats on my new single speed.
- Buy the cheapest bike I could find in Halfords and hope it had the muscle to carry me to the finish line.
- Take to social media and see if someone would lend, rent or give me a bike.
- Pack a bag and walk the rest of the way.

As it turned out, Andrew Smith wasn't just a bike mechanic but an engineering marvel. Dyson, Mitsubishi, Boeing and NASA should be fighting over this man's signature, because for 90 minutes, while I paced around the store like an expecting father in a maternity ward, he brought my bicycle, and my entire trip, back to life.

Rohloff hubs are so complicated that 99 per cent of mechanics wouldn't risk their reputations – or their wages – on trying to fix one. But with the help of a few German YouTube videos, he did just that. He then tightened up my brakes, replaced the inner tubes and realigned the saddle and headset. He got me back on my way, quickly and efficiently, through no other instinct than to simply play a small part in my big adventure. He only charged me £30. I would have happily paid ten times that.

For the rest of the afternoon, I had a spring in my step. I was in a corner of Britain that I barely knew, but strangers felt like old friends. I was alone, but far from lonely.

———

I pushed on into a biting headwind. The North Sea growled and howled and belched fizzing whitecaps on to the pebbled beaches of Horden and Dawdon. Tree trunks swirled in the churning shallows. A Dobermann looked reluctant to leave the warm boot of its Subaru.

By the time I reached South Shields, my ears roared, and when I stopped at a petrol station to eat, I caught sight of my reflection in a petrol-station window. Scraggly and bedraggled, I resembled Worzel Gummidge. I couldn't remember the last time I'd washed my clothes. Goodness knows what sort of fetid odour I must have been giving off.

I had no idea where I'd end up that night, yet luck seemed stacked in my favour. I'd received a message on Twitter from a stranger – Claire Thorburn – who had been following my adventure around the country.

> Welcome to the north-east. I've arranged for you to stay at a pub in Blyth tonight. Our shout. Get some food too. Tomorrow you can camp at our place in Bamburgh. Let me know how you're getting on.

It always seemed to be the way. When things were going badly, they became very bad, often very quickly. But when things went well, generally they went extremely well. When I first started travelling in my late teens, I was naturally wary of offers like these. What's the catch? I would wonder, somewhat suspiciously.

A decade and a half on, however, and I'd learned that the world was a good place, filled with good people who liked doing nice things for one another. Of course, no one wants to be seen as a freeloader or exploitative of someone's kindness, but it seemed crazy to shiver in a tent when a warm room was available.

This was also one of the reasons why I'd set off on the trip in the first place: to regain a wonder for a life unplanned. Because it was the wonder that had all but vanished.

FORTH:
SMOKING LIKE A KIPPER

Watching TV in your dirty pants, however, can only be so wondrous. But after almost cycling the entire length of the country, I figured that I could adopt a laissez-faire approach to personal hygiene without giving myself too much of a hard time. In the evenings I took a strange pride in using the fewest possible calories. My clothes festered where they fell, and I dared not rummage too deep in my panniers. They were now – almost certainly – the breeding ground for a new tropical disease that would give Ebola a run for its money.

It was a delicious night, out of the wind, between soft sheets with scarcely a blemish, let alone a bodily fluid. I'd held back on alcohol and, an hour before sleep, turned the lights down low and my phone off. I was determined to come out stronger, to return home a better, and hopefully easier, version of me. Not only for myself, but for Alana, too. If I simply fell back into my old ways, then what was the point?

I only possessed finite reserves – of energy, of patience, of concentration. Sure, I could occasionally push myself beyond what I thought was physically possible, but in doing so I opened myself up to injury. Sometimes of the body, but almost always of the mind. Just because I *could* cycle 100 miles, didn't mean that I *should*. Just because I *could* survive without a night's sleep, didn't make it right.

I slept for 5 hours without as much as a snort, then drank decaf coffee until the street lights clocked off. Dawn broke across the North Sea, bright and silvery, like the shiny underbelly of a marlin. There was barely a scar on the eastern horizon, just a single giant container ship heading north, maybe south. To Scotland, maybe Spain.

I imagined the crew that might be taking breakfast on board. Filipino deckhands, Greek mates, a grizzly Norwegian skipper with a beard like Captain Birdseye. Dozens of transient souls, all on adventures of their own.

Northumberland's dunes hissed in the wind. Waist-high beachgrass tussled in clumps. No peregrine falcons, but fulmars, kittiwakes, gannets and terns. Clean and empty, it was hard to imagine why anyone would join the masses in Cornwall when you could have a northern beach entirely to yourself. I followed a cycle path and didn't pass a single person for 2 silent hours. Then, on an empty stretch of sand away to my right, I saw a shape so alien, so out of place, I had to take a closer look.

The carcass of a minke whale, perhaps 25 or 30 feet long, was rotting in the summer sun and oozing a putrid goo, part fishing chum, part farm slurry. It gave off an odour so grotesque that it resembled nothing else on Earth. I edged closer, through ankle-breaking rock pools and across patches of greasy seaweed.

It had two barnacled pectoral fins the size of washing machines and a tail fin that stretched as wide as a family saloon. Ugly but magnificent, its gurning grooved jaw had been pecked and dismantled by a thousand tiny beaks.

I couldn't get within 50 feet without retching. And that felt more than close enough. Although it looked like the whale's skin had been broken and breached, I wasn't prepared to push my luck. Whale blubber isn't porous, therefore when its heart stops beating, methane, carbon dioxide and nitrogen can build up quickly. Cadavers often swell up, like massive offal balloons.

There have been several infamous explosions over the past century. In Oregon in 1970, a few idiots decided to blow up a dead whale with dynamite. By all accounts, they used far too much, and chunks the size of coffee tables flattened cars 2 miles away. In 2013, a YouTube video went viral when a 45-foot-long sperm whale exploded in the Faeroe Islands and almost killed the imbecile that had been cutting it open. But perhaps the most notable tale of all played out in Taiwan in 2004. A 60-tonne sperm whale with – according to the *Taipei Times* – a 5-foot penis, was being transported through the city of Tainan when it unexpectedly blew up, covering hundreds of people, cars and shops with its pungent innards.

Even upwind, the smell was too much, so I continued down the beach. A couple with a particularly hungry-looking Labrador were bounding toward the whale with reckless abandon.

"I wouldn't get too close," I said, with all the authority of David Attenborough.

"Should we tell someone?" said the woman.

"Tell who?"

"I don't know, the RSPCA?"

"Why? It's dead. What exactly are they going to do?"

"I think people should know."

I left the pair to take selfies beside its bulbous tummy. If a whale dies on a beach and no one puts a photo of it on Facebook, did that whale die at all?

———

I reached Bamburgh sometime around late afternoon. Its medieval castle had loomed large on the horizon all day, but when I finally saw it from beneath, it was almost too vast to comprehend. Grand turrets rose up from a mount of steep, impenetrable grass. A Union Jack blew stiff in the breeze. The North Sea snarled and frothed ashore in shire horse-sized waves.

The village beneath was busy with tourists dawdling with ice creams. On the outfield of an immaculate cricket pitch, a mob of pensioners in white coats knocked croquet balls from one hoop to another. It looked and felt about as *Midsomer Murders* as you could get.

Claire Thorburn had told me to ask for her at the castle gates. I assumed that she worked for the property in some capacity, which she did, kind of. However, it quickly transpired that she and her husband, Francis Watson-Armstrong, didn't just live in Bamburgh. In fact, they owned the very castle itself. And when she'd said I could camp at their "place", what she really meant was that I could pitch my tent in the castle grounds.

Francis was busy dealing with a Pinewood Studios film crew that was still on site from the night before. We shook hands and passed pleasantries, but he looked exhausted and had to "get back home to feed the dogs". He was just 22 when he inherited the castle from his father, but in 2001 took the decision to relocate to a nearby farm. "It sounds nobby to say I own it," he told the BBC in 2019. "I'm more like its current keeper. I just keep it standing."

The couple turned out to be some of the friendliest, most generous and down-to-earth people I'd ever met. Claire gave me a quick tour of the castle before it closed; through an armoury filled with 1,000-year-old swords and seventeenth-century crossbows. Then into the teak-lined King's Hall that echoed with the heels of umpteen opulent events. We snooped around staterooms where royalty had slept, then finished off at the castle's gift shop.

"Grab whatever you want," said Claire, as she threw fudge, chocolate, crisps and fizzy drinks into a paper bag. "Hold on," she said, marching over to a fridge. "You might as well have all these sandwiches, too. Keep your energy up. I've loved following your journey from afar. This is the least we can do."

Before Claire joined Francis back at the farm, she showed me where I could camp – a patch of wonderfully flat grass, beneath a sandstone windmill, about a hundred feet above the cricket pitch.

"What has this period been like for you here?" I asked.

"The challenge is immense in a normal year," said Claire, her blonde, shoulder-length hair twirling in the wind. "But Covid made things doubly hard. We'd just had our best ever year. In 2019 we had 170,000 visitors, but then the rug was pulled from beneath us."

Owning a castle was clearly as much a burden as it was a privilege. Pandemic or no pandemic, it still cost several hundred thousand pounds a year, just to keep the building and its surroundings in shape.

"This 2,000-year-old castle is doing its best to fall down all around us," said Claire.

"The work must never stop."

"Only now, for example, are we starting to realise that the way it was rebuilt in the Victorian era, with steel and sandstone, doesn't do at all well in the salty sea air."

"It must be a huge concern."

"We have a massive responsibility, and we don't want things to fail on our watch."

Despite the worry and stress, however, Claire told me that she never stopped appreciating just how lucky they were. And while many of us spent our lockdowns cooped up in houses and apartments, Claire and Francis might have experienced the most unique quarantine on Earth.

"It was a bit like Christmas Day. Over and over again."

"I don't think I'd like that."

"There was this kind of bleak emptiness, a vacuum of quiet. It was a very frightening place to be at times, but it gave us an opportunity to realise exactly what we have here. It really sharpened our love and appreciation for this place."

Claire left me at the castle in the company of "Dave the Moneyer" – a 67-year-old Anglo-Saxon impersonator with a bushy grey beard, glasses with lenses the size of pennies and a costume made from stained rags. The castle website described Dave as "quite a character" which, I would quickly learn, was underplaying things somewhat.

He spent his summers living in a wooden hut, covered by a linen-and-leather canopy that he'd weatherproofed with lanolin, pig fat and fish oil. By day, he helped visitors mint their own coins, but by night he drank ale beside a fire, and I was only too happy to keep him company.

I immediately warmed to Dave. He was a kind man with a big heart and an insatiable appetite for chewing the fat. Over the course of just a couple of hours, our conversation drifted from the Channel 4 archaeology show *Time Team*, to family planning, ghost sightings, the national inflation of the price of fish and chips, the annual depreciation of his Mercedes Transporter van and the onset of his Parkinson's disease.

"A positive mental attitude and lots of sea air," scoffed Dave, as we drank Guinness from rusty tankards. "I'm planning to keep my van going for another ten years, then I fully expect to be leaving this planet in a box!"

The hut was warm and cosy. The only issue, however, was that it would have been unauthentic to have a wood burner with a flue. Without one, the hut became a sooty hot box, and I was soon smoking like a kipper.

There was only so long I could tough it out, so I thanked Dave for his company and ran off to bed. The night was crisp, and the sky effervesced with a billion twinkling stars. It seemed like a good idea to sleep in my bivouac instead of putting up a tent while half-cut. I couldn't see a single cloud; north, south, east or west. What could possibly go wrong?

I woke up a few hours later, being rattled by wind and drenched in drizzle. It was now far too blustery to put the tent up, but thankfully the windmill door had been left ajar and I sat out the rest of the night in a dusty room filled with old radiators, mouse droppings and cans of motor oil.

I was itching to cross the border into Scotland, but Holy Island, or Lindisfarne, was just a 10-mile detour and it felt criminal not to see it while I was passing. By a stroke of luck, the tide was low, allowing me to cross the sand causeway that separates it from the Northumberland mainland. And I'm glad I went, if only for the people watching.

The island was aswarm with day trippers, most of whom were moving so sluggishly they were at risk of falling over. Hundreds more were arriving on coaches, dressed as though they were about to embark on a three-year natural-history film shoot. One man had a telephoto lens that was bigger than his wife. Most were wearing gaiters, just in case they encountered a lost rattlesnake.

I quickly decided that I couldn't be around crowds while I was on such a personal and, at least comparatively, fast-paced journey. I locked up my bike, practically jogged to the castle for a 5-minute look, then retreated as quickly as possible. I'm sure it's a wonderful place to be at times – perhaps in a raging winter storm – but nowhere on the planet, in my opinion, is such a "must see" that it's worth sharing with thousands of other people.

The same could be said for Berwick-upon-Tweed, a twee little town filled with tea rooms and bookshops. Half a dozen people on Twitter had told me to stop and have a look around, but when I arrived it was so packed with other humans that I couldn't muster the energy to trudge around looking at the soles of someone else's shoes. I'd wanted to have lunch in a nice little café, but most had long queues outside them. Instead, I settled for a sandwich at the nearby Morrisons.

Some people will call me a philistine, but the great joy of travelling by bicycle is that you rarely feel the need to stop and look at anything in particular. You're hoovering up sights, sounds, tastes and smells, every single second. The journey *is* the experience, not the physical waypoints you might plot along the route.

That's why, for me, the greatest joy came a few miles later when I spotted three Saltires flipping and flapping on the wind. Riding beneath them gave me a buzz of exhausted pride that I'd only ever felt when I completed a marathon. I was still a long way from the finish line, but at least I was now on the home stretch.

It hadn't rained in Scotland for weeks, but within half a mile of crossing the border I was soaked. Thankfully, it only lasted 10 minutes, and when the clouds parted the land throbbed with luscious petrichor, so thick and moreish the air tasted of watermelon.

The next 20 miles turned out to be some of the most picturesque in Britain. Part lazy coast road, part empty single track, the route climbed and fell through meadows of sunbathing cows then plunged into hidden coves.

At the top of blustery hills, I could see further north into Scotland, but also back south, to Lindisfarne and beyond. The pasture in between had been stained mauvy-red by thousands of bell-shaped foxgloves and a million delicate sea pinks.

———

The fastest man to cycle around the world, Mark Beaumont, had arranged for me to meet a friend of his, Markus Stitz, the first person to complete a loop of the planet on a single speed. I found him waiting for me in Dunbar, outside the birthplace of the Scottish-American naturalist, John Muir.

Originally from Germany, Markus had been living in Scotland for more than a decade. Lean and athletic, he'd cycled 21,000 miles through 26 countries, in just one gear. It was incomprehensible. I'd struggled with 30 miles. "On some mountain roads you can't do a full turn of the crank," he told me. "You just have to do a fraction of a turn, over and over."

I followed him through golf links and around East Lothian's pebbled shores. Seams of cream, black and red volcanic rock had formed layers beneath the grassy cliffs. They resembled giant lasagne sheets specked in ragu and cracked black pepper.

Markus had grown up in Berlin while it was still behind the Iron Curtain. Had that inspired him to explore more? I wondered.

"I was ten when the wall came down. Until then, I had very restricted freedoms. Throughout my life, freedom became an incredibly important thing to me."

"A bit like running away."

"It almost certainly played a part in me wanting to explore."

"How did the pandemic make you feel?"

"It reminded me a lot of being a child again. If we're not careful, we can really take freedom for granted."

As we cycled through golden barley fields that whistled and bristled in the breeze, Markus was clearly at ease. For him – and for me – being outside was the simplest of all simple joys.

"I think the pandemic made us a lot more conscious of our relationship with the environment. As individuals we are only small, but we still have an important role to play. Without green spaces to enjoy, life would be a horrible time. I hated being cooped up in my apartment in Edinburgh."

"Did that impact your mental health?"

"Without the space to ride my bike I would have been absolutely miserable."

Unable to travel as far and as wide as usual, Markus began mapping cycle routes much closer to home.

"Lockdown in Edinburgh felt like a never-ending Sunday. I cycled to keep my spirits up."

"With Mark Beaumont? You two have covered some serious miles over the years!"

"We did some amazing winter rides, at night and in the snow. Bike touring is booming."

"The lockdown effect."

"I think its popularity has been amplified by the pandemic because it's an activity that gives people breathing space from the world. I always come back from my trips seeing things in a totally different light."

I left Markus in North Berwick and pitched my tent on the grassy dunes surrounding Yellowcraig beach, 2 hours east of Edinburgh. Butterflies fluttered beneath the russet sunset. Gannets skipped over glassy shallows garnished in sprigs of kelp.

The sun barely set on that midsummer night, and by 2 a.m. a wood pigeon was cooing loudly on a nearby branch. Thankfully though, the sunrise turned out to be just as impressive as the sunset. Streaks of amethyst washed through the tussled grass, like purple rinse reinvigorating a pensioner's grey perm. I was packed up by 4 a.m. and eating breakfast in Edinburgh by 8 a.m.

———

Alana's parents' friends Jane and Stephen had kindly offered to let me rest at their house for the day and night. I'd only ever met them once, at a family lunch, but they turned out to be generous and chilled-out people who were only too happy to let me empty their fridge and use their washing machine and shower.

Jane had recently retired from working in education, while Stephen was a professor of biology at Edinburgh University. After sleeping in a tent, their three-storey Victorian town house was like a palace. Complete with marble worktops, high ceilings and long shelves filled with novels with stressed spines, their home was neither too big nor too small. For me, it epitomised the middle-class dream that Alana and I aspired to. I messaged Alana: "This house is mega."

I'd been apprehensive about gatecrashing on them, but I can't have felt too uneasy because I napped through the afternoon, an almost unprecedented feat. In the early evening, we drank wine in their immaculate garden, then ate plates piled high with fresh salad, home-made bread and wild salmon fillets. "I could get used to this," I joked. "Certainly beats cereal bars and noodles."

———

They waved me off the next morning. I felt as clean and as healthy as I'd ever been. And for the first time in living memory, I smelled of washing detergent and expensive shower gel, not dried sweat and mouldy bananas.

Edinburgh pulsed with a nervous energy. It was the summer solstice, and the mercury was set to rise to a Balearic 25°C. "Taps aff" weather, if ever you'd seen it.

There was also the small matter of a football match. At 8 p.m. that evening, England would host Scotland at Wembley, in their first meeting at a major tournament for 24 years. "Come on Scotland! Come on Scotland!" cheered a group of teenage boys and girls, as they waited for their school bus. By the time I'd reached the north-west outskirts of the capital I'd counted 28 men in kilts, nine of whom also had Saltires painted on their faces.

Before crossing the Firth of Forth at Queensferry, I called in on the travel writer Robin McKelvie, a blonde-haired, blue-eyed Scot in his late forties, who'd kindly offered to fill me up with Tunnock's teacakes. His garden sloped north toward the banks of the estuary. The Forth Bridge was so vast, and so close, it practically cast a shadow over the writing shed he shared with his two cats, Bobby and Molly.

Robin had been a supporter of my journey right from the off and despite having never met in person, I knew from our correspondence that we'd get on. He was a youthful and enthusiastic man, with the energy reserves required of any successful freelancer. He'd also found a way to balance travel writing with a family life.

"I used to work hours that would make a junior doctor blush. But then the pandemic came along, and it became something of an existential crisis. What on earth does a travel writer do when no one can travel?"

"Grab a bike and cycle around Britain?" We laughed.

"For years I'd wondered what I might do with my life if I had more time, but then, suddenly, I had it."

Robin invested hundreds of hours into his garden. He grew flowers and vegetables, built furniture and a wood store. "I wasn't a writer any more; I was a builder, a digger. I whistled to the same robin, and it always whistled back."

"It sounds like you've had your own eureka moment?"

"I learned to hold and cherish nature in a way I'd seldom experienced before."

"And you didn't have to go to the Serengeti or the Amazon."

"I found a state of pure mindfulness, right here in my back garden. Some people pay hundreds of pounds for what I discovered for free."

Fifteen years my senior, Robin urged me to never lose sight of what really mattered in life.

"Spend as much time as you can with your family. I wish I'd taken more proper weekends off, every single week. Would we have paid off quite as much of the mortgage? Probably not. But family is everything. I've also set new resolutions: a maximum of one foreign trip a month. And never cancel on your friends. Even if a last-minute offer comes in to go to the Maldives or Thailand; tough. Real-life relationships are number one, otherwise you'll always be that guy who is defined by his job."

He then instructed me to sit on a beanbag in the bottom corner of the garden. It was dappled in an acne of warm summer light. "This is kind of my forest bathing spot. I'm going to leave you here for twenty minutes. I want you to just chill out. No phone, no thinking about where you've got to go next. Just try and simply be."

I closed my eyes. My mind whirred. I drifted from people to places, from memories to fantasies. My ears latched on to the discordant pattern of vehicles hitting the same loose metal plate somewhere on the bridge. Clunk, clunk, clunk. A passenger jet roared overhead, igniting a daydream about the hundreds of people on board. They're off to Iceland, I assumed, before fast-forwarding through images of glaciers and volcanoes, my mind's eye spinning like the reels of a fruit machine.

I felt self-conscious, as though I could see myself from a few feet away. One of those poseurs who meditates cross-legged in busy parks. I wanted to get up and move around, to give in to the temptation of familiar, frantic thought.

But then one of the cats walked over, dropped on to its back and started purring for a belly rub. With its warm fur between my fingers, I made the effort to breathe. Six breaths in, 12 breaths out. Shallow at first, high into my chest and shoulder blades. But with every inhalation I visualised my diaphragm relaxing, perhaps by 0.1 per cent each time.

Something heavy, probably a bee, landed on my nose, then flew away. My tongue glided through the gap between my incisors and inner lip, picking up remnants of sweet milk chocolate. When my mind wandered, I pictured my hand on the cat's tummy. To have jerked away would have scared it, and to have thrown in the towel would have filled me with shame.

So, I dozed. It might have been 20 minutes, it might have been an hour, but when Robin returned, the flesh on my cheeks hung lighter than usual. For a few short minutes, Queensferry was the centre of my universe. The anaesthesia of sleep had produced a mental clarity that I was desperate to have more of in my life.

"Just go easy on yourself," said Robin. "I don't really know you, but you're moving at a hundred miles an hour. Don't forget to cut yourself some slack occasionally. Find the time to just be."

From that moment on, I vowed to spend 20 minutes a day in silence, at least for the rest of my ride. Not "meditation", not "prayer", just silence. Whatever rush I found myself in, I had to make time to pause, to breathe, to come out stronger. I would be a civilian again soon, a friend, a fiancé. A road man no longer.

———

I crossed the Forth Bridge and cycled north-east, through place names I only knew from BBC 5 Live's classified football results, as read by the Scottish broadcaster James Alexander Gordon. To me, his voice was the sound of the 1990s. My 1990s. "Dunfermline Athletic, one. Cowdenbeath, one," I said aloud, satirising his calm enunciation. "Raith Rovers, four. East Fife, two."

The afternoon grew warm and muggy. Hundreds of acres of potato and raspberry fields looked luscious and ripe for picking. I tried my best to avoid the Lomond Hills – they sounded exhausting – but by the time I reached Cupar, a pretty little town with pansies in window boxes, I'd climbed almost 3,000 feet.

Every shop, café and bus stop buzzed with pre-match nerves. "This morning, 150 lads set off on three coaches," said a woman outside Argos. "They were already blootered when they left at 5 a.m. God knows what state they'll be in by kick-off!"

It felt mischievous to be behind enemy lines. Most of the banter was in good nature, but I decided to stay mute all the same. "We'll stick it up those English bastards!" screamed a grizzly man carrying two pints of cider into a busy pub garden. Meanwhile, every café, bar and restaurant blared out the unofficial ditty of the Tartan Army, the 1977 hit "Yes Sir, I Can Boogie" by the Spanish band Baccara. A song so catchy that its rhythm and lyrics will remain indelibly etched into my inner brain forever.

My loose plan had been to cycle all day, then find a pub near a beach somewhere north-east of Dundee. I could tally up 80 or 90 miles, watch the game and "wild camp". If England scored, I'd try not to blow my cover. If Scotland did, I'd jump up and high five my faux compatriots. But then, with about 60 miles on the clock, Jane messaged me.

> Hope you're getting on OK. Our friends Dave and Wendy live in Tayport, just south of Dundee. They've said you can camp in their garden and watch the game. Head to the lighthouse next to the river. (They're English)

It would have been stubborn, and rude, of me to ignore such a kind offer, especially one that immediately piqued my interest. A lighthouse. Another lighthouse. From Muckle Flugga to Bishop Rock, and now to Tayport, these beacons had illuminated my way. Better still, this one had been thrust into my lap, not by design, but by divine intervention.

I arrived just before 7 p.m. and found Dave, a reader in structural biology at Dundee University, enjoying an early evening cigarette in his garden beside the river Tay. On the far side of the water, Dundee's church spires caught the first reddish embers of a waning sun. But high above us, a 79-foot whitewashed lighthouse, designed by Robert Stevenson and built by Trinity House in 1823, seemed to sway in the fleeting clouds. It was enough to induce vertigo.

Wendy, a gynaecology consultant, arrived home not long after. She'd retired the year before, but returned part-time to help the NHS in its hour of need. She looked utterly exhausted. Goodness knows what sort of drama she must have dealt with that day. The journalist in me was desperate to quiz her about the long hours and her struggles on the frontline. But the polite house guest held back. This was her night off and her safe space. She didn't need me rabbiting on.

Instead, we chatted about Brexit, the weather and house prices, the staples of modern British conversation. We ate chicken fajitas with fresh guacamole and grated cheese as warm light streamed into a living room of dark teak furnishings, Persian rugs and a wood burner enjoying a few months' downtime.

As it turned out, neither of them had much knowledge of or interest in football, but they humoured me all the same. It was just a shame the game finished 0–0, barely a scoreline to get the pulses racing. "You know you don't have to camp?" said Wendy, as we cleared the dirty dishes. "Because we've got four spare rooms. You are more than welcome."

I looked at the empty beer bottles on the coffee table, then out to the swirling river Tay. Once again, total strangers had taken me in, filled my belly and left me warm with their kindness and generosity.

"Well, if you insist," I said, before stumbling off to a room filled with cuddly toys, musical instruments and a pair of pink ballet shoes hanging on the back of the door.

CROMARTY:
SWIMMING IN SYRUP

The forecast was dreadful. Drizzle and 20 mph headwinds for at least the next few days. It would have made sense to divert inland and avoid the worst of it rolling in off the North Sea, but I'd travelled this far by mostly following the coast of Britain and I didn't want to look back on my deathbed and regret cutting off the "nose" of Scotland.

With a bellyful of toast and marmalade, I set off cautiously, into a dank and ugly fug. It was hard to imagine Dundee any other way. Grey walls, grey road, grey rain. I passed a church welcoming a christening party. A toddler looked nervous. About to be plunged into Nikwax, no doubt.

In a strange way, though, the bad-weather days nearly always became the most efficient. I ploughed on, powered by petrol-station food and dance music. By the time I reached Montrose, 35 miles north-east of Tayport, I'd eaten 30 Jaffa Cakes and four bananas and had listened to an hour-long Carl Cox mix three times on repeat.

The A92 – the main road running up the east coast of Aberdeenshire – swept through a tableland of oilseed rape. Almost ready for harvest, millions of yellow stamens burped mustardy pollen into the mizzle, so cloying it was like swimming in syrup.

The afternoon brought torrential rain, cold and fierce. I had to take shelter in a barn filled with steaming cows and their suckling calves. As the roof rattled above us, they emitted a familiar, sentient warmth. But soon my teeth were chattering. There was no way I could camp out without killing both my laptop and my spirit. So, I set myself the challenge of reaching Aberdeen by nightfall. If I could make it, I'd reward myself with a hotel and a curry.

I'd like to say the journey was a gruelling ordeal, but if I'm honest, the miles took care of themselves. Visibility was poor, which meant my imagination couldn't drift off to the horizon and beyond.

Earlier on in my adventure, this might have triggered a state of panic – I'd been wary of being alone with my thoughts, with my friends, for fear of what I might discover deep within. But life felt different now. Less intense, nowhere near as overwhelming. As the mist drew in around me, I fixated on the patch of road just a few feet ahead. Simple and rhythmic, a meditative daze engulfed me. Even with a headwind, I moved at 14 mph.

I held off booking accommodation until the bitter end, and for £30 bagged a four-star hotel, right in the middle of Aberdeen. It felt like I'd hit the jackpot, but I then made the mistake of sitting down in the first curry house I found. The menu looked more like a catalogue at Sotheby's. Every waiter was dressed in Gucci, Armani or Dior. Every dish appeared from the kitchen with flashing lights and sparklers.

You might assume that the further north you go in Britain, the cheaper things become. This is a myth. According to the human-resources consultancy firm Mercer, Aberdeen is the third most expensive city to live in in Britain after Birmingham and London. The North Sea oil and gas boom saw to that. Four of the five occupied tables were taken up by single men with unkempt beards.

The meal was so expensive that, in a strange way, I wanted it to be terrible, so that I could grumble about the cost to Alana. It was, however, one of the most delicious things I'd ever eaten, and it was served with the pomp and razzmatazz of Cirque du Soleil.

The previous year had made me so miserly and tight-fisted that I found it hard to spend money. The constant stress of a mortgage that was going unpaid and a bank account that had hit the red ground me into a state of morbid austerity. But now that a trickle of money was rolling in, I had to force myself to start living again rather than simply surviving. The economic fightback was on, one outrageously priced bhuna at a time.

I slept well, showered and packed up, then took full advantage of the complimentary breakfast and bottomless black coffee. Inevitably, nature called shortly after, and I returned to my room. What happened next, however, was one of the most traumatic few minutes of my life.

It felt as though I was shitting a serrated steak knife covered in broken glass. At first, I put this down to the spice from the night before, but when I looked between my legs, I was horrified to see a toilet bowl filled with bright-red blood. For 20 minutes, I struggled to stem the flow, while simultaneously relieving my heavy bowels. With toilet roll stuffed between my arse cheeks I jumped back in the shower, then dried myself off with a hairdryer.

Surrounded by bloodied tissues, there was no ignoring the fact that I was quite seriously injured. I was already filthy, but the last thing I needed was an open wound, down there.

What would Alana say or do in this situation? I thought to myself. She'd tell me to stay calm and think about it rationally. What had happened? And why? I pondered these questions as I slowed my breathing, cutting off the anxiety at source, before it could course through my body and mind.

I'd clearly made myself so dehydrated again that my intestines had been deprived of the water required to soften my stools. If I was honest with myself, this was entirely self-inflicted. I'd grown so fixated on reaching the finish line that I'd assumed my body could simply take care of itself. Meanwhile, I'd been filling it to the brim with biscuits, cakes, bread and beer.

I patched myself up the best I could then stopped at the nearest shop to buy as much fibre as I could carry. Six apples, a bag of prunes, a head of broccoli and a box of bran flakes. Too little, far too late, but at least it felt like I was taking some control.

"Good morning. How are you today?" asked the sprightly teenage girl behind the till.

"I'm bleeding from the arsehole!" I was tempted to reveal, but I didn't have the heart to ruin her day, too.

———

Dark and gloomy, my journey was at risk of seeming pointless again. It was the thirty-fifth day of the second leg and I was still cycling in the wrong direction, for no other reason than a commitment to an entirely arbitrary route. Annoyingly, I couldn't even see the sea from the cycle path. I could have been anywhere.

I skirted around meadows flooded with daisies and cut through muddy farms conquered by chickens and geese. I barely saw a human for 4 lonely hours. I also didn't have as much as a sliver of mobile phone reception, at a time when I needed it the most.

After 50 solitary miles battling into a headwind, I reached Fraserburgh – the biggest shellfish port in Scotland – and collapsed on to a bench beside a few bustling fishing boats. I could have cried, if it wasn't for all the burly men in overalls.

Just as I was starting to feel physically bulletproof and psychologically free, a hurdle had been placed in my way. I only had myself to blame, but I felt cheated by the world. "Why did this have to happen to me?" I said aloud, over and over. In normal times, I enjoyed being alone, but suddenly, I hankered for company.

I had to find a second wind. Without one, my trip would end there and then. I was so sore that I found it hard to sit on the saddle, and the more I cycled, the less I could tell if the moisture between my legs was sweat or blood.

Finally, I had enough mobile phone signal to reach Alana. Her soft voice cascaded through my ears and down to my aching heart. She was cock-a-hoop. After a year of cancelled contracts and hundreds of emails of rejection, she had a new client that would help pay our bills. But it was about so much more than money. It was about identity and belonging. A feeling of being in control.

"So, what did you want to tell me?" she asked. At which point I brought the mood down with a thud. I could hear her grimace down the phone. "OK, well, you know it's nothing serious, don't you? You've been here before. Stay calm and think about it rationally."

It was all I needed to hear. I'd put my body through hell, and it was only natural that something like this would happen again. I promised her that I'd strive to eat more fruit and vegetables, drink more water and less beer. "Don't worry," she said. "You'll heal. You did last time. Just take it easy. You're not in a race!"

I finally turned west, and for the first time in 400 miles I had the wind at my back. Maybe it stopped raining, maybe the sun burst through the heavy clouds. I don't quite remember. All I know is that my body was numbed by love, by the intangible anaesthesia of knowing that someone, somewhere, cared.

I'd been determined to camp. It seemed crazy that I was lugging a tent and sleeping bag around the country and not using it more often. But by the time I reached Pennan, the small seaside village where the 1983 Burt Lancaster film *Local Hero* was shot, Alana had booked me into a hotel 12 miles further down the coast.

You can't wild camp while you're in this state. You need to be clean.
Don't try and be a hero. Anyway, I'm celebrating. It's paid for.

Fresh and salt-beaten, Banffshire was easily one of the most striking corners of Britain. Villages clung to cliff sides. Boats huddled together in little harbours. The North Sea crashed ashore in stocky rollers, with frothy shoulders as broad as heavyweights. As a cyclist, though, the hills were too much, too steep. Some had 20 per cent gradients and were impossible to ride.

This corner of Scotland also seemed lonelier than the rest. It wasn't on a thoroughfare to anywhere and the car parks at trail heads sat eerily empty.

If I'm honest, I was relieved that Alana had booked me a hotel, because if I'd stubbornly slept in a forgotten cove, all on my own, I don't know where my imagination might have wandered. I was paranoid of sepsis. Of the body and the mind.

I finally made it to the Fife Lodge Hotel in Banff at just after 7 p.m. I'd cycled another 80 miles and climbed close to 3,000 feet. If I'd gone directly, and not followed the coast, it would have been 55 miles and half the ascent. It had certainly felt like a fool's errand at times, but at least it was over now. I was less than 200 miles from John o'Groats. For some of it – hopefully – I'd have the wind at my back.

The hotel had only recently changed hands and the scent of fresh paint filled a reception room adorned with tartan carpets and stained teak furnishings. A hum of tourist chatter filled the restaurant, but I settled into a soft leather armchair in the bar and ordered a pint of dark ale, a veggie burger, a side salad and an extra plate of steamed greens.

After a year of mixed messages from Westminster and Holyrood, the new owner seemed jaded. "There have been so many inconsistencies and hypocrisies from politicians," said John Cox. "We had a wedding recently in which they weren't allowed any music, singing or dancing. I've heard stories about people having quiz nights after their wedding meals because there was nothing else to do. But then you watch the TV and see thousands of football fans all sitting next to each other. It all seems very unfair."

According to the research agency CGA, the hospitality sector lost £80 billion in the first 12 months of the pandemic alone, down 64 per cent on the previous year. The UK's biggest hotel chain, Premier Inn, reported a £1-billion annual loss, while more than 2,500 British pubs called last orders for the very last time. Why would anyone want to enter an industry in such dire straits?

"I had a gut feeling that things would change, and people would be desperate for normal life again."

"And it paid off."

"There was a pent-up demand for getting out and seeing friends and family."

"This place must mean a lot to people."

"Hotels also play a major role in local economies. If we don't strive to keep these places, then people take their disposable income to other towns and villages. Take weddings, for example. Not only is it a huge market for us, but there's also a big spin-off to people like florists and taxi drivers."

"Despite the hardships of the previous year, what lessons have you learned for the future?"

"I'll never be complacent in business again, that's for sure. It's essential that we constantly change with the times."

After dinner, I stripped in front of the bathroom mirror. Wide at the hips, narrow at the shoulders, I resembled a pear. My face was raw and gaunt, and my palms were calloused from gripping the handlebars too tight. It was hard to determine if I was in full fitness or on the verge of illness. It wasn't until gone midnight that the day's adrenaline finally ran dry, and I nodded off, dreading the pain that might unfold the next morning.

At the start of my journey, all I'd wanted was to be away. But now, so close, yet still so far from the end, I fantasised of home. The predictability of the afternoon light rounding from one side of our flat to the other. The silky touch of my writing desk and the familiar creak it made when I scrawled in a notebook. The way my favourite coffee mug sat snug between my thumb and forefinger.

The journalist wanted a rousing climax, a pay-off, a twist. But life rarely has the arc of fiction. Instead, the day just crept on, 1 mile at a time, 1 passing hour after another. Squalls rolled in and soaked me to the skin, then the sun emerged and turned my skin and clothing crisp.

I finally holed up in Nairn, in a pub particularly popular with golfers and Boorman–McGregor types. On one side of the bar, three men in polo shirts were "absolutely knackered" from their 27 holes (with a buggy). On the other side, two couples in black leathers droned on about how tired they were from driving Land's End to John o'Groats (in a week). "I've cycled 3,000 miles!" I wanted to scream. But instead, I just supped my orange juice and lemonade in silence, and doodled profanities on to the back of a beer mat.

Nairn was a windswept and affluent town. I spied on a dozen people playing bowls, then on couples sharing bottles of rosé in cosy wine bars. VisitScotland sold the destination as "one of the sunniest and driest places in Scotland", which seemed a bit like describing Novosibirsk as one of the most tropical cities in Siberia. Nevertheless, it was a pleasant place to rest my head and I woke up early the next morning to the chirp and cheep of sparrows, tits and chaffinches. I felt well rested but ached from the back of my neck to the ends of my toes, via all the unspeakably tender crannies in between.

There was barely a wisp of cloud in the sky and by the time I reached Inverness, a city I'd only ever seen dusted in snow, I was down to a T-shirt drenched in sweat. With fair winds, four paracetamol and three ibuprofen in my system, I crossed the Moray Firth on the busy A9 then turned north-east toward the Black Isle.

The road swooped just a little, up and down like a spine, but mostly it meandered through the pit of a windless valley, hemmed in by fields of wheat and barley. There was hardly a soul to be seen, just the occasional runaway ewe or a farmer in a tractor with big muddy tyres. Having cycled so far, through so many different landscapes and conditions, the Black Isle was heaven.

Contrary to its name, however, it isn't an island but a peninsula, surrounded by water on three sides. And in order to carry on north, I had to cross the Cromarty Firth on a little passenger ferry, alongside a single car and five other tourists.

Known by many locals as the oil-rig graveyard, I counted nine of the 30,000-tonne steel Goliaths. As drilling in the North Sea continues to slow, more will inevitably arrive. Many of us would agree that a world less dependent on fossil fuels is a marvellous thing, but to see them up close, rusting like the dreams of proud men, they were a brutal harbinger of unemployment and economic decline, just as much as symbols of a greener, brighter future.

———

Twitter had, once again, come up trumps and, via a contact at the local tourist office, I'd been offered the chance to camp at Easter Airfield, an unlicensed aerodrome a few miles south-east of Tain. It would mean ending my day early, but instinct urged me to go there. I could make up the distance the next day.

Within 5 minutes of arriving, I'd found my host, David Edes; a balding man from the north-east of England with a grey beard, dressed in a red and white chequered shirt and baggy jeans held up by braces. "I've been waiting for you," he said, with the slightest hint of the Bond villain. "I was thinking of going flying, if you fancy joining me?"

My instinct had come good, and soon we were strapped into a single-prop Cessna and idling at the top of an empty runway. After a few final checks, David fired up the throttle, released the brakes and sent us roaring across the asphalt. Up, up and away, back toward Cromarty Firth.

Radio chatter crackled into our airwaves. Beneath us, a flock of sheep cantered around a craggy pasture, shape-shifting like a murmuration of starlings. From the cockpit we could see all the way back to Banff and beyond. Two days' worth of blood, sweat and graft, captured in one epic picture.

The oil rigs were now less like giants and more like LEGO toys. We flew a few hundred feet over their helipads, cranes and towers, then took a sweeping 180-degree arc, swooping us over North-Sea shallows that glowed a Caribbean blue.

Bouncing in and out of thermals, I was keen to find out if David's life had changed much. "Not really," he said. "The interest in flying has remained about the same during the pandemic."

"I suppose it's the sense of freedom?"

"What I love the most is that you can go out and be totally alone."

"But surely it's incredibly expensive?"

"People see flying as an expensive hobby, but if you only go once a week, it's no more expensive than drinking or smoking every day."

"A lot healthier, and more fun I expect, too."

"It works out at about £2 a minute."

Flying northward, back in the direction of the airfield, David pointed out the twists and turns ahead of me, as though tracing his finger over a paper map. "I'm very lucky," he said, as we began our descent. "But I've worked very hard for that luck."

As the plane's wheels skidded back to Earth, my heart quaked. "You know you don't have to camp unless you really want to?" he said, as the propeller whirred to a halt. "I've got to head home now, but I'll leave you the keys to the shepherd's hut. It's only recently been built as somewhere pilots can stay overnight. You'd be very welcome."

Throughout my journey around Britain, I'd always strived to tell the stories of the people I met as honestly and as faithfully as possible. And the fact that David's life hadn't changed all that much was a story in itself, as significant as the people who'd lost everything.

About my parents' age, he – like them – was much better prepared for the unexpected. He had investments, assets and a pension. Lockdown had been a bit of an inconvenience, but it certainly wasn't the existential crisis felt by me and many of my peers.

As a freelancer I'd always brushed off the idea of pensions and savings. "My pension is my future success," I'd tell my financially scrupulous dad, much to his frustration. But the pandemic, coupled with my journey around Britain, had given me a wake-up call I never expected. I had to plan better and save harder. However boring and adult it was to admit it, my future life, death, physical and mental well-being depended upon it.

———

I spent the evening in a local pub, nursing a pint. I was fed up with being a stranger, the weird loner at the end of the bar. Without Alana, my friends and family, I had no identity, no soul. I was ready for the dull and the tedious again, for different clothes and a belly that hung over the waistband of my boxer shorts.

Back at the airfield a mild southerly wind whipped through the grass and rattled the corrugated-iron roof of the shepherd's hut. According to Google Maps I was 95 miles and 3,000 feet of ascent from John o'Groats. I set my alarm for 4.30 a.m. then drifted off to the *Shipping Forecast*. "Tyne, Dogger: south. Six, occasionally eight. Fair, good… Cromarty: south. Seven, occasionally eight. Fair, good…"

I slept terribly. Rather than resting, I spent most of the night waiting for my alarm to sound. Nevertheless, I was so eager to finish, that I loaded up the bike and hit the road. It was high summer in the Highlands yet thick plumes of bright-white steam bellowed from my mouth and nostrils.

After a mile I was so cold that I stopped and threw on almost every item of clothing I wasn't already wearing. Three pairs of dirty socks, thermal long johns, two extra T-shirts and the gloves I'd lugged all the way from Scilly. I even cut neck and arm holes in a bag for life but stopped short of using my bloodied cycling shorts as a makeshift beanie.

For over an hour it felt as though the dawn might freeze my bones to dust, but then a bright orange sun rose out of the North Sea and illuminated a trillion pinheads of dew. When the warmth finally hit my shoulders and legs, I came alive, and so did the land around me. A pair of hares kicked up mud as they sprinted from one side of a turnip field to another. Gannets and guillemots emerged from a dark wetland that steamed like soup. Black shapes ringed the northern horizon. Maybe ospreys, probably buzzards.

I'd been warned against cycling on the A1, the road that skirts along the north-east coast of Scotland. "It's very busy," I'd been told in the pub the night before. But all things are relative and one man's "busy" is another man's "quiet". In the first 2 hours of the day, I passed just three other road users: an articulated lorry with an invisible driver, a nurse in PPE, and a clean-shaven cyclist with brand new panniers and untanned legs.

We shared the customary nod as we passed, but 50 feet down the road both glanced back. He looked appalled. Was this his destiny? A chapped-lipped, grimy road man with a tangled beard and a Tesco bag as a waistcoat?

As the morning grew older, the road became busier, but by no means intimidating. I did, however, pass more touring cyclists than I had done in all the previous 3,000 miles. This was a Land's End to John o'Groats (LEJOG) bottleneck, frequented by couples on tandems, OAPs on e-bikes, big pelotons followed by minibuses, and the occasional self-supported desperado. Part of me felt compelled to stop and chat, but a much bigger part wanted to be invisible. I'd had hundreds of these conversations before and they were nearly always a massive waste of time.

"Where are you going?"

"Land's End. You?"

"John o'Groats."

"Cool."

I quite enjoyed the mystery, the wonder of passing someone and not getting the full story. We were all out there for our own unique reasons. That was enough for me.

Under a hot sun and with the wind at my back, I crept north. The A1 picked up pace but not so fast that I'd have diverted inland to avoid it. This route saved me 30 miles, but also allowed me to follow the coast. It was pretty, too. Pine, larch and fir trees crowded the roadside. Gorse-ringed lochs mirrored the cotton-wool clouds above. Occasionally, furry creatures would scuttle across the grey and scramble into the shadows.

I stopped at a café in Helmsdale for a late lunch; a vegetable pasty and a bowl of spicy carrot soup. I felt fit and determined and was on course to hit John o'Groats sometime that evening. Local chit-chat swung from one mind-numbing subject to another, but then it turned to the prospect of an impending storm and my ears pricked up. "Full-on *dreich*," said a man with a big bushy beard, as he stuffed a slice of Victoria sponge into his face. At which point I turned to Google. *Dreich*: "wet, dull, gloomy, dismal, dreary or any combination of these. Scottish weather at its most miserable."

The *Shipping Forecast* had stitched me up like a kipper. Or, more accurately, I'd done it to myself. I'd naively assumed that the morning's southerly winds and high pressure would hang around all day. Wrong. I probably should have checked the forecast on my phone, too. But if I'm honest, ignorance had been bliss. And if I'd known a storm was rolling in, it wouldn't have changed a thing.

By the time I'd paid, a few spots of drizzle had already settled on my saddle and panniers. Then, within just a mile of setting off, the rain was so fierce that I had to take shelter under a knotted old yew tree with a canopy that dipped at the rim like an umbrella.

A torrent of water roared down the road, washing twigs, leaves and feathers along in its dirty ripples. The sky above was as black as coal. I had no option but to continue, grinding up switchbacks with 18 per cent gradients, my teeth chattering, my nose streaming with snot.

To make things even worse, the wind then rounded by a hundred degrees or so and gusted in from the north-east – exactly the direction I was headed. I kept telling myself to push on, one rotation after another, but as I slowed to just a few miles per hour, the prospect of reaching John o'Groats that day became increasingly unrealistic.

I was forced to lay up in Lybster, once a busy herring port, and now a popular stop off on the route of the North Coast 500. I couldn't afford the hotel, but instead paid £50 to stay in an old man's spare room. Covered in liver spots and dandruff, he reminded me of my late maternal grandad. Kind and gentle, but also as deaf as a post, even with two hearing aids he could barely hear a thing. "Make yourself at home!" he shouted, over a TV so loud it rattled the windows.

At first, I was furious that I'd had to stop, but after a hot shower and with my clothes drying beside a radiator, I calmed. Ten years before, maybe even ten months before, I'd have stubbornly persevered through gritted teeth and driving rain, then curled up in a bus shelter to "sleep" – that was what proper adventurers did. Now, though, I felt like I had nothing left to prove. It was the distance that mattered, not the time it took to get there.

───

The next morning was even wetter than the night before it, but the wind had dropped and at least the forecast held hope: 5 hours of solid rain followed by an afternoon of sunshine and clear skies. All I had to do was sit in the saddle and soak it up.

If I'd raced, I could have probably got there in 2 hours. Instead, I tried to slow down a little, to be mindful of my surroundings; the clatter of raindrops, the scent of oily lanolin rubbed against fence posts. I was quickly soaking wet again, but I didn't really care. I was at the bleak forehead of mainland Britain, the trail head of countless public, but also very private, pilgrimages.

I passed teams of cyclists in matching jerseys and gangs of motorcyclists communicating via headsets built in to their helmets. Almost every lay-by was filled with some sort of narcissist with a smartphone. At times, one of them was me.

But then, a few miles from the finish line, I spotted a lonely old man burdened by a heavy rucksack, taking shelter in the porch of an abandoned bungalow. Intriguing and out of place, I slammed on my brakes. "Are you OK?" I yelled, before joining him in the dry.

Seventy-year-old Anthony Hennigan was about to finish his third LEJOG, completed solo and unsupported, entirely on foot.

"I've never taken a single lift."

"Never? Not at all? You sound even more stubborn than me!"

"I almost got arrested once because I refused to get into a police car. When the officer was about to cuff me, I was forced to play my trump card."

"Which is?"

"I'm a retired detective chief inspector for West Yorkshire Police."

After 30 years in the police force, investigating homicides, drug deals and all sorts of heinous crimes, he felt compelled to hit the road. "It's hard to put into words quite why I feel the need to do this, but I think it's because I need to rid myself of those memories and experiences. This is a breath of fresh air in so many ways. It's also a great leveller; any status you have elsewhere in life becomes irrelevant. I'm just a human and a traveller, nothing else."

His three journeys around Britain had raised almost £30,000 for Sue Ryder, Cancer Research and Children in Need. He was once given £250 in a pub car park, but it was a 10p donation from a homeless man that meant the most. "In the context of his situation, that 10p was worth a lot more to him. What made it even more special was that he handed it over with a smile. I can't tell you how rare that is."

We shook hands and I set off into the rain. As he disappeared behind me, John o'Groats finally came into view.

FAIR ISLE:
EMBRACE THE RAIN

I queued up for one of those awkward photos with the town's famous signpost. Land's End: 874 miles. New York: 3,230 miles. Edinburgh: 273 miles. Orkney: 8 miles. Shetland: 152 miles.

"You've done what?" shrieked a woman with an American accent, before ordering her teenage son to take a photo of me for Facebook. For the next 10 minutes I felt like a paparazzi-harassed A-lister, but when the limelight faded, I finally got to reward myself with a cup of tea and a massive slab of chocolate cake.

I was there. Finally. I'd cycled more than 3,000 miles around mainland Britain, during an unprecedented pandemic. In the process, I'd seen, heard and experienced the very best and worst of life.

Physically I was haggard, but in my mind, I felt light and free. It's one of the oldest clichés in travel, but my journey wasn't about the finish line and a photo for Instagram. It was about all the people, the places, the ups and the downs that had come before it. John o'Groats was a place, just like any other.

Up until this point, my plan had been vague. But now that I'd reached the end of the road, I had a choice to make. I could either begin the long schlep home via a series of taxis, trains and coaches, or perhaps I could just keep going. For a little longer, at least.

"It would be nice to have you back," said Alana, whom I immediately called for counsel. "But what's another few days in the grand scheme of things?"

"You don't mind?"

"You'll be unbearable if you don't end it properly, and it would probably make a more satisfying story? Maybe you could write a book?"

"I'm not sure if anyone would want to read it."

"I guess a lot depends on when the next ferry is?"

———

Twenty minutes later, I threw my bike and panniers on to the foredeck of a slippery boat, the only service running between John o'Groats and Orkney that day. The water was so choppy that instead of sitting in the warm cab I opted to linger at the exposed aft deck with my eyes fixed to the horizon, much like a pensive sea dog.

Consumed by the fear of throwing up, the journey rushed by and we made landfall at the southern tip of South Ronaldsay about half an hour later. The fact that it took the skipper four attempts to dock really should have set alarm bells ringing; when the boat departed and left me alone at a desolate and empty jetty, the strength of the wind was like nothing I'd experienced before.

I set off northward, with the vague notion of reaching Kirkwall later that evening. With a bit of luck, I might even get there in time to catch the overnight ferry to Shetland. Within less than 2 minutes, however, I'd decided this was not just wishful thinking but pure poppycock. It was almost impossible to balance on the bike, let alone make any considerable progress. It took me well over an hour to travel just 3 miles.

When I stopped to wolf down some emergency biscuits, I found a dazed oystercatcher sheltering in the grass at my feet. I hadn't seen a single car so assumed it must have been thrown into a fence post by the wind. Instinctively, I picked it up and held its floppy body to my chest. With an orange beak as long as two chopsticks and red eyes like spotless ladybirds, it radiated a beauty so pure, I might have cried. If only my tear ducts hadn't been wind dried.

Goodness knows what I must have looked like, but when a couple in a camper van sneaked up behind me and asked if I needed a lift, they didn't bat an eyelid. "We can carry your panniers!" they shouted. "Lighten the load a little!"

But I refused. Stupidly, stubbornly, I refused. "I'll crack on!" I yelled back, with a pack of Hobnobs in one hand, and my feathered mascot in the other. "I've come this far... I said I've come this far!"

I eventually rolled into the village of St Margaret's Hope at 8 p.m. and bagged a single room above the only pub, the Murray Arms. It was warm and noisy, with the scent of seared scallops and dark ale in the air. I splashed out on both then soaked under a hot shower. My cheeks had been blown raw. My ears throbbed like car alarms.

Besides the steady flow of tourists, the pub was home to a team of nine, mostly Eastern-European scallop divers. They'd persevered through a challenging year and were now reaping the rewards on the other side.

"We were selling to the very best restaurants in London," said their boss, Fred Brown, whom I met later in the bar. "But when they closed, everything dried up. It was very difficult for the divers because we were forced to cut down to just one and a half or two days a week."

"But you stuck it out."

"Thankfully, things started picking up. We're now selling to Marks & Spencer."

"That's a massive achievement."

"We're now working at beyond 2019 levels. A lot of people have money in their pockets and are desperate for a degree of normality."

The wind and rain were so atrocious the next morning that it was after 11 a.m. by the time I felt brave enough to set off. The main road between Burwick and Kirkwall climbed and plummeted like a rollercoaster.

The only advantage of being at the foot of a looming ascent was getting the brief opportunity to hear myself think.

After so much rushing around, I had far more time than I needed. The ferry to Shetland wasn't for another 12 hours, so I made an effort to ride slowly, however masochistic that seemed. This would soon be over, and I felt pangs of both happiness and grief. However challenging the journey had been at times, it had become my normality, my routine, my daily medicine. I was ready to finish and return to some sort of humdrum, but I was apprehensive for the imminent transition between road and desk.

It was, therefore, important to gently wind down, rather than slamming on the brakes abruptly. The mind and body required time to cool, before taking on the next challenge – be that another big expedition, a massive life event or simply changing a light bulb.

Crossing the Churchill Barriers, I battled to stay upright. Waves crashed into the causeway and sent icy white water fizzing across the road. Sometimes it missed me, often it didn't. In the churning shallows, the burly, rusted hulls of German shipwrecks sat motionless, unfazed by the commotion around them.

After 3 hours I finally descended into Kirkwall. Amazingly, 255 days – 70 of which I'd spent cycling – had elapsed since my first visit, a time I spent mostly alone on windswept beaches or chatting to people at an awkward distance. Back then, the sense of paranoia, in both Kirkwall and in me, was palpable and itchy. Many islanders had been wary of outsiders and a single Covid-19 infection would have been enough to send curtains twitching.

Now, however, much had changed. The town was dealing with a fresh outbreak of the virus. A thousand tests had been distributed. Five hundred people were at home isolating. Nevertheless, the streets were busy with tourists. The pubs were open, and multigenerational families laughed over big lunches and bottles of wine. I spent the afternoon in a windless suntrap, simply basking in the sound of chit-chat and footsteps.

Some big businesses had folded, but others had flourished. The Kirkwall Hotel, for example, had used the third national lockdown to undertake a refurbishment that should have taken five years. The pandemic had also been an opportunity for many budding entrepreneurs to try out new ideas.

"I thought if I don't do it now, I might never do it," said Kristian Cooper, the tall, bearded owner of Sea Kayak 59 Degrees North, whom I met in the harbour. "One great thing to come out of this is how people learned to see their own country from a different perspective. Adventure tourism feels like a whole new sector up here. I'm now busier than I could have ever imagined."

Ironically, it had taken a pandemic for many of us to wake up to the healing powers of fresh air and exercise. Activities such as hiking, bicycle touring and sea kayaking were no longer niche, but mainstream. "There is definitely a bigger awareness for the environment and everything we have around us. In a strange way, being locked up in our own homes, but also in our own country, really showed us what we'd been missing."

When the wind finally dropped, I took a lazy ride from Kirkwall to the Halston ferry terminal, the industrialised harbour where I'd arrived, in the black of night, all those many months before. It felt surreal to be retracing my tracks, to be pedalling in rewind, but as a warm sunset spat pink and orange embers at cranes, shipping containers and forklifts, I felt at peace. In fact, it became one of those oddly grounding moments that rarely occur in life. This was precisely where I was meant to be. And this was exactly what I was meant to be doing.

Before boarding the ferry, Dave Flanagan, the surfing journalist I'd met at the Bay of Skaill, the previous year, arrived with a couple of cold beers. In an odd way, it was like meeting one of my oldest and dearest friends. When I'd set off from Orkney, what now seemed like a lifetime ago, I'm sure he'd sensed a pain bubbling up inside me. A pain that I myself had not yet fully felt, or realised.

"Looking back at this time," I asked, "do you think the islands should have done anything different?"

"I think it was right for Orkney to distance itself as much as possible. There was a collective desire to protect the welfare of the community."

"And even more so on a group of islands?"

"Islands by their very nature are vulnerable places. A lot of businesses struggled with the lack of visitors, but if Covid had really taken hold here, then it could have been absolutely devastating."

Since our last meeting, Dave had been busier than ever. Closed international borders had made Orkney one of the most exotic places available to British travel writers and film-makers. He'd also found the time to write two children's books. Was he hopeful for what comes next? I wondered. Not only in his life, but in all of ours.

"Watching your journey from afar really showed me that all of us have gone through so many similar things. The most heart-warming thing for me was seeing just how many people welcomed you. All our worries and concerns seemed so universal. I just hope we don't all fall back into our old habits. Because it was the humanity that shone through. We are all the same. We are all in this together."

———

I boarded the ferry, dropped on to a bunk bed, then woke up 5 hours later. With sticky eyes I looked out of the porthole. The sun had risen out of the sea but was hesitating in the conduit between horizon and sky. Through it, black wisps raced from north to south, the zigzag filament in a light bulb.

Soon we were rumbling into Lerwick. I could see church spires and slate roof tiles, parked cars and gravestones. I was eager to hit the road, but I'd agreed to meet Emma Williamson, the A&E nurse and open-water swimmer I'd met briefly on my first visit.

I was hoping she'd forgotten that I'd promised to join her for a swim, but when the ferry doors opened, she was the first person I saw, stood with a bright-blue beach towel in one hand and a spare pair of goggles in the other.

Ten minutes later I had sand between my toes and my nipples were as hard as nails. "Just take it real slow," said Emma, as we edged into the frigid shallows at Lerwick's Bains Beach. "If you go in too quick, you'll get cold shock, and this is meant to be my day off."

On my first visit I was left awestruck by Emma's grit and resolve, not only in cold water, but also on the frontline of the NHS. Long before the vaccine, she'd risked her life to save others. I wondered what lessons she'd learned in the nine months since we'd last met.

"I think Shetlanders feel even more independent," she said, splashing the near-Arctic water on to her face and shoulders. "Not being able to get off-island made us feel even more together."

"And you, specifically. How did it make you feel?"

"As an individual I think I'm a lot less inclined to leave now."

"Not even for a holiday?"

"I used to love going away somewhere warm, but I've not felt that. I feel really at peace here."

Despite the positives, Emma was concerned about the long-term impact on her three teenage sons. "I, and a lot of people my age, really quite loved lockdown. We loved the peace and having the islands to ourselves. But for the younger ones, I think this period could leave a lasting impression. My eighteen-year-old didn't get to go out for a pint on his birthday and my middle son has left school without ever sitting a proper exam. I've not been too worried about myself, but for the young ones it's healthy for them to get off-island and see what's out there."

The water was so cold I could feel my heart skipping beats. I waded in to testicle depth, took a giant gasp of air, then insisted Emma head on without me. "I'll just swim around here," I lied, and when she turned her back, I splashed my face and hair, to make it look like I'd been fully submerged.

"You wimp!" yelled a woman from the jetty.

As I waited for Emma to swim a lap of a replica Viking longship anchored a hundred feet or so out to sea, I pondered Bressay, the dumpy green island on the horizon. It was the place where I'd learned that Sarah had died nine months before. Since that swirling, sleepless night, it had appeared in a dozen of my intense and haunting dreams. Even from a safe distance, it terrified me.

A loop of Britain later, and it was hard to tell if I'd come to terms with her death or if she, and indeed all my lost loved ones, would occupy my busy mind forever. Entranced by the island, cold water lapping at my waist, many of the emotions I felt on that momentous night flashed through me. Horror, shame, loneliness, anger.

What had changed, however, was my perception of those emotions. My battle with anxiety and all the physical symptoms associated with it had taught me to appreciate that negative feelings are entirely normal. When bad things happen to us in life, our bodies and minds will react in ways that are unpleasant.

Life isn't, and won't be, a procession of wonderful events; there will be bad days, too. Therefore, in many ways, a protracted adventure, like cycling for thousands of miles, becomes a fitting allegory for life itself. To enjoy the sunshine, I had to embrace the rain.

———

It was a relief to see Emma emerge from the dark water. White and pink, with a thick scar down her right thigh, this was her natural habitat.

"This is so important to me because it connects me to Shetland. It gives me a sense of the fish, the birds and the seaweed; all the things that I share this place with."

"You sound almost evangelical. This place is like your church."

"I don't feel spiritual, but I do feel a connection with nature. Being in water – I suspect a lot like being on a bike – means you only concentrate on what's just in front of you."

"I need my bike, just like you need the water."

"It resets my head. We all need something like this. It's all about finding the thing that works for you."

After bacon rolls and cups of tea, I set off north, through Lerwick's grey suburbs and out into empty and austere valleys. It was neither warm nor cold, wet nor dry. Bubbles of mizzle, less than 500 feet wide, marched in from the Atlantic, then fizzled out over the North Sea. The sun was flirtatious and teasing. There one minute, gone the next. The road was empty, but not as lonely as I remembered it. No humans in sight, just sheep and fulmars.

I might have made it to the top of Shetland in a long and gruelling day, but I was done with that lifestyle, done with the rush. So, I diverted to Hillswick, to St Magnus Bay and the hotel that had faced closure nine months before.

To my great surprise, it wasn't just open, but bustling. The air was heavy with laughter. A dozen staff rushed from one table to the next with trays of drinks and second helpings of roast potatoes. I gorged on a lunch of local lamb with mint sauce and fluffy Yorkshire puddings, then retired to the bar to catch up with Richard Grains, the fisherman I'd met right at the start of my journey.

"This whole experience has definitely made me realise just how lucky we are to live up here. When I'm working out at sea, I look back at the land and the colour of the rocks and feel very fortunate. On the downside, though, a lot of people have realised the same thing and are buying up homes here. The housing market has boomed, and I wonder if young people will be able to afford to buy here."

Richard had weathered many storms, but through all of them he'd pinned his hopes on a brighter future. Without that, what did he have? Indeed, what did any of us really have? Most of all, he'd never stopped appreciating all the things he had in his life, rather than pining for the things he didn't.

"Whatever happened to those lobsters you were hiding for Christmas?" I asked.

"I was a bit dubious about what they'd fetch. But it ended up being very, very good. It was the best Christmas we ever had. We made about £2 or £3 extra per kilo. It was just a pity we didn't have more!"

Richard headed home for a rare evening off, but before I crept away to bed, I wanted to hear from the landlady, Andrea, who was cashing up in the office. The first time we spoke she was contemplating closing the business, at least for the winter, but maybe forever.

"Financially, it was a disaster," she admitted. "I'm desperate to retire. I didn't realise just how tired I was until I had nothing to do. But then I had more time to cuddle my grandchildren and I realised just how much I'd been missing."

On one hand, Andrea believed they'd been lucky, because no one close to them had died of Covid. But on the other hand, her elderly mother grew "desperately lonely", and then her brother died of a heart attack. "He spent eighteen months trying to avoid Covid because he thought it would kill him. Then last month he dropped down dead. That's not fair."

I woke up early the next morning, restless and eager to move. This was my very last day and my body craved movement. As I hoovered up a plate of scrambled eggs, beans and toast, my right leg jumped up and down involuntarily – not an anxious tick, but unbridled lust for the finish line.

A force-6 gale tore in from the east, but the sky was electric blue with flecks of silken cloud. I set off northward, with Emma's words still echoing in my ears: "It's all about finding the thing that works for you."

Emma had found swimming, others had discovered music, art, drama, literature, metal detecting, horticulture and religion. For me it was cycling. Without it I wasn't human. And with every passing mile, and every fleeting smile, I'd been soothed. Not healed or cured, but placated. And that was all that mattered to me. For now, at least.

As the wind swirled around me, I simply turned the pedals, one rotation after another. Focussing on the tarmac just beyond my nose, the miles dissolved, and when thoughts raced into my head, I set them free, to snag on the barbed wire with strands of natty wool.

I crossed into Yell, then took a ferry across Bluemull Sound to Unst and Belmont, the half-moon beach where I'd spent my first frosty night, cocooned in a tent, tainted by the scent of my own frozen urine. All those months before, I'd wondered where my journey might take me. Even Land's End seemed out of my reach.

To have gone full circle was a dream. Not in a corny or inspirational sense, but because it all seemed so unreal. The road curled around inlets I half recognised. I passed seagulls I might have seen before. Was this déjà vu or memory? It didn't matter. I had sea and sand coursing through my veins. Pollen in my ears and salt on my lips.

I was battered and bruised, sure: a swollen tongue from too much sugar, muscles that screamed and suntan lines that threatened to brand my skin forever. But my lungs – my once labouring, broken lungs – had wriggled free from their shackles and were now expanding deeply into the bulbous hollow of my tummy. I could breathe. By Jove, I could breathe!

— ⁓ —

According to a paper published in October 2021, in the medical journal *The Lancet*, depression and anxiety disorders increased by more than a quarter worldwide in 2020. In Britain, a record number of children and adults sought help from the NHS for problems like panic attacks and eating disorders. Record numbers of people reported feeling lonely, while 78 million prescriptions for antidepressants were dispensed in England, a 5 per cent rise on 2019.

According to the Department of Health and Social Care, mental illness remains the single largest cause of disability in the UK, contributing up to 22.8 per cent of the total burden, compared to 15.9 per cent for cancer and 16.2 per cent for cardiovascular disease. In England, this costs the taxpayer £105.2 billion a year.

On paper, the data was startling, but the picture on the ground was more nuanced, and in many ways more severe. On my journey around Britain, I was told time and again, by farmers, artists, swimmers, fishermen and musicians, people with homes and people without: when the pandemic is finally over, the next crisis will be in our heads.

———

Our modern lives have become so complicated. Most of us live beyond our means. We buy cars and sofas we can't afford, then let these debts weigh heavy on our shoulders. Consciously and subconsciously, social media, peer pressure and the workplace are constantly pushing us to work longer and achieve more.

I, like many people, had allowed myself to become distracted. But my time on the road, with rain in my hair and sun on my back, gave me the freedom to recognise what was truly important in life. Where I wanted to be, where I wanted to go. And significantly, who I wanted to be on that journey with.

By boiling life down to just eating, drinking, exercising and "sleeping", I quickly realised that all the other stuff was just extra. Having the time and the luxury to think is surely the greatest, and most valuable, commodity any of us will ever have.

But journeys like mine shouldn't be seen as eccentric escapades for the few. They should be a rite of passage, for young, old, rich and poor. Rather than dishing out antidepressants and writing sick notes, GPs should be handing over bicycles, tents and cagoules. The solutions to many of our problems won't be found in stuffy NHS offices, but will be discovered out there, in the wind and the rain, on pilgrimages of mind, body and soul.

———

Rather than march out to the headland at Hermaness like before, local fisherman Kevin Tulloch met me in Burrafirth, the hamlet where Britain's asphalt finally ran into grass. With my bike lashed to the back of his boat, we steamed northward through a jagged fjord, escorted by a squadron of shrieking seagulls. The water was still and glossy, but the scarred cliffs that loomed above us had been ravaged by a million storms.

To the north-east I could see the radar station where I'd snooped and the rocky path I'd climbed to get there. But then, as we escaped into the churning confluence of the Atlantic and North Sea, Kevin cut the engine and we bobbed in silence.

Muckle Flugga Lighthouse and the guano-covered island Out Stack grew bigger as the current sucked us closer. This really was the end of the line. The exclamation mark right at the top of Britain.

From here on in, life would become more complicated. There were no manuals or maps to follow. All I could do was improvise the best I could, and swerve around the giant oaks that would inevitably crash into my path.

Whatever came next – a global crisis, the loss of a job, the death of a loved one – I would be better prepared. I'd simply grab my bike, and I'd hit the road.

EPILOGUE:
RICH SUMMER GREEN

I'd spent 75 days on the road, spread across nine strange and sometimes tragic months. I'd cycled 3,427 miles through 55 counties, consumed 750 litres of water, 250 cups of coffee, 170 pints of beer and burned more than 400,000 calories.

I'd properly interviewed about a hundred different people, but had enjoyed fleeting encounters with several hundred more. I'd sold just enough articles, and had made just enough money, to start paying our mortgage again. I'd lost two friends but had gained a future wife.

My journey was over, but not quite complete. I took a taxi back to Lerwick, jumped on a ferry and embarked on one final leg: to Bressay.

I climbed to the summit of the island, then descended toward the Gorie bothy, the little house I'd escaped from at the crack of dawn all those many months before. On that traumatic autumn night, it had creaked and groaned with cold, hard death. But now it throbbed with new life. The greenhouse was packed with courgettes and tomatoes. The potato patch bloomed with plumes of rich summer green. Little lambs looked for warmth and milk between their mothers' woolly legs.

As the fire hissed and popped, I drank tea and ate biscuits with golden midsummer light streaming through the windows, wondering if soon, just maybe, a little robin might swing by to say hi.

ACKNOWLEDGEMENTS

If you've made it to this page, then I thank you, dear reader, for joining me on my 3,427-mile journey around Britain. I thank you for tolerating my tangents, enduring the lows and celebrating the highs. I hope there were laughs, and some – but not too many – tears.

The challenge of cycling around the country was nothing in contrast to finishing this 103,000-word book, and it brings me immense pride to think that someone – besides my mum – might be reading these words. So, thank you for parting with your hard-earned cash to fill your brain with my waffle.

When I set off on this adventure, I had no idea what might become of it. But more than any other journey in my life, this was something I felt compelled to do. I would not hesitate to do something similar again in the future. Travel is good for the soul.

Without the hundreds of people I met along the way, this would have been a much shorter, significantly more boring book. To all the kind characters mentioned in the previous pages, I will be eternally grateful for your time, words of inspiration and generosity. At a moment in our history when we were told to keep our distance, I was continually met with love and hope – most of which came from "strangers" I now consider friends.

A special thank you must go to Oliver Smith at *The Telegraph*. Without him saying, "This is a totally crazy idea, but I'll take some articles," then this would have remained just another silly daydream that never came to fruition. And to David Nicol, Steve Mathieson and Adam Civico in Shetland – your support at the beginning and end of this journey was more than I could ever have asked for.

Thank you to Tim Ecott for being the first person to read my manuscript and book proposal, right back in the dark days of lockdown, and to Debbie Chapman at Summersdale for taking a punt on me. A special mention should also go to Ross Dickinson, the brilliant editor who helped me knock several drafts into shape.

Thank you to all the journalists, travel writers and adventurers who took the time to read proof copies of this book. Your kind words fill me with immense pride. You are all people I've looked up to on my road to this point. If I can ever repay the favour somehow, just shout.

Thank you to Alana's parents, Ruth and Tim. Without your kindness and generosity during this past couple of years, I have no idea what we might have done. A big thank you must also go to Grand John and Pepe. The Red House in Suffolk became our lifeline and refuge.

It's hard for me to put into words just how hard my parents, Richard and Maureen, have had to work during their lives in order to give my sisters and me opportunities that they never had. I'd struggle to say these words out loud, but I want you to know that I love you dearly. All the help you've given me over the past three and a half decades has led to this. I hope this book makes you proud.

And now, finally, to Alana. If you've read the preceding few hundred pages then you'll know just how lucky I am to have her in my life. Throughout all of those challenging moments, she remained – almost always – optimistic, upbeat and level-headed.

During those sometimes dank and depressing days, Alana wasn't just my girlfriend, but my gym buddy, shrink and soulmate. Thank you for always encouraging my crazy ideas, and for also reminding me to "chill the fuck out" from time to time.

I would never have got here without you, and even when we were hundreds of miles apart, you were with me.

ABOUT THE AUTHOR

Simon Parker is an award-winning travel writer and broadcaster who has reported from over 100 countries. He has documented climate change in Svalbard for the BBC World Service, scored a half-century for the Guatemalan cricket team on BBC Radio 4's *From Our Own Correspondent*, and cycled 300 miles beside the US–Mexico border for *The Telegraph* (before almost dying of heatstroke in the Chihuahuan Desert).

In 2016 Simon sailed and cycled from China to London for the BBC, via the Pacific, the USA and the Atlantic. He has driven a rickshaw the length of India, cycled the length of Scandinavia for his *Earth Cycle* TV show on Amazon Prime, and hiked every commercial route to Machu Picchu for *The Telegraph*.

When he's not almost killing himself on an assignment, Simon shares his time between the Cotswolds and Cape Town.

For more information visit www.simonwparker.co.uk

You can follow his adventures in real time on social media:

Twitter: @SimonWIParker

Instagram: @simonwiparker

Facebook: simonparker1987

PUBLIC SPEAKING

Simon has spoken at hundreds of schools, universities, members' clubs, corporate and public events all over the world, including The Frontline Club, Royal Geographical Society, Cambridge and Oxford Universities and Tedx.

His multimedia presentations include:

Riding Out: Cycling 3,427 Miles around "Pandemic Britain"

To coincide with the publication of this book, Simon will be speaking at a number of theatres and festivals around the country. This is a presentation of short films, stories and photos from his journey, followed by a Q&A.

A Reporter's Adventures in Over 100 Countries

From Namibia to Nepal, the Pacific to the Andes, this talk travels the globe via films and photos from his adventures in six continents.

The Fragile Arctic

Simon looks back on assignments in Greenland, Svalbard, Finland, Sweden and Norway while making content for the BBC, Amazon Prime, *The Independent* and *The Telegraph*.

For public speaking enquiries visit www.simonwparker.co.uk

Testimonials:

"An excellent public speaker."
Laura Gane, The Frontline Club

"Simon is a fantastic young man who has dozens, if not hundreds, of funny and highly interesting anecdotes from a life spent living nomadically as a journalist around the world."
Lisa Curtiss, Journalism Studies Course Leader, Solent University

"Not only fascinating and engaging, but carried an inspiring message about acknowledging who you are. Instead of conforming to 'normality', Simon has chosen a life which suits who he truly is – something we could all learn from."
Phil Sanger, Director, Vault IP Law Firm

"Simon's presentation had all the elements that our audiences enjoy: interesting anecdotes, great images, and, of course, some physical suffering. The content of his talk was so well illustrated with skilfully made video clips and still images showing the people, countries and personal body-punishing hardships involved."
Gordon Macfarlane, Secretary, Royal Scottish Geographical Society, Glasgow

IMAGE CREDITS

Have you enjoyed this book?
If so, why not write a review on your favourite website?

If you're interested in finding out more about our books, find us on
Facebook at **Summersdale Publishers**, on Twitter at **@Summersdale** and
on Instagram at **@summersdalebooks** and get in touch.
We'd love to hear from you!

Thanks very much for buying this Summersdale book.

www.summersdale.com